POPULATION AND SURVIVAL

POPULATION AND SURVIVAL

The Challenge in Five Countries

Georgia Lee Kangas

PRAEGER SPECIAL STUDIES • PRAEGER SCIENTIFIC

New York • Philadelphia • Eastbourne, UK
Toronto • Hong Kong • Tokyo • Sydney

Library of Congress Cataloging in Publication Data

Kangas, Georgia Lee.
  Population and survival.

  Includes index.
  1. Developing countries—Population. I. Title.
HB884.K36   1984   304.6′ 09172′4   84-8271
ISBN 0-03-071871-6 (alk. paper)

Published in 1984 by Praeger Publishers
CBS Educational and Professional Publishing,
a Division of CBS Inc.
521 Fifth Avenue, New York, NY 10175 USA

© 1984 by Population Communication

456789 052 9876545321

Printed in the United States of America
on acid-free paper

Dedicated to Lenni, Sara, and Tanya

Acknowledgments

The book was edited by Julie Lauren and updated by John Laing, Sandy Lieberman, Wendee Walberg, and myself. Anne Marie Marti provided research assistance and Lenni Kangas obtained valuable up-to-date publications and reports on the family planning activities in the five countries. In addition, valuable comments on the book were provided by Kingsley Davis and Parker Mauldin.

Contents

List of Tables

Introduction

The population of the world now stands at 4.7 billion
people. A billion were added during the last 13 years and
another billion will be added in the next 12 years. It took
from the beginning of history until 1830 for the population
level to reach 1 billion. The second billion arrived by 1930,
and by 1960 there were 3 billion people on the planet. The
principal reason for this increase in population has been the
reduction of disease during the first half of this century.
Couples are not having more children--fewer children are dying.
Unfortunately, many countries have not been able to bring the
birth rate into equilibrium with the death rate due to a number
of physical, cultural, economic, political, and religious
reasons.

In the developing countries, almost one-half the population
is below the age of 17. If all couples have replacement-size
families of two children, the populations of these countries
will increase 80 percent. In most of these countries, couples
would have to have a one-child family for the next 30 years in
order for the population to stabilize at the existing level.
If somehow, parents reduce by half the number of children they
are currently having within the next 30 to 40 years these populations will still increase two and a half to three times their
current size.

The daily life of each reader of this book is profoundly
affected by population growth in the underdeveloped countries,
as is every aspect of life in the United States, including such
factors as national security, employment, inflation, availability of raw materials, and the ethical decisions of who will live
and who will die on the planet as a whole.

There are no major famines today. However, the fossil-fuel
system needed to maintain subsistent agricultural production in
the developing countries will eventually compete with American
life styles. There will be direct competition for a barrel of
oil produced in the Middle East. India will need the oil to
produce grain and America will need the oil to fuel its auto-
mobiles. If there is famine in India or Bangladesh, North
Americans would have to choose between a manageable price for
fuel or the survival of children in Asia.

People in the United States have vital national security
interests and heavy financial commitments in both Egypt and the
Philippines. If, due in part to rapid urbanization or uncon-
trolled population growth, the population problem destabilizes
these countries, the impact on the United States would be pro-
found. If, due to a disenfranchisement of the middle class,

unabated inflation, and a lack of jobs, Mexico becomes the
next Iran, there would be a flood of refugees and illegal
immigrants into the United States.

Employment of minorities is already profoundly affected by
the refugees and immigrants coming into the United States. In
1983, there were 3.2 million births and 1.6 million deaths--
the United States grew by 1.6 million people. In addition, an
estimated 1 million legal and illegal immigrants entered the
United States, giving it the highest population growth rate
among the developed countries. In an effort to focus on the
problems of population growth, Population Communication was
founded in 1977 to communicate the urgency of this issue to
national leaders, to develop motion picture and TV screenplays
with population and family planning themes, to disseminate the
latest information on family planning techniques to doctors in
developing countries, and to promote the concepts of population
stabilization using surveys and publications. In addition,
Population Communication assists developing countries in formu-
lating population policies and programs that incorporate rewards
(incentives) and constraints (disincentives).

In 1982, Population Communication commissioned Georgia
Lee Kangas to write a book; the resulting work is unique. To
date, no reports or publications have adequately described the
cultural, historic, religious, economic, and political setting
of the population problem. Nor has there been a first-hand
account of professionals actually working on these programs.
Most books on the population problem describe the situation
as hopeless or overdramatize the impact of family planning
problems in lowering birth rates. Population and Survival:
The Challenge in Five Countries provides a dramatic insight
into both the failures and successes that have occurred in
family planning during the last 20 years. It challenges the
reader to consider population as the single most important
problem facing India, Mexico, Philippines, Egypt, and Bangladesh today.

In the absence of rapid development, couples will continue
to have twice as many children as are required for replacement.
Completed family sizes are resulting in doubled populations in
18 to 33 years. In countries such as India and Bangladesh
there will be no hope for the level of development required
until couples begin to have one or two children. The Indians
have three choices: starvation, coercive sterilization, or
positive rewards for the one- or two-child family. Without
incentives now, many millions, even hundreds of millions of
people will probably starve to death. Even with incentives
there is no guarantee that famines can be prevented. The technology and research to determine the type of rewards that can
provide the maximum benefit for children and their parents is
urgently needed.

A well-planned combination of rewards provides for an
enrichment of life and greater freedom of choice. The rewards

are needed to substitute for the negative motives for having children. Parents want children to work as cheap labor and support them in old age. These attitudes can be compensated for by reinforcing the positive motives for having small families, such as better educational opportunities and improved access to health facilities. Increasing the interval between births will definitely improve the health of mothers and their children. Incentives can help couples discriminate between family sizes, decrease the ambivalence toward a specific family size, develop the discipline required for a reduction. Different inducements can shift the emphasis from the selfish motives parents perceive for large families to the values that protect and enhance the welfare of the individual child.

In the short run, children will benefit from increased educational opportunities, improved health care, and the additional attention parents of small families are able to provide. In the long run, if couples have replacement-size families, the very depressed populations may be able to avert large scale famines. As long as populations continue to double every 18 to 33 years and parents want four or five children, famine is inevitable.

In her 20 years of observing family planning programs and studying population policies in Egypt, the Philippines, and India, Georgia Lee Kangas became deeply concerned about the effects of population on development. She felt that a book which explored more than just the demographic aspects of the population problem would make a significant contribution. Her objective in writing this book was to be honest about the shortcomings of the programs and, at the same time, provide hope for actions that can be taken to achieve population stabilization.

She believed that without committed leadership, nationally and internationally, there is no hope for solving the population problem. Her hope was that this book would make a contribution to a better awareness of the problem in the United States and in each of the five countries described here.

STATEMENT ON POPULATION STABILIZATION

In preparation for World Population Year in 1984, Population Communication requested that national leaders from every country in the world sign the following statement. Population Communication challenges readers of this book, after having completed the book, to reread the following statement and re-evaluate their attitudes and opinions on worldwide population stabilization.

Mankind has many challenges: to obtain a lasting peace among nations; to preserve the quality of the environment; to conserve natural resources at a sustainable level; to advance the economic and social progress of the less developed nations; and to stabilize population growth.

At present there are 76 million more births than deaths on our planet each year. If present birth rates continue, by the year 2000 there will be 100 million more births than deaths. A billion people have been added in the last 13 years and the next billion will be added in 12 years.

Degradation of the world's environment, income inequality, and the potential for conflict exist today because of over-consumption and overpopulation. If this unprecedented population growth continues, future generations of children will not have adequate food, housing, medical care, education, earth resources, and employment opportunities.

We believe that the time has come now to recognize the worldwide necessity to stop population growth within the near future and for each country to adopt the necessary policies and programs to do so, consistent with its own culture and aspirations.

To enhance the integrity of the individual and the quality of life for all, we believe that all nations should participate in setting goals and programs for population stabilization. Measures for this purpose should be voluntary and should maintain individual human rights and beliefs.

We urge national leaders to take an active personal role in promoting effective policies and programs. Attention should be given to setting realistic goals and timetables; encouraging active participation of communities in designing and implementing their own programs; and developing appropriate economic and social policies.

We call upon donor nations and institutions to be more generous in their support of population programs in those developing nations requesting such assistance.

Recognizing that early population stabilization is in the interest of all nations, we earnestly hope that leaders around the world share our views and join with us in this great undertaking for the well-being and happiness of people everywhere.

Robert W. Gillespie
Population Communication

POPULATION AND SURVIVAL

Chapter 1

India: Racing on a Treadmill

India is a world in itself, a vast subcontinent of stark contrasts between the remnants of its past and the realities of its overpopulated present. It is a small universe of human diversity, a microcosm of humanity in conflict with itself.

One of the world's oldest civilizations, India must now count time as its worst enemy. The world's largest democracy must combat the tragedy of a social system thousands of years old, based on inequality between man and the limited resources of the country. And this nation's primary battle must be waged against the one element pervading all Indian life, art, and aspirations: the traditional ideal of fertility.

Much has happened, but little has changed since the veteran India-watcher, Martin Hürlimann, observed in 1966:

> Today the name 'India' no longer merely conjures
> up vague images of a strange and distant land; we
> have seen the apostles of non-violence taking to the
> sword, and we have heard the twin voices of national
> pride and personal humility; extremes of materialism
> clash with extremes of idealism, the urge to contem-
> plation and self-abnegation with the urge to action,
> the backward pull of age-old traditions with a
> desire to move forward. Political, economic and
> social problems are mounting alarmingly and continue
> to mount even as attempts are made to solve them.
> A rapidly increasing population . . . is trying to
> discover what role it can play in the twentieth
> century and in the great family of nations. For
> India is in the throes of a revolution which goes
> to the very roots of her being. Despite her great
> antiquity as a people, despite the fact that she had
> already developed a culture and way of life of her

*own thousands of years ago, she finds herself today
confronted by a world which no longer permits isolationism. A people that once lived outside time is
fighting to gain its historical identity.*

Against a backdrop of occasional violence, widespread
illiteracy, severe poverty and unemployment, and rampant undernutrition that has kept starvation on its doorstep, the nation
adds 15.3 million people to its population each year. However,
with recent trends in agricultural technology, and good weather
for the past four years, India has been able to feed its population.

In mid-1984, the population of India stood at 714 million,
nearly 80 million more than the mid-1978 populations of North
America (256 million) and Latin America (378 million) combined.
And despite its preeminence as the first nation in the world
to adopt a national family planning program (in 1951), the
nation's population is continuing to grow at the rate of 2.23
percent per year. If this growth rate continues, and the
country's crude annual death rate of 15 per 1,000 remains
steady, India's population will double in just under 31 years.

Today, India is second in population size only to the
People's Republic of China, which in mid-1982 had an estimated
population of 1 billion. If India's current growth trends
persist, however, in 1998 the country will have more people
than China does today.

To say that India's social, economic, and political future
is in jeopardy is to vastly understate the problems facing it.
Overpopulation limits efforts at national development. The
overwhelming reality of its size frustrates attempts to describe its socioeconomic and demographic characteristics and
problems. With a land area just under 1.3 million square miles
(about two-thirds the size of Europe, excluding the Soviet
Union), India ranks as the world's seventh largest country.
The density of its population, however, means that 15 percent
of the world's population is crowded into only 2.2 percent of
the world's total land area.

Just one of India's 22 states and nine union territories
--Uttar Pradesh, with a mid-1984 population of nearly 12 mil-
lion--could itself be considered the world's seventh largest
country in population size. The nation's second largest (and
equally poverty stricken) state, Bihar, had a mid-1984 population of nearly 77 million, which would qualify it for eleventh
place, just ahead of Mexico. On top of this, extreme cultural,
regional, and geographical differences impose developmental
constraints of their own.

HISTORICAL AND CULTURAL BACKGROUND

The origins of India's earliest inhabitants are lost in
the mists of prehistory. Three major racial groups have

emerged in India today: the Dravidians, the Mongols, and the
Indo-Europeans who in their sacred scripts use the term *Aryan*,
which despite its misuse in modern times, actually comes from
the word *Arya*, "freeborn" or "noble." It is generally agreed,
however, that from the great mass migrations before the dawn
of history, that of the Dravidians proved to be the largest,
and their culture dominated the area long before the arrival
of the first Indo-Aryans brought Hinduism to the subcontinent.

About 1500 *B.C.*, successive waves of Indo-Aryans began to
arrive from Persia. As they settled in and conquered the last
of the fortified towns in the Mohenjodaro civilization, a number of kingdoms were established in various parts of northern
India. The Persians' sacrificial cult beliefs began to expand,
and the socio-religious synthesis that is Hinduism found its
first roots.

The Rig Veda, the oldest of the many Indo-Aryan texts
(Vedas) held sacred by Hindus, was composed around 1200-100
B.C. It depicts the Persian invaders as shepherds and warriors
organized in family groups and village communities. The arts
of plowing, pottery making, and weaving became known to them
only after their contact with the ancient Indus civilization.
That contact, however, also gave rise to a much less progressive social system: slavery was introduced to India. Upon
meeting the dark-skinned and militarily weaker Dravidians, the
lighter-skinned Indo-Aryans quickly made them their slaves.
And India's caste system was born.

Hinduism and the Caste System

The Indo-Aryans, who wrote and adhered to the teachings of
the Vedas, saw themselves as members of a single "genus of
respectable men" (*arya-varna*) and as "the humans" (*manusa*).
Their code of conduct included the offering of sacrifices to
the Vedic gods (*devas*) and the fighting and enslaving of their
"natural enemies," non-Aryan "nonhumans" (*dasyu-varna*), who
were considered by their birth and morality to be fit only for
service. The concept of a ranking system involving more than
two birth groups appeared only after 1000 *B.C.*, when descend-
ants of these early Aryans began to settle in the upper Ganges
region and build a more complex society of towns and states.
The revered Hindu lawgiver, Manu, made it the sacred duty of
every couple to beget a large number of children. In the case
of a husband's impotence, a wife was encouraged to engage in
extramarital relations for the purpose of increasing the fold.
As the society grew in size and complexity, the Vedic texts
became more elaborate in the specifications of moral lineage
and conduct, culminating in the moral code book, *Dharma-sastra*,
composed by the Manu School between 200 *B.C.* and 200 *A.D.*

According to the Rig Veda, the four major caste divisions
or hereditary social groups sprung from the body of a primeval

god, Prajapati. From his mouth came the *Brahmins*, from his
arms the *Kshatriyas*, from his loins the *Vaisyas*, and from his
feet the *Sudras*. Although all of these *varnas*, or castes,
shared one original natural substance, the body of Prajapati,
they were thought to be born to different stations and occupations as symbolized by the parts of the original code body from
which they emerged. The nature of these differences was delineated by the concept of Vedic sacrifice, which was seen as
vital to the maintenance of the natural and moral order of the
cosmos.

Sacrifice required exchanges between gods and men. Gods,
the wielders of *brahma* (divine power), were seen as the
ultimate source of bodily existence and well-being; men were
the suppliers of the food necessary for the gods' sustenance.
The ritual offering of food through sacrifice thus created a
bond between gods and men; it also created a ranked relationship between them. Only pure food was sacrificed to gods by
men; after they had "eaten," the gods returned their "leavings"
for men to eat. Men came to regard their own food leavings as
contaminated by saliva and therefore as impure and valueless to
others of their caste.

Rank in this ancient moral order was thought of as being
based less on established possessions than on generosity. Gods
were of higher rank than men not so much because they possessed
divine power, but because they were incomparably generous in
bestowing that power on men. Because they could not return
this gift, men were of lower rank. Men could give the gods the
most valued foods, but they could not equal the value of the
divine power contained in the gods' gift to men. And this
relationship was extended to the various "natural genera" within the Vedic society as a whole; it formed the basis for
explicitly mandated relationships between the castes.

Thus the Brahmins, the possessors of divine knowledge
passed from the mouth of Prajapati, became the preeminent
priestly group. They taught the Vedas, performed animal
sacrifices for the Kshatriyas and Vaisyas, and accepted gifts
from them in exchange. In the process, they acquired such
privileges as exemption from taxes and personal inviolability.
The claims of purity of birth that added to the Brahmins'
prestige were later only occasionally challenged on the grounds
that learning is the primary criterion of being a Brahmin.

The Kshatriyas, thought to be endowed with royal (but not
divine) power, became the princes, landowners, and military
leaders. Their mission in life was to fight enemies, give
gifts and food to the Brahmins, and protect the Vaisyas. In
exchange, the Kshatriyas received a share in the leavings of
the sacrifice from the Brahmins and wealth from the Vaisyas.
The Vaisyas, born from the loins of Prajapati, were a more
subservient group thought to possess great productive power.
Their mission in life was to produce wealth for the Brahmins
and Kshatriyas through agriculture, commerce, and animal

herding and to give a share of their earnings in taxes to the Kshatriyas in exchange for protection. Eventually, the Vaisyas became artisans and traders. The business of the Sudras, as the Vedas make abundantly clear, was to serve the three higher castes.

The lowly Sudras, having emerged from the feet of Prajapati, were considered to be "once-born," while the Brahmins, Kshatriyas, and Vaisyas, having become godlike humans through a second, ritual birth during sacrifice, were considered to be "twice-born." The once-born Sudra (servant) was not to hear the sacred Vedic words spoken in the temple, nor was he to sacrifice directly or receive the gods' leavings. Instead, Sudras were to exchange with the twice-born in the same way that the twice-born exchanged with the gods.

Over time, these four main castes broke up into subcastes; there are now some 3,000 subcastes throughout India, each with its own code of conduct, idea of *dharma* (divinely prescribed duty), concept of virtue and list of taboos, and communal laws. Given the existence of these virtually autonomous communities within communities in India today, it becomes clear that Hinduism is as much a way of life as a religion, and that the nation's struggle to maintain a strong yet democratic form of federal government becomes a struggle against the traditional nature of Indian society.

From Caste to Outcaste

As caste occupations and spiritual duties became firmly delineated and enforced, a new social class arose. Non-Aryan Sudras, whose work and dietary habits brought them into contact with substances considered to be polluting by the Brahmins, became "outcastes" or "untouchables."

The most damning of the occupations and dietary "lapses" leading to untouchability were, and still are: taking of a life for a living, a category including, for example, butchers and fishermen; killing or disposing of dead cattle or working with their hides (tanning, leather working); work that brings a person into contact with "unclean" emissions of the human body; and eating the flesh of cattle or of domestic pigs and chickens in violation of Hindu vegetarianism, a category into which most of the primitive tribes fall.

Traditionally, untouchables have been denied access to temples, to most schools, and to wells from which higher castes draw water; an untouchable may handle raw food destined for the table of a caste Hindu, but may not participate in its preparation or serving. Even the shadow of an untouchable was formerly considered to be polluting to a caste Hindu; in southern India, some untouchable groups were forced to live a nocturnal existence.

The violent personal and group persecution of untouchables, the lowest strata of society and therefore the scapegoats for

its ills--persecution which continues even today--led to early
revolts by some Hindu sects. As these sects broke away from
Hinduism, new religious communities were formed; over the years,
many untouchables have sought some degree of freedom through
conversion to Christianity, Islam, or Buddhism. It was, in
fact, a widespread revolt against the rigid and ruthless caste
system that gave rise in the sixth century B.C. to Buddhism and
Jainism.

Buddhism Conquers Hinduism

     Both Siddhartha Gautama, who later became a *buddha* (en-
lightened one) and founded Buddhism, and Vardhamana (later
known as Mahavira, "great hero"), who founded Jainism, were
born to the Hindu Kshatriya caste. Their followers included
many princes--and in the case of the Jains, merchants--all of
whom joined Gautama Buddha and Mahavira in their renunciation
of the Hindu caste system, ritualistic sacrifices of animals
and divine control by the Brahmins. Both preached nonviolence,
and since trade and commerce did not involve killing, Jains
eventually became the great financiers of western India, while
Buddhists tended to excel in the mercantile trades.
     As Buddhism rapidly spread through the Ganges Valley to
the Punjab, to Afghanistan and even south beyond the Vindhya
mountains of India, Hinduism fell away before the radiance of
the benign "living god," Buddha. It would not be until a
thousand years later that Hinduism would experience a revival
that would again put the Brahmins in charge.
     The Jains also lost ground to Buddhism and with it the
protection of powerful princes. Nevertheless, the Jains have
survived to this day in India as a relatively small yet active
and highly disciplined community.
     Between 180 B.C. and 200 A.D., Sakas, Parthians, and
Kushans from the region now known as Iran, and Greeks made a
series of invasions into India. Although these people added
to the ethnic diversity of India, they did little to change
the basic culture of the society into which they were assimilated. Until Christian and Mohammedan invaders began to
arrive later from the west, all of India was cut off from the
rest of the world.

The Hindu Revival

     The birth of Christ set off a swelling tide of deism
throughout the world. In India, the old Vedic gods Brahma
and Indra were replaced by Vishnu, the Penetrator or Protector,
who also reveals himself as Krishna and Rama, legendary figures
probably based on actual princes who lived during the Vedic
period. Beside Vishnu stands the equally powerful Siva, the

god of dancing, destruction, and death, whose fertility is symbolized by the lingam, a stylized phallus. The principal gods, their consorts, and acolytes began to take on innumerable forms. Siva's wife Parvati, for example, is also the fearsome mother-goddess Kali Durga.

As Arab invaders occupied Sind in the northwest in 712 A.D. and Muhammad Ghuri conquered major parts of northern India between 1193 and 1206, Islam nudged out Buddhism where it had been strongest, in the areas now known as Pakistan, Bangladesh, and Kashmir.

In response to the advent of Islam, Hinduism took on a new emotionalism. Temples became larger; their carved exteriors and interiors became more elaborate and often erotic. The lingam, symbolizing Siva's strength and fertility, became the central focus of countless sculptures representing the pantheon of gods. In a paroxysm of revival, Hinduism became dedicated to fertility, the life force.

While many of the Muslim conquerors showed great tolerance toward Hinduism, many did not. Particularly in northern India, Hindu temples were sacked and destroyed along with Buddhist monasteries.

From Mughal to Viceroy

Beginning at the end of the twelfth century, Muslim forces stepped up their campaigns to extend Islamic domination over India. Hindus, fighting to preserve their caste laws, were often ruthlessly persecuted as new dynasties were founded and new kingdoms were established deeper in the Hindu Deccan. There were now two Indias.

It was left to the Mughal Babar, a descendant of Genghis Khan, to amalgamate the two Indias of the Hindus and Muslims into a united Indian state. After conquering Delhi in 1526, Babar founded a dynasty destined to become the most powerful in India since that of the Buddhist emperors.

For two hundred years, the mighty Mughals ruled from the Himalayas to the Deccan Plateau in central India. The era was marked by courtly opulence, artistic splendor, and extraordinary religious tolerance.

But the Mughal Empire, glorious and powerful as it was, was not India. During the sixteenth and seventeenth centuries, the Portuguese, who had brought Christianity to India, were followed by Dutch, English, and French traders. All of these groups were seeking to control India's lucrative spice and silk trade with the West. To this end, the newcomers established trading posts in the country's coastal regions and competed with each other for control over the various rulers outside the Mughal Empire. The competition was intense and often bloody; the Hindu strongholds did not fall easily.

As the Mughal Empire declined, the new Christian invaders gained important footholds in India. The Portuguese had con-

quered Goa in 1510 and the Dutch were entrenched in the country's southern coastal regions. But it was the struggle
between the French and English that was to result in the
ascendency of new and entirely culturally alien masters over
India. The French finally retreated, and a charter granted
by Elizabeth I to a group of London merchants gave them a
trading monopoly with India. Thus the East India Company was
able to expand steadily and systematically into a major enterprise which England was prepared to defend with all her might.

In the beginning, it appears that England's interest in
India was much less imperial than commercial. England's
strategy was to play rival Indian states off against each
other to gain British control over trade in the area, thus
strengthening London's position as a center of world trade.
This, of course, necessitated the use of both military and
political weapons, which eventually resulted in the submission
of the warlike Mahrattas, Sikhs, and Rajputs to British suprem-
acy. Members of these once proudly independent groups became
the fierce elite of the Anglo-Indian army.

The British Era

In 1858, the British governor-general in Calcutta was
elevated to the position of Viceroy of India. With England's
rule thus established over India, Queen Victoria assumed an
additional title in 1877, that of empress of India. It was
not until December 1911, however, that a British monarch set
foot for the first time on Indian soil. The occasion was the
crowning of King George V as emperor of India and the announcement that the empire's capital would be transferred from Calcutta, where the viceroy had resided, to Delhi. A new capital
was designed, and a complex of breathtakingly magnificent
government buildings formed the foundation of New Delhi's
present urban sprawl.

Although British control over India would last for 90
years, only about three-fifths of the country was under direct
British rule. The rest of the country was ruled by Indian
princes in 562 states; the dominion of these princes, however,
was subject to British authority.

From the very beginning, a strong enmity existed between
the English and their colonial subjects in India. A relatively
cohesive administration, characterized by a strong and efficient
civil service, was instrumental in India's emergence as an
independent and increasingly modern state. But that same civil
service is now viewed by many progressive Indians as a firmly
entrenched, old-fashioned and self-serving system which presents
a major stumbling block to modern development. Throughout
their oftentimes heavy-handed and violent control, the English
failed to recognize the fact that their tenure of control in
India was limited. A few liberals sympathized with Indian

yearnings for independence and did their best to see that an eventually independent India would be strong enough--administratively, at least--to withstand future attempts at imperialistic invasion.

The Indian National Congress (later to become the Congress Party of Nehru) was founded in 1885. From initial efforts to achieve better representation of Indians in the administrative services, the congress went on to fight for freedom from foreign rule. Between 1919 and 1939, the association of Indians in provincial governments was gradually increased. But reforms usually came too late to satisfy the Indian leadership and the public they served. An essentially nonviolent civil disobedience or noncooperation movement became a vital element of the struggle for freedom and produced perhaps the most unlikely of heroes. Mohandas Gandhi, the diffident man who came to be known as Mahatma (the great soul) to millions of his countrymen, became the backbone of the movement.

Gandhi and the Struggle for Independence

Gandhi's childhood home was steeped in Vaisnavism (worship of the Hindu god Vishnu) with a strong tinge of Jainism. He thus took for granted *ahimsa* (noninjury to all living things), vegetarianism, fasting for self-purification, and religious tolerance. His father, who had little formal education, was dewan (chief minister) of the capital city of a small Gujarati principality and later the dewan of a larger princely state, Rajkot. He was adept at juggling relations between the capricious princes, their long-suffering subjects, and the headstrong British political officers then in power.

Having earned a law degree in England, Gandhi eschewed the notion of trying to set up a law practice in India, in favor of a move to South Africa. He was totally unprepared for the racial discrimination and persecution that was to be heaped upon him, a non-European--as it was upon the large Indian commercial communities in Durban and Pretoria. These experiences became his moments of truth. Henceforth, he would devote his life to the defense of the dignity of man in general, and of Indians in particular.

In 1920, Gandhi refashioned the 35-year-old National Congress Party into an effective political instrument of nationalism. From annual meetings of upper-middle-class Indians, the congress became a mass organization with its roots in small towns and villages. Gandhi's program of nonviolent noncooperation with the British government extended boycotts from English manufacturers to other institutions operated or aided by the English in India: legislatures, courts, offices, and schools.

The program electrified the nation, erased the fear of foreign rule, and led to the arrests of thousands of Satya-

grahis (those committed to "firmness in truth"), who defied
laws and cheerfully lined up for prison. Eventually, Gandhi
himself was tried for sedition and sent to prison. Upon his
release he found that the Congress Party had split in two.

In 1931, Gandhi attended the Round Table Conference in
London as the sole representative of the Indian National Congress. The conference, however, was a sore disappointment;
rather than focusing on the transfer of power from the English,
it concentrated on the problem of the Indian minorities.

Disillusioned by growing evidence that Congress Party
leaders were not truly dedicated to the principle of nonviolence, Gandhi resigned from the party in 1934. Having turned
from political activity, he took up the cause of building the
country "from the bottom up" by promoting literacy among
India's rural population, developing such cottage industries
as spinning and weaving to supplement the earnings of the
underemployed peasantry, and evolving a system of education
best suited to the needs of the people. His respite from
political life, however, was short-lived.

With the outbreak of World War II, the nationalist struggle
in India came to a crisis. Gandhi abhorred fascism and all it
stood for, but he also despised war. The Indian National Congress, on the other hand, was not committed to pacifism; it was
prepared to support the British war effort so long as Indian
self-government was assured.

The British equivocation on the transfer of power to the
Indians and the encouragement given by high British officials
to conservative and communal forces promoting discord between
Muslims and Hindus forced Gandhi in the summer of 1942 to
demand an immediate withdrawal of the English from India.

Over the next two years, trilateral negotiations among
leaders of the Congress Party, the Muslim League, and the
British government culminated in the Mountbatten Plan of June
3, 1947. In mid-August 1947, the new sovereign states of India
and Pakistan were formed.

The partition of India and the fragmentation that continues to plague the country today are seen by many as proof that
the democratic principles to which Gandhi dedicated his life
are antithetical to the very foundations of Indian society.
The greatest irony, however, is that Gandhi's light should have
been extinguished not by a foreigner or a Muslim, but by a
fellow Hindu.

On January 30, 1948, only a few days after Gandhi's final
fast had halted rioting in India's capital city, and as he was
on his way to evening prayer in Delhi, the gentle nationalist
and idealistic champion of nonviolence was shot to death by a
young Hindu fanatic.

INDIA TODAY

The national unity for which Gandhi gave his life still
eludes India. The mass migration of Muslims from India to the
newly formed Pakistan at the time of partition left the country with an overwhelming (83 percent) majority of Hindus of
all sects. About 11 percent of the population is Muslim, while
Christians make up about 2.6 percent, and Sikhs 1.9 percent.
Buddhists now make up only 0.7 percent of the population; most
of these are neo-Buddhists, Harijans primarily in Maharashtra,
who adopted Buddhism during the late 1950s. The highly urban
Jains comprise about 0.5 percent of the population, and are
concentrated in the western states of Gujarat, Rajasthan, and
Maharashtra. Other religious groups making up less than 0.4
percent of the population include the Parsis, who practice
Zoroastrianism and are known for their enterprise and low
fertility. The Parsis are concentrated on India's west coast,
with 70 percent of their members in greater Bombay.

On top of this religious diversity, India's vast regional
and linguistic diversity creates a picture of extreme hetero-
geneity. The 1961 census reported more than 1,650 languages
considered to be mother tongues, many of them dialects spoken
by small groups of people.

Hindi, a northern language, is spoken with minor variations
by about 30 percent of the population and was designated the
official administrative language of the country following independence. English, however, continues to be used, in addition
to Hindi, for all parliamentary business and for communication
between the central government and states that have not adopted
Hindi as their official language. Fourteen other major languages specified in the constitution were reported in 1971 to
be the mother tongue of nearly 58 percent of the population.

The administrative problems posed by such language variation was alleviated somewhat by a redrawing of state boundaries
in 1956. This resulted in major linguistic groups being drawn
together under the same administrative jurisdictions. However,
serious communications problems remain.

Overall administration by state governments is as uneven
as one would expect in a country harboring sharply contrasting
degrees of development, caste, and cultural cohesion. One
approach to analyzing basic standards of living would be to
disaggregate India into thirds and give the top spot to those
states that are most modernized and developed across the board.
These would include Punjab, Haryana, Maharashtra, Kerala, and
Tamil Nadu. Here, people enjoy a level of state-provided
services on a general par with people in Thailand and the
Philippines.

At the bottom are such states as Uttar Pradesh, Bihar,
Orissa, Rajasthan, and Himachal Pradesh. The delivery of all
services in these states, whether it be credit to farmers,
irrigation water, educational facilities, or family planning

and health services, tends to lag measurably behind the
national average and far below the performance level achieved
by the top third. Here, the level of state-provided services
is minimal, undeveloped, and about on a par with some of the
less developed countries in Africa. In the middle is a wide
range of states in which services provided are generally equal
to those found in Egypt and the least developed parts of Indonesia, but better than those existing in neighboring Pakistan
and Bangladesh.

While trying to get a handle on India's diversity, it is
important to remember that India is very much a dual economy,
with roughly 15 percent of its population solidly ensconced in
the latter part of the twentieth century in terms of modernization, education, economic mobility, and access to material
wealth. The other 85 percent, however, are generally illiterate, tradition bound, superstitious, increasingly landless,
and frequently hungry, and have little hope of rapid improvement in their life quality.

Scheduled Castes, Scheduled Tribes, Scheduled Discrimination

The Indian caste system has a well-earned reputation of
being the scourge of democracy and development. It locks the
individual in and development out. What the Westerner views
as Indian arrogance is actually an ingrained sense of station.

Upward mobility to most Indians means the acceptance of
karma, adherence to dharma, and the expectation that the next
life will be better. A person's occupational range, marriage
partner, education, and social privilege are all determined
in varying degrees by his or her ancestry. But, with rank
prescribed by the potential for generosity, the caste system
provides a system of social security for child-mothers with
infants slung on their hips as well as self- or family-
mutilated persons who work the streets, hands outstretched,
murmuring "Baksheesh, baksheesh" (money, money). In this
atmosphere, ubiquitous beggars thrive; sometimes they earn
more than the nation's underemployed poor. But giving is a
matter of duty, rather than of compassion. There is, in fact,
no word in Hindi or any other Indian language for compassion.
The nearest Western expression for Hindu-inspired generosity
is noblesse oblige.

B. R. Ambedkar, regarded as the "father of India's constitution" and the greatest Harijan (untouchable) leader
outside of government, finally came to the conclusion that
Harijans (listed in the constitution as being among the
"scheduled castes," while tribal Hindus are designated "scheduled tribes") could never receive just treatment if they remained in the Hindu fold.

Today, 15 percent of India's population, 110 million
people, fall into one or another of the scheduled castes

designated by India's constitution. While about 82 percent of
India's 1971 population lived in rural villages, the percentage
of scheduled castes living in rural areas was 89.3. In some
states (i.e., Punjab, Bihar, Orissa, Assam, and West Bengal),
more than 90 percent of the Harijans lived in rural areas.
Landlessness is the major economic problem facing the nation's
Harijans today; in 1971, only about 9 million Harijans had
landholdings, and these were all less than five acres in size.
The major social problem facing Harijans today, however, is
still persecution. Stuart Auerbach (1982a) reported in the
Washington Post:

> *India ended 1981 with its second massacre of*
> *untouchables in six weeks, causing Prime Minister*
> *Indira Gandhi to plead for greater security for*
> *harijans and threatening the rule of her chief*
> *minister in India's most populous state of Uttar*
> *Pradesh, where both recent attacks on harijans*
> *occurred.*

> *In the latest attack, four or five armed men*
> *at dusk on Wednesday December 30, 1981 entered*
> *the village of Sadhofur, about 15 miles north*
> *of the tourist center of Agra, where the Taj*
> *Mahal is located, and started shooting at hari-*
> *jans. In 15 minutes, they killed 10 persons--*
> *including five women and two children--and*
> *severely wounded two others . . .*

> *The killings in Sadhofur followed by exactly*
> *six weeks the Nov. 18 unprovoked daylight slaying*
> *of 24 untouchables, including seven women, in the*
> *village of Deoli, 18 miles to the north.*

> *While these mass killings are an extreme*
> *manifestation of anti-harijan activities, attacks*
> *on untouchables in modern India are increasing*
> *rather than subsiding. [According to government*
> *figures released in March 1981] the number of*
> *'atrocities' against untouchables has tripled in*
> *the three years beginning in 1976, and are con-*
> *tinuing to climb. . . .*

> *Indian sociologists have noted that most of*
> *the attacks on untouchables come either from*
> *small landowners, who fear that their economic*
> *security will be threatened if the large landless*
> *harijans assert their rights to such things as*
> *minimum wages, or from low-caste Hindu laborers.*

The potential political ramifications of the continuing
persecution of Harijans, particularly in Indira Gandhi's home

state of Uttar Pradesh, could be severe for the prime minister.
In 1980, Gandhi toppled the Janata Party government of Uttar
Pradesh on the grounds that police attacks on untouchables
proved that the state government was unable to maintain law
and order. Moreover, as Auerbach also points out, some politicians charge that the recent conversion of 2,000 Harijans in
the southern state of Tamil Nadu was engineered by the oil-rich
Islamic states of the Persian Gulf, who had bought the untouchables' loyalty in an attempt to launch a psychological attack
on India by diluting the hold of its Hindu majority on the
nation. Most observers, however, believe the Harijans converted because they were tired of their miserable lot in life.

While little has been done to upgrade the lives of the
scheduled tribes since the mid-1960s, India has been running
what many call the world's largest affirmative-action program.
In 1961, the literacy rate of the scheduled castes was half
that of the general population's literacy rate of 28 percent.
In 1966-67, however, the government launched a program of
government-sponsored university scholarships for members of
the scheduled castes with funds to cover 90,000 such scholarships.

Although these scholarships enabled chosen representatives
of the scheduled castes to climb the educational ladder, many
found their university degrees did not offer them either economic or social mobility. Even the most highly educated Harijans often found themselves doing work at their educational
level while being paid at their caste level, and still being
subjected to the discriminatory rules applied to the majority
of uneducated Harijans.

The Educational Picture

According to the 1981 census, only about 36 percent of all
Indians are able to read and write. Literacy among males (47
percent) is almost twice as high as among females (25 percent).
Low as these figures are, they nevertheless reflect a substantial, if slow, advance over the literacy situation at the
time of the 1951 census, when a mere 17 percent of the total
population (24 percent of males and 8.0 percent of females)
were reported to be literate.

Literacy rates tend to understate the case of literacy
somewhat, since these rates are based on total population
numbers, which include growing numbers of pre-school-aged
children under five. On the other hand, the fact of rudimentary literacy should not be taken as an indicator of educational achievement: a person who is able to make out street
signs and write up a grocery list, for example, is not necessarily able to read a newspaper. (The ability to read a newspaper, in any case, is of little importance to the nation's
rural population, nearly all of whom have no access whatsoever
to the nation's 850 or so daily newspapers.)

Even basic literacy, however, opens the door to awareness. But, as the literacy trends presented in the following table make clear, that door has been opening very slowly over the past two decades.

TABLE 1.1 *Literacy Rate 1901-81*

Year	Percentage Literacy		
	Total	Males	Females
1901	5.4	9.8	0.6
1911	5.9	10.6	1.1
1921	7.2	12.2	1.8
1931	9.5	15.6	2.9
1941	16.1	24.9	7.3
1951	16.7	25.0	7.9
1961	24.0	34.4	13.0
1971	29.5	39.4	18.7
1981	36.1	46.6	24.8

Source: Visaria and Visaria, 1981.

Despite the rise in literacy, however, the nation's high annual population growth rates of 2.0 percent during 1961-71 and 2.23 percent during 1971-81 mean that the actual number of illiterates in the total population as well as among population aged 10 and over increased. Between 1971 and 1981, the number of illiterate persons in India grew from nearly 387 million to more than 440 million.

Educational progress in the country was relatively rapid between 1950 and 1970, when the number of primary schools more than doubled from 540,000 to 1.1 million. In 1979-80, education received 11.6 percent (nearly Rs. 30 billion, or $3.3 billion) of the 15.1 percent of central and state development budgets allotted for human resources development (education, health, and family planning). Capital expenditures for human resources development, however, tend to be deferred when resources become scarce: under the Indian government's sixth

Five-Year Plan (1980-85), education and health command only 3.0 percent each of the national budget. Nevertheless, the government continues to emphasize the need for increased and higher-quality education, particularly at the primary level. It is also developing a program to increase literacy at the adult level.

Many rural children have no access to primary-school facilities whatsoever; primary enrollment in 1979-80 was 69 percent of children in the 6-14 age bracket, as compared with a mere 22 percent in the early 1950s. But many obstacles stand in the way of further progress.

In July 1980, Roger Grawe of the World Bank found that 70 percent of all primary-school students drop out of school before grade 5. Because of this high dropout rate, literacy remains low among young teenagers, particularly among girls. Moreover, the high incidence of children required to repeat a grade adds to the dropout rate because, even without school fees, other school expenses are more than many poor families can afford. Attitudes toward education by the nation's rural poor are also often negative because of their dependency on child labor. These attitudes will probably change only in the presence of rising rural incomes from increased opportunities for adult employment, particularly among rural women, whose lives and attitudes are severely restricted by their lack of education.

In addition to the predominance of male over female literacy and an urban literacy rate that is persistently about twice that of the rural level, sharp variations exist between the states. Literacy rates in 1981 ranged from 69 percent (74 percent of males and 65 percent of females) in the progressive, communist-led state of Kerala to only 26-27 percent in the heavily traditional and economically depressed states of Bihar, Jammu, Kashmir, Rajasthan, and Uttar Pradesh. In the latter four states, where the status of females is particularly low and early marriage is the norm, the proportion of literate females is a mere 11-15 percent.

While India suffers from lack of education at the bottom of the socioeconomic scale, it suffers from overeducation in the upper-middle and upper classes. Education, the time-honored mark of the Brahmin, has come to be regarded as the prime status symbol for all high-caste Hindus and upper-class non-Hindus. And the status increases according to the degree of educational achievement. The nation's upper classes are swarming with Ph.D.s; even those failing their doctoral examinations will often advertise their respectability by following their names on business cards with such notations as "Ph.D. (failed)."

The inability of the country to absorb such large numbers of highly educated people and to provide incomes commensurate with their expectations has led to large emigrations of people destined for positions in foreign universities and as engineers, doctors, public health administrators and medical technicians. United Nations agencies and the World Bank, for example, draw heavily on India's abundant reserve of highly trained but underemployed people.

The Status of Women

It might be assumed that a nation with a woman at its helm is a nation with enlightened views regarding sexual equality. In the fragmented Indian society, however, where social atti- tudes, like the quality of life itself, depend on who you are and where you live, this generalization stands up no better than any other.

While a thin stratum of high-caste and financially privi- leged women enjoy a wide range of educational and occupational opportunities, the typical Indian woman leads a life proscribed by male domination that has caused a historical blurring of religion and law. Although the sacred Hindu texts regarded men and women as being equal in God's eyes, the ancient lawgivers reduced women's status to that of chattel. According to sociol- ogist Chandrasekhar (1965):

> The nonparticipation of nearly half the total
> population in the life of the community and the
> nation is a source of colossal wastage. Today,
> the sole function of these women is to produce
> unwanted babies and suffer from improvident
> maternity, but once they are given the benefits
> of purposeful and rational education, an economic
> revolution can be set in motion. The women of
> India can then become intelligent homemakers and,
> when necessary, able breadwinners. They will
> refuse to be herded into the married state to
> become victims of the dowry system, and they will
> plan their families and take pride in healthy and
> happy children rather than in costly ceremonies
> and jewelry.

In the nearly 15 years that have passed since Chandrasekhar made the above observations, India has made significant strides toward economic development while securing military dominance over southern Asia. There have been few changes, however, in the status of women.

Today's typical Indian woman remains uneducated, bound to a domestic role, subservient to men throughout her life, and physically weakened by a life of neglect (which results in mal- nutrition and extreme vulnerability to disease), and by a primary, culture-dictated function that results in repeated pregnancies.

Although female infanticide is no longer sanctioned by society, India's male-to-female ratio of 1,069 to 1,000 makes

it one of the few countries in the world to have an excess of
males (or a deficit of females). The United States, by way
of contrast, has a ratio of 950 men to 1,000 women.

Except in Kerala, where the status of women is relatively
high, males outnumber females in all of the states of India.
In 1981, there were 11-14 percent more males than females in
the northern states of Assam, Punjab, Uttar Pradesh, and
Haryana, and 23 million more males than females in the country
as a whole. According to Visaria and Jain (1976), "The primary
factor responsible for the excess of males appears to be the
higher risks of death suffered by women due to high maternal
mortality and the neglect of females, both in childhood and in
adult ages."

To Hindus, childlessness is a sign of extreme weakness;
it is preferable to have female children than no children at
all. But while the scarcity of employment opportunities for
women and the dowry system mean that female children grow up
to be economic liabilities for their families, the value of
male children to the family is at once economic and spiritual.
The ceremony called *sraddha*, which is conducted following a
person's death and includes the splitting of the deceased's
skull and lighting the funeral pyre to release the soul, can
be performed only by a son. In the absence of a son, the
ceremony cannot be performed; in the absence of sraddha, a
soul is not likely to attain salvation.

The death of a husband has also traditionally been accompanied by supreme sacrifice on the part of the wife, who is
bound to him both in life and death. *Suttee*, the suicidal
(although not always voluntary) burning of a wife either on
her husband's funeral pyre or by self-immolation, has, until
modern times, served as proof of a Hindu wife's devotion to
her husband. Although that practice is dying out, another
traditional manifestation of the low status of females in India
is still to be seen: the selling of females into slavery is
still not uncommon among the poorest and most backward segments
of Indian society.

A far less cruel form of servitude is also widely practiced in India. Among the higher castes and more affluent
families, it is common to import a poor "country cousin" to
join her wealthier relatives as a serving-girl. Since most
Indian servants are untouchables, and therefore cannot serve
food to people of caste, food service is facilitated by the
presence of a serving-girl of caste. In exchange, the girl
receives the benefits of free food, lodging, medical care, and
clothing, and often receives primary-school privileges as well.

Marriage, Divorce, and Widowhood

In India there is almost as much diversity in marriage
customs as there are castes, subcastes, and noncastes. Some

caste communities require members to marry only within their subcaste, sometimes only within their own kinship groups; others require members to seek marriage partners of the same caste, but from outside of their particular community. But whether a couple's marriage is arranged by their parents (still the most common practice) or the couple marries for love (an increasing phenomenon among urban, educated groups), Indians in general agree on one point: marriage is a family affair.

Marriage is still as much a financial exchange (and there-fore, bond) between families as it is a preservation of blood-lines and a Hindu sacrament. A female's marriageability is dependent on the size of her dowry; the larger it is, the better the bride's family's chances are of making an auspicious mar-riage for her. Her dowry may consist of money, property, and/or livestock; among poor families, a bride's dowry may be paid by labor extended by members of her family to her bridegroom's family. In exchange, the bride's family shares, through the extended-family system, in the social status and political and economic influence of the bridegroom's family.

Except among the hill tribes, where sex is casual and polyandry common, a bride's virginity is as crucial to her marriageability as a dowry. A nonmarriageable female becomes a social and economic burden to her family; the poorer a family is, the less the birth of a female is welcomed. Generally, the older a female is at the time of marriage, the greater is the size of the dowry expected of her. For this reason and to ensure the bridegroom of a virginal bride, marriages are still sometimes contracted during early childhood with the wedding rites taking place just before or as soon as the girl reaches puberty. Another reason for young, arranged marriages is the shortage of females relative to men. This makes it a parental duty to find suitable husbands for their daughters, while the prospects are still good.

While the legal age at marriage is now a minimum of 18 for females and 21 for males, the average age of females at the time of marriage is 17 years (it is about five years older for males). This religious and social custom of early marriage, which perpetuates childbearing by children, is one of the root causes of continuing high fertility and population growth. Kerala's relatively low birth rate, for example, is undoubtedly due in large measure to a high literacy rate among females and, as a consequence of female education, a high average age at marriage of 20.9 years for women and 26.3 years for men. In Bihar, Madhya Pradesh, Rajasthan, and Uttar Pradesh, on the other hand, low female literacy rates prevail, and the average age at marriage is a low 15 to 16 years for women and under 20 for men.

Birth rates also vary according to religion, with the Muslim population exhibiting a consistently higher-than-average fertil-ity rate. This is generally attributed to the Muslims' belief that Allah will provide, as well as to the extremely low status

of women, the relatively high incidence of illiteracy, and the
general poverty in Muslim areas.

Marriage among Indian women is almost universal. In 1980,
56 percent of all females between the ages of 15 and 19 were
married, and 89 percent were married by the time they were 24
years old; by age 50, only 1.0 percent of Indian females have
not married. By way of contrast, only 10 percent of Sri Lanka's
females were married by the age of 19, and only 46 percent by
age 24 in 1980. The incidence of sustained widowhood in India,
however, is very high, although declining: between 1931 and
1971, the percentage of widows in the population fell from 16.0
to 8.8. The traditional Hindu ban on widows' remarriage was
overturned by law in 1856 and is now strictly observed only by
the higher castes. But remarriage is difficult for widows with
surviving children because of problems surrounding the inheritance of land and other fixed assets held by a joint family.
However, declining mortality rates are succeeding in reducing
the number of widows in India, while increasing the overall
fertile period among India's married women between the ages of
15 and 49.

Although divorce occasionally takes place among most of
the non-Brahmin castes, most divorces in India occur among the
country's Muslims and scheduled tribes. Divorce is permitted
by law with the consent of the local councils of elders and
occasionally with the approval of the local *panchayat* (village
council).

Public Health

By 1981, 48 percent of India's population (51 percent in
rural areas and 38 percent in urban areas) lived below a poverty
line based on the ability of a family merely to purchase enough
food to maintain an adequate nutritional standard. A far greater proportion live under overcrowded, inadequate, and unsanitary
conditions. About 55 percent of India's nearly 600,000 villages
lack electricity. More than 100,000 villages lack safe drinking
water, and existing water supplies throughout the country are
dwindling rapidly from the demands of a growing population.

Sewage facilities are practically nonexistent outside of
the large urban areas. The casual urination and defecation
habits of all but the upper- and upper-middle-class Indians have
turned even the cities into open cesspools of disease. Sources
of firewood, upon which three-quarters of the population depends
for over 70 percent of their energy needs, are becoming critically short, as are supplies of alternative dung and crop resi-
due fuels for the rural poor. And with the burgeoning demands
for more and more food, even arable areas are being eroded:
population pressures are pushing more and more people into the
nation's cities; sprawling urban centers are exploding onto
vital croplands.

For 30 years, the Indian government has been struggling with a variety of schemes to help the states provide just minimum health care for the majority of their rapidly growing population. Even in the face of India's bureaucracy, a number of public health inroads have been made. With the assistance of the World Health Organization (WHO), smallpox has been eradicated. Malaria, however, which by 1970 had been brought under control with the assistance of a U.S. contribution of $90.1 million, has been steadily rising since 1975. To find an answer to the persistent malaria problem, India and the United States signed an agreement on December 9, 1981 to cooperate in the development of a malaria vaccine. Meanwhile, cholera has virtually been controlled, but other communicable diseases, such as tuberculosis, intestinal parasites, and poliomyelities, persist. The lack of rural refrigeration facilities drastically reduces the effectiveness of cold-chain vaccines used, for example, in anti-polio campaigns.

Today, pneumonia and diarrheal infections constitute the prime contributors to the nation's high annual death rate of 15 per 1,000. At the root of these diseases, however, are the triple scourges of overpopulation, poverty, and malnutrition, all of which appear to be highly resistent to decades of concern and programs delineated in successive five-year plans for development. Meanwhile, even minimum health care and family planning services remain beyond the reach of the bulk of India's rural population. As Dr. Saroj S. Jha, head of the Department of Preventive and Social Medicine at Topiwala National Medical College in Bombay, pointed out in 1978:

> *Any improvement [in health care] over the past 30 years has been slow, and largely confined to large cities and urban areas where medical services are concentrated and sophisticated health care is available on practically every doorstep.*
>
> *Attempts to correct this situation have concentrated on improving the health care delivery system by increasing the number of health centres, modifying job requirements (making single purpose health workers multipurpose) and strengthening the paramedical component of health teams by recruiting village health workers.*
>
> *It is unlikely that these programmes will succeed unless a complete overhaul of medical and paramedical education and training is also carried out.*
>
> *The present system of medical education in India continues with minor modifications the British pattern set 140 years ago. A doctor graduating from a medical college in India today is hopelessly ill-equipped to meet the health needs of the rural population. Cloistered within the four walls of*

his college and hospital, he emerges suited
merely for solo practice, or for work in British
or American hospitals. The doctors so trained
can certainly not organize or deliver health
services to a group, a society or a community. . . .
The result is that the majority of primary health
centres in India--first established in 1952 to
provide an integrated preventive and curative health
service to the rural population, with the accent on
the preventive component--are manned by doctors with
very little appropriate training. . . . It is no
wonder that the doctors who are products of such
training have reduced health centres to mere treat-
ment centres, catering to a select few who reside
in its vicinity. With a few exceptions, very little
effort is made in the fields of nutrition, maternal
and child health care, family planning and health
education. . . . Very little practical work is
taught, with little or no field experience. Stu-
dents graduate as doctors quite incapable of
inserting a loop [IUD] or performing a simple
vasectomy [or even instructing a woman about how
to use birth control pills correctly].

By mid-1980, 5,400 rural primary health centers (PHCs),
each staffed by two or three doctors and a complement of
auxiliary nurse-midwives (ANMs) and lady health visitors (LHVs)
to serve about 100,000 people, had been established under the
aegis of the Ministry of Health. Some 39,000 subcenters also
have been set up to provide health and family planning services,
and a major goal of the government's Comprehensive Rural Health
Program is to bring the number of subcenters up to 117,000 to
reduce the service load of each subcenter to about 5,000 people.
Eventually, each of these subcenters will be staffed by two
multipurpose workers (MPWs).

Females employed as MPWs are being trained as ANMs. At
present, each ANM is responsible for the health needs of 10,000
people. Male MPWs, all of whom are former workers in the fields
of malaria or smallpox control, sanitation, or family planning,
are being retrained as paramedics, and will assume responsibilities in all these areas. *Dais* (midwives) are also being
trained in the arts of hygienic deliveries, general health
maintenance, and family planning motivation. The plan is to
train one *dai*, who is unsalaried but paid Rs. 2 (1 rupee ≃ $0.1
U.S.) for each birth reported, for each village of about 1,000
people.

A major innovation of the rural health scheme, beginning
in 1977, has been the training of community health workers
(CHWs) at the village level. These *rakshaks* who are appointed
by their villages, work part time, are paid Rs. 50 ($5) a month,
and are given the responsibility of promoting community par-

ticipation and self-reliance in health care among the 1,000 or
so people in their own villages.

The widespread reliance on traditional and relatively
expensive forms of health care has created a deep-seated suspicion of modern medicine. People who shy away from city oriented
physicians have full confidence in primarily rural-based ayur-
vedic doctors (whose practice is based on the Ayur-Veda, the
Hindu book of health and medicine), homeopaths, unani practitioners, and other nonphysicians. Moreover, since less than 30
percent of the nation's hospital beds are located in rural
villages and, even when available, hospital care is usually
sought only as a last resort, hospitals have gained the reputation of being a place where people go to die.

Although the matter is often discussed, the government has
not managed to devise ways of enlisting the services of ayur-
vedic doctors in key public-health campaigns, including family
planning. As trusted, responsive community members, they could
be particularly effective as family-planning educators and
service providers.

Meanwhile, overpopulation, nutritional ignorance, and
poverty continue to show up in severe, widespread malnutrition
and extreme vulnerability to disease, particularly among women
and children under the age of three. According to population
experts (Gulhati and Gulhati, 1978),

> This situation is unlikely to change with the
> introduction of community health workers who are
> largely men. Their access to women will be
> inhibited by cultural factors and customary taboos.
> And yet it should be obvious that women are the
> group most directly affected by large numbers of
> pregnancies and by population pressure at the
> household level. The Committee on the 'Status of
> Women in India' reported appalling disparities
> between the sexes within households, where the
> women 'serve the family first and eat last . . .
> in poor families this results in still greater
> malnutrition of women.' The main health problems
> of women remain high maternal mortality and mor-
> bidity, lower life expectancy at birth, mental
> disorders, a high suicide rate and malnutrition.

Rampant malnutrition among women is, in turn, passed on to
their infants in the form of low birth weight, inadequate and
low-quality mother's milk, and low immunity to disease. Between
1951 and 1971, the infant mortality rate fell from 146 to 129
per thousand live births. By 1981, however, the infant mortality rate stood at a distressingly high 134 per thousand live
births. It has become clear that the reductions previously
achieved in infant mortality were due not to increases in curative services, but primarily to the eradication of smallpox and

efforts to control other endemic communicable diseases. Meanwhile, the country's crude death rate of 15 per thousand has
changed insignificantly from 1970, when it was 15.7 per thousand
per year. In fact it might be even higher: according to
Visaria and Visaria (1981), it is probable that deaths (particularly those of infants) were underreported by 5-10 percent
for the period 1971-81. If so, the country's reported crude
death and infant mortality rates would have to be adjusted upward.

Again, as in the case of marital age and fertility, infant
mortality rates vary dramatically from state to state. Kerala,
for example, boasts the nation's lowest annual infant mortality
rate of 55 per thousand live births, while Uttar Pradesh has
the highest at 185 per thousand. By way of contrast, neighboring Sri Lanka's infant mortality rate is 42 per thousand, while
Pakistan's and Bangladesh's are even higher than India's at 142
and 139 per thousand, respectively. The United States has an
infant mortality rate of 13 per thousand.

Much of Kerala's success at lowering its infant mortality
rate is due to good birth care. About 53 percent of the babies
born in rural areas in 1976 and 1977 were delivered in hospitals
or clinics or by trained midwives. On the other hand, less than
7.0 percent of the 1978 rural births in Uttar Pradesh (and 24
percent of rural births in India as a whole) were professionally
attended. Although there is a controversy among demographers
over the relationship between infant mortality and birth rates,
it is generally true that women living in areas with a high
infant mortality rate tend to give birth to more children.
Whether this is due to a desire to replace an infant that has
died or to a fear that an infant *might* die is really an academic
point. In any case, Kerala's annual birth rate of 26.4 per
thousand, as opposed to Uttar Pradesh's birth rate of 40.3 per
thousand, is undoubtedly due in great measure to the prevalence
of infant deaths, particularly since they reflect overall health
care and general development, including female education and
relatively good nutrition patterns.

While malnutrition is a fact of life for hundreds of millions of Indian women and children, starvation also stalks the
land. Starvation is endemic among such homeless, indigent
Indians as the 1 million people in Calcutta and 500,000 people
in Bombay.

Mass starvation, however, has periodically been averted
following poor crop years by waves of food shipments from the
United States and Canada. Although India is considered to be
food-grain self-sufficient today, minimal grain reserves and
the increasing food demands of a population growing at the
annual rate of 2.23 percent mean that just one poor crop year
can open the door to the specter of widespread starvation. The
severe monsoon failure of 1979-80 brought about such a year: a
17 percent drop in food-grain production meant that, by early
1981, India suffered from an aggregate per capita food supply

gap estimated at 10 percent of total consumption, based on dietary adequacies prescribed by WHO/FAO. Moreover, extreme disparities exist in food availability among income groups and individuals.

To help alleviate malnutrition among primary-school-age children, major school-feeding programs have been set up by both CARE and Catholic Relief Services in rural areas with high numbers of scheduled tribes. The hope is that these programs, which dispense U.S. food surpluses on a soft-loan basis under U.S. Public Law 480 (PL 480), will also enhance school enrollment rates, particularly for girls.

PL 480 food has also formed the backbone of a number of nutrition-intervention schemes attempted by the government of India: the Applied Nutrition Program, the Special Nutrition Program, the Integrated Child Health Scheme, and various other state-level schemes. Although these programs demonstrate the government's continuing concern over the nutritional status of India's poor majority, little of that concern has been translated into action. Extreme poverty and a cultural bias against females in this vastly overpopulated country create a strong and ever-expanding chain of human suffering. As Fullam (1978) reports:

> [Even] where nutritional status is marginal, a pregnancy may tilt the balance and precipitate a woman into an overt state of malnutrition . . . women may carry a baby to term with little or no gain in weight and actually lose weight while lactating. Such women are 'literally milking the flesh off their bodies for children,' in the words of Dr. F. T. Sai, former Assistant Secretary-General of the IPPF [International Planned Parenthood Federation]. While family planning cannot compensate for food deficits, it can, by enabling a mother to space her children, help her to conserve her physical resources which would otherwise suffer progressive depletion through successive pregnancies.
>
> A study in India of malnourished children found that 61 percent of the severely malnourished children examined were fourth or later children. It has been calculated that without any other improvements in income, medical care or food supply, a three-child family norm in areas of poverty would reduce the incidence of overt protein-calorie malnutrition by at least 60 percent.

In India, where the average completed family size decreased only from 5.7 children in 1971 to 5.3 in 1981, the three-child family norm is a long way off. Meanwhile, the heavy concentration on public health measures aimed at the control of communi-

cable diseases has raised life expectancy in India from an
average of 20 years in the 1920s to about 50 years in 1981.
Why, then, aren't equally vigorous and humane family planning
and maternal and child health measures--now beyond the reach
of the vast majority of the Indian population--being directed
toward the nation's number one public health problem, overpopulation?

Administrative Organization

At present, India is divided into 22 states and nine union
territories. The number of states and state boundaries, however, can be altered by the national Parliament. Although the
executive power of a state is vested in the governor, the
political organization beneath the governor varies from state
to state: some states have a bicameral legislature, while
others have only one House, known as the Legislative Assembly;
some union territories also have legislative assemblies and
councils of ministers, while others are administered directly
by the central government.

The chief units of administration, however, are the districts; in early 1976, the country was divided into a total of
387 districts. These, in turn, are divided into subdivisions
called *taluks* or *tehsils* (villages and towns).

The head of the district, called the collector or the
deputy commissioner, acts both as the principal revenue-
collecting officer and development officer. A district magis-
trate, assisted by magistrates of the taluks or tehsils, is
responsible for maintaining law and order. In urban areas,
the local self-governing institutions are called municipal
corporations or committees; in rural areas, they are known as
district boards and village panchayats. In addition to the
panchayats, which consist of villagers elected to handle the
village's civic needs, each rural village also has an informal
but influential council of elders.

Since independence in 1947, India has functioned as a
parliamentary democracy, based for the most part on the British
model. The constitution, adopted in 1950, provides for a bicameral Parliament. Members of the *Lok Sabha* (House of the
People) are directly elected for five-year terms. The elected
members of the state legislative assemblies and of some of the
union territories elect the members of the *Rajya Sabha* (the
House or Council of States), the upper house of Parliament,
for two-year periods. The leader of the majority party in the
Lok Sabha becomes the prime minister, who is the functional
head of the government and selects other ministers or cabinet
members from party colleagues. The president, who is elected
by the members of both Houses and the state legislatures,
functions as the ceremonial head of the government and acts on
the advice of the prime minister.

The central government has exclusive responsibility for defense, foreign affairs, railways, communications, currency, banking, and insurance. The states control such areas as law and order, local government, agriculture, education, public health, sanitation, and other developmental functions. Family planning which, until 1976, was not mentioned specifically in the constitution, has been lumped with health since independence, and left up to the individual states. Although family planning is still regarded as a facet of health care, a constitutional amendment in 1976 took the responsibility for family planning programs from the states and put it in the hands of the central government. Financial assistance for health and family planning programs run by individual states continues to sift downward from the central government to the state level.

The bulk of elastic taxes (income taxes, corporation taxes, and excise duties) are collected by the central government; portions of some of these revenues are transferred to the states. The states also raise revenue from sales and purchase taxes, stamp duties, motor vehicle taxes, electricity duties, and land taxes.

The Planning Commission, which is chaired by the prime minister, reviews state proposals for projects and policies for the five-year development plans. It also provides funds for selected projects and programs. The plans are then discussed and approved by a National Development Council composed of the chief ministers of the states and the prime minister to ensure broad agreement on major policies.

As has happened several times in the past, the central government can assume all or any of the functions of a state government when its constitutional machinery breaks down. The constitution also empowers the president to declare an emergency whenever national security is threatened by war, external aggression, or internal disturbance. During such an emergency, the government is permitted to abridge the fundamental constitutional rights of the people and Parliament, and together with the union executive (consisting of the president, vice-president, and cabinet), assume the power to make laws and issue orders infringing on those rights. Parliament can also legislate on the areas normally under exclusive state control and issue directives on the exercise of state executive power. Thus, under a state of emergency, it is possible to convert a federation of states into a single, centrally administered state.

The first emergency declaration, made during the border conflict with China in October 1962, remained in effect until 1968. A second emergency, ordered in December 1971 during the war with Pakistan, lasted until June 1975, when another emergency was declared to meet the threat of internal disturbances.

Lining Up for Nonalignment*

Asked to name the country that came closest to India's foreign policy, Indira Gandhi once said, "Yugoslavia." By way of explanation, the prime minister said that Yugoslavia pursued a socialist policy and, like India, steered clear of both the Soviet and U.S. blocs. It was therefore able to go about the business of building its economy without getting caught in the superpowers' cross fire.

The concept of noninvolvement via nonalignment, which underlies India's foreign policy today, was the brainchild of Indira Gandhi's father, Jawaharlal Nehru. When Nehru, the secular leftist head of the Congress Party, became India's first prime minister, the winds of the post-World War II cold war were directing independent nations into either the Soviet or U.S. bloc. Nehru rejected the curious but almost universal notion that a country's freedom depended on the surrender of at least a portion of its freedom to one of the superpowers. Nehru argued that collective security for a smaller nation would translate to collective danger if the two superpowers decided to go to war.

Nonalignment was not viewed by Nehru as isolationism, but rather as a way to ward off hostilities and gain the peaceful respite necessary for developing nations to build their economies, with the help of whomever was willing to tender appropriate assistance. Nurtured by the nonviolence preached by Buddha (563–483 *B.C.*), the Emperor Asoka (273–232 *B.C.*), and Mahatma Gandhi (1869–1948), the Indian people stood behind the charismatic Nehru's zealous advocacy of peaceful solutions to international problems.

Nehru's reasoning also won the early allegiance of Tito, Nasser, and Sukarno. He succeeded in organizing the first Afro-Asian Conference at Bandung, Indonesia, in April 1955 and, much to his later regret, managed to introduce Chou En-lai to the delegates. In September 1961, he convened the historic Meeting of the Nonaligned Third World in Belgrade. From the very beginning, however, India's leadership of the nonaligned world was challenged as much by the Indian leadership's diplomatic naiveté as by the world's misunderstanding of Nehru's political motives.

---

*Unless otherwise indicated, all of the quotations and much of the information in this section are drawn from Nayar (1971). An outstanding Indian journalist, sometime government press officer, and astute political observer, Kuldip Nayar has enjoyed extraordinary access to both public and private conversations between Indian and foreign political leaders.

India's policy of nonalignment first came into question in October 1956 at the United Nations, when it was the only non-aligned nation to side with the Soviet Union in its invasion of Hungary.

Increasingly strained relations between India and China finally collapsed in 1959, when Nehru granted asylum to the Dalai Lama, who had been forced to leave Lhasa to escape the terrorism that followed China's invasion and subsequent control of Tibet in 1950-51. Subsequently, having restrained the Dalai Lama from setting up a government in exile in India on the advice of India's ambassador to China, Kavalam Madhava Pannikkar, Nehru found himself opposed by the West as well. The United States charged that Nehru had bought peace by allowing China to occupy Tibet.

Eventually, misunderstanding of Nehru's zeal for peace led the West to criticize India's nonalignment policy as being soft toward Communism. (Nehru, a longtime admirer of Fabian philosophy, accepted the Marxist interpretation of history, although in his autobiography, Nehru wrote that he resented the Soviet Union's "regimentation and unnecessary violence.") Nehru was both surprised and hurt by this criticism from the West; he had thought that since India had opted for democracy at the time of independence, its status as a democratic, nonaligned nation was beyond question. He championed peace both in the name of economic development and as an end in itself. But what Nehru and subsequent Indian leaders failed to recognize is that in today's world, foreign and economic affairs lie on two sides of the same bed.

By 1961, however, Nehru's popularity as a peace-loving man was riding high; India's reputation as a dedicated moral state seemed secure. During a visit to the United States in November 1961, Nehru told then Foreign Secretary Manilal Jagdashbhai Desai, who was about to leave for a meeting at the State Department in Washington, to "Tell them not to go to Vietnam. They will get stuck there." Nehru not only felt the United States had no business in Vietnam, but that U.S. involvement there could very well set off a confrontation between the United States and the Soviet Union that could lead to World War III.

Then, without warning, on December 18, 1961, Indian troops attacked the Portuguese colony at Goa, on India's southwest coast. Adlai Stevenson, then U.S. Representative to the U.N., vehemently denounced India's action as "the use of armed force by one state against another and against its will."

New Delhi's pronouncements had become its Achilles' heel, a situation that became even more apparent during the escalation of the long-simmering border dispute between India and its increasingly hostile neighbor, China. When India's exhortations for a peaceful solution to the problem failed to weaken China's territorial claims, India matched Chinese border posts with military posts of its own. The Indian Army, however, was woefully inadequate; having initially rejected the idea of

military assistance from either of the superpowers on the
grounds that the acceptance of such aid would compromise
India's nonalignment policy, Nehru was dismayed to discover
that none of India's nonaligned friends were willing to jump
into the fray. India's eventual request for a massive arms
buildup from the United States was rebuffed by a White House
special assistant who, according to Nayar (1971), remarked,
"So you couldn't last out even two days. Churchill fought the
war without any weapons for two years."

Even more damning to India's posture against the Chinese
threat was the conviction of India's procommunist defense
minister, Vengalil Krishnan Krishna Menon, that China would
not launch the attack that India had learned was planned for
October 20, 1962. The attack, however, was made right on
schedule; in about an hour, an entire Indian brigade of 3,000
men was wiped out. As the Chinese army swept southward,
knocking out one Indian military post after another, Krishna
Menon, brooding over endless cups of tea, remarked, "How could
I have known that they would come like an avalanche?"

The bloody Chinese offensive lasted for one month; it
finally ended with a unilateral Chinese declaration of a
cease-fire. China had made its point, which was made humili-
atingly clear soon after the October 20 attack. Surprised by
the Chinese military action, then Minister for Home Affairs
Lal Bahadur Shastri said over and over again, "We are the
ones who in fact introduced Prime Minister Chou En-lai to the
Nonaligned Powers in Bandung!" When this remark reached Chou
En-lai, he reportedly observed that he was surprised at the
"effrontery of a third-rate power like India claiming to
introduce to the world the prime minister of a first-rate
power like China." Thus signed in warfare and sealed in verbal
insult, the enmity between India and China has lasted to this
day.

Soon after a beloved but disillusioned Nehru died of a
stroke on May 27, 1964, and Shastri became prime minister, the
even older enmity between India and Pakistan began to flare up
into a conflagration over the disputed territory of Kashmir,
which had been divided between the two countries at the time
of partition. Pakistan, which India viewed as being overly
friendly toward China, had been receiving massive arms assistance from the United States and the Soviet Union, both of whom
had promised that the arms would not be used against India.
China, meanwhile, had assured Pakistan that Chinese troops
would be poised to counter Indian and internal Hindu threats
to East Pakistan (which was separated from West Pakistan by
more than a thousand miles of Indian territory), should Pakistan decide to assume its "rightful control" over Kashmir,
which like Pakistan was a predominantly Muslim territory.

Shastri, a diminutive man whose critics charged had a
"napoleonic complex," repeatedly tried to negotiate a no-war
pact to avert what he felt would be a disaster for the entire

subcontinent. Finally, however, Shastri ran out of patience with Pakistan's rejections of Indian goodwill. As he explained later to *Statesman* editor Kuldip Nayar (1971), who had formerly served as his press officer:

> *Pakistan mistook my desire not to fight as a sign*
> *of weakness; it thought that I will never go to war*
> *and it tried to take undue advantage in Kashmir.*
> *When it did so, I was convinced that Pakistan was*
> *not serious about good relations and peace with*
> *India. I decided to act.*

In the winter of 1964, Peking informed Pakistan of its intention to "eject interlopers from the south of China." It suggested that this action, scheduled for September 1, 1965, would act as a diversion for Indian troops and create an opportunity for Pakistan's taking of Kashmir. In reply, Pakistan moved a division of U.S.-supplied Patton tanks to the Indian border, and began infiltrations into Kashmir. After Rawalpindi launched a heavy attack in the Akhnur-Jammu sector on September 1, 1965, Shastri ordered the Indian Army to march into Pakistan on September 6.

Eventually, the U.N. intervened by sending Secretary-General U Thant to both Rawalpindi and New Delhi. What turned the tide, however, was pressure from Soviet Premier Kosygin during a period of frantic shuttle diplomacy, plus a realization by both countries that British and U.S. military and financial assistance, which had been suspended to both Pakistan and India during the period of hostilities, would not be resumed until a mutual cease-fire had been signed. And on January 10, 1966, just a few hours before Shastri suffered a fatal heart attack, India and Pakistan signed the Tashkent Declaration, which charged both sides to settle their differences "through peaceful means."

Open hostilities had ceased, but the stage had been set for a future all-out war with Pakistan, and India's increasing friendship with Russia and simultaneous estrangement from the United States. The irony, of course, is that Nehru's policy of nonalignment had ended in de facto alignment, and that the peace he had so vigorously sought had proved elusive. Meanwhile, the nation's economic buildup had been stymied by the very international political forces Nehru had resisted, but which his own sermonizing had done so much to inflame.

Indira Gandhi Steps Forward

With Shastri's death, "the Syndicate" (the political bosses at the head of the Congress Party founded by Nehru) was thrown into a panic. The nation's economy was reeling from the accumulated effects of Nehru's favoring of industrialization over

agricultural development, enormous military spending on a succession of wars, and bureaucratic corruption. While cabinet
ministers were living like princes, and princes (maharajahs)
were living like kings, unemployment, inflation, and food
deficits were causing great unrest among the nation's hungry
majority; communism was finding increasing acceptance. To
bring the nation under control and thus insure the party's own
survival, the mutually suspicious Congress Party leaders cooperated with each other long enough to come up with the name of
the one person who would have both wide voter appeal and a
sense of loyalty to the Congress Party.

The party's kingmakers were right on only half of Indira
Gandhi's qualifications for prime minister: the aura of Nehru
the Peaceful that clung to his relatively unknown daughter
appealed to the masses as much as her caste (despite the fact
that she was the widow of a Parsi, Feroze Gandhi, Indira Gandhi
was a Brahmin) appealed to powerful Brahmins who feared that
the influence of Thakurs (non-Brahmins) in government was
getting out of hand. Once in office, however, Gandhi proved
that, unlike her father, she owed allegiance to no one. The
party bosses had drastically underestimated the pride, ambition,
and personal strength of the woman they had made prime minister.

The Congress Party's ideology was summed up by the 1962
election manifesto: "The fundamental problem in India is not
only to increase greatly the living standards of the people but
also to bring about progressively social and economic equality."
At the time of the general election in 1967, the party went a
step further by promising to every individual "a national
minimum comprising the essential requirements in respect of
food, clothing, housing, education and health."

Unlike the Congress syndicate, Gandhi felt that campaign
rhetoric should be turned into action; she believed that the
return of the Congress majority to Parliament and most state
legislatures meant that the people wanted to move to the left.
Accordingly, she endorsed a ten-point program, which was
adopted on May 12, 1967, and called for social control of
the banks; nationalization of general insurance; progressive
take-over of export and import trade by state agencies; state
trading in food grains at the wholesale level; organization of
consumer cooperatives in urban and rural areas; effective steps
to curb monopolies and concentration of economic power; provision of minimum needs to the entire community by the earliest
feasible date; ceilings on individual holdings of urban property; prompt implementation of land reforms; and abolition of
the princes' privileges as well as privy purses (which by 1971
totaled Rs. 480 million, or about $101 million a year).

When the party bosses seemed to stand in the way of the
government's achievement of these goals, Indira Gandhi broke
with them. As for charges that she was playing the Communists'
game, she said that it was the party bosses who were making the
people look to the Communists for succor. "If I don't do any-

thing to take the wind out of the sails of the Communists,"
said Gandhi, "the entire country will go red" (Nayar, 1971).

Although the prime minister claimed to be using socialism
to attack communism, she was beginning to cement relations
between India and the Soviet Union, at the expense of India's
relations with the United States. In a meeting with President
Eisenhower, Nehru had been offered the same quantity of arms
($2 billion) that the United States had supplied to Pakistan
in 1954 in a bid to "contain communism" on the subcontinent.
Nehru, however, had refused to become involved in the superpowers' arms race. But times and the Indian leadership had
changed; having gained the approval of a surprised Soviet
Union by refusing to condemn the Soviet Union's aggression in
Czechoslovakia in August 1968, Gandhi proceeded to secure
sophisticated weaponry from Russia, including five submarines
for the fledgling Indian navy.

In July 1969, claiming that the Congress Party had spcken
of socialism only because "that was what went down well with
the masses," and that the Congress Party had "no faith in
progressive measures," Indira Gandhi relieved Morarji Desai,
a self-proclaimed socialist who nevertheless appeared to the
masses to be a rightist, of the Finance portfolio. Having
thus rid herself of a finance minister who had been placed in
her cabinet by the party bosses against her wishes, she began
to divest herself of all other vestiges of control by those in
the party whom she considered to be hypocritical and old-
fashioned. Within hours of accepting Desai's "resignation"
on July 20, 1969, Gandhi nationalized 14 major Indian banks,
which were already under "social control," or close scrutiny
by the government's Reserve Bank of India.

Bolstered by Soviet approval of the nationalizations and
by communist support within India, Gandhi then went about the
business of engineering the election of the innocuous V. V.
Giri as president to replace Zakir Husain, who died on May 3,
1969, thus assuring herself of the prime minister's post at
least until 1972. Her next step was to take on the entire
apparatus of the Congress Party itself.

Weakened by internal squabbling and dismayed by Gandhi's
independence, the old party bosses finally came to a momentous
(and as it turned out, final) agreement. The party, which had
ruled India for the 22 years since independence, fell under
the spell of Gandhi oppositionists led by Desai and, on November 12, 1969, expelled their most prominent and unmanageable
member, Indira Gandhi. These bosses had controlled the party
for so long, and were so confident of their strength, they
expected their pronouncement to be the end of Gandhi. They
were, of course, wrong again.

Gandhi's ouster deepened the split in the Congress Party.
While pro-U.S. Sadashiv Kanoji Patil, from the rich mill area
of Bombay, claimed that Gandhi was in cahoots with--even a
puppet of--the Soviet Union, procommunist V. K. Krishna Menon,

surprisingly enough, pleaded for party conciliation. He feared that India might disintegrate if the Congress Party were to split permanently. Gandhi, however, was in no mood for reconciliation: she was determined to be her own boss. The party split in two: the old-liners became the Congress Party-O, the the Party Organization; the new party of Gandhi became the Congress Party-R, the Party of Requisitionists.

The division of the enormous broad-based Congress Party strengthened Gandhi's own position, but also strengthened oppositionist party forces both to the right and to the left of the Congress-R. On the right were such parties as the Jana Sangh, a Hindu chauvinistic party confined largely to north India; the Swatantra, a rightist party founded in 1963 to oppose the Congress Party's deviation from Mahatma Gandhi's ideals of service and selflessness; and, eventually, the Janata Party, a socialist party headed by Morarji Desai, who bolted from the Congress-O after failing in his bid to be elected Syndicate head.

On the left were such communist organizations as the pro-Chinese Marxist Party, the Communist Party of India (CPI), and the radical-terrorist Naxalites, a pro-Mao group formed as a rebel separatist movement at Naxalbari, near the Sino-Indian border. Although the CPI and other pro-Chinese communist parties were distressed by what they viewed as Gandhi's pro-Soviet stance, they joined pro-Soviet forces standing behind the prime minister and, in fact, continued to form much of her base.

Since the presidency in India is primarily a ceremonial post, somewhat akin to England's royalty, the prime minister holds both reins of government. Until 1971, however, Gandhi's seat in the Indian government was shaky.

The Indian-Pakistani War

Despite several (some say half-hearted) attempts at reconciliation, the enmity between Muslim Pakistan and Hindu India, which had been simmering and occasionally erupting since partition in 1947, boiled over in 1971. West Pakistan proceeded to exploit East Pakistan. It also occupied half of the princely state of Kashmir.

The two portions of Pakistan flanked a 1,000-mile stretch of Indian territory. And, despite Pakistan's partial control of Kashmir, India always claimed it as de jure Indian territory vital to Indian defense. Meanwhile, Kashmir continued to think of itself as a separate if not entirely autonomous state.

While India continued to claim nonalignment and prove it by accepting foreign aid and technical assistance from the United States and military hardware as well as financial aid from the Soviet bloc, Pakistan had clearly swung over to the side of the United States. Pakistan was maintaining its close friendship with China, while reaping the benefits of America's concern over and interest in China: U.S. arms and financial and technical assistance had been flooding Pakistan for a decade. Against this background, India's support of a movement among East Pakistanis for autonomy found an ever-deepening response in Pakistan's new capital city, Islamabad. The now militarily strong Pakistanis had lost their previous fear of India's size and might.

In March 1971, Pakistani troops swept into East Pakistan to quell a revolt by the Indian-backed pro-autonomy Awami League. The fighting soon escalated to a full-scale civil war; thousands of East Pakistanis were ruthlessly and systematically massacred. It was, however, an attack by Pakistani bombers on the Indian-Kashmiri capital of Srinigar and a bombing run on the Agra airport on December 3 that brought India openly into the "civil war."

On December 16, 1971, the Pakistani army met its Waterloo at the East Pakistani capital, Dacca. With the surrender of the Pakistani army to India, the liberation of what is now known as Bangladesh (Bengali Homeland) was won. Support given to Pakistan during the war by the United States and China, however, caused the rift between India and those two countries to deepen.

On the heels of columnist Jack Anderson's publication of a secret National Security paper outlining President Nixon's instructions to then Secretary of State Henry Kissinger to do whatever he could to tilt the balance of power against India, Indira Gandhi did some tilting of her own. Following India's victory over Pakistan, the mammoth and highly influential U.S. Agency for International Development (USAID) program in India, with all staff, consultants, and dependents, were unceremoniously thrown out of India. Even the nation's leading private school, the American International School, which educated exceptional Indian students as well as U.S. citizens and other foreign nationals, was threatened with nationalization and forced to divest itself of its Indian and foreign components. Most importantly, the precipitous cutoff of U.S. financial aid to India acted as a symbolic signpost to the near future when an increasingly heavy-handed approach to the nation's economic-population imbalance would bring development within a democratic framework to a halt.

Political Costs of Stability

By 1975, inflation and unemployment had gotten out of hand. While labor unrest and production slowdowns were causing critical consumer shortages and three poor crop years in a row had resulted in a food crisis, the oil price hikes of 1973-74 were eating at the nation's balance of payments. The worldwide recession had reduced the demand for Indian exports.

In early June, a court found Indira Gandhi guilty of several technical violations of India's election laws in 1971; her tenure as prime minister was thrown into jeopardy. On June 24, 1975, the prime minister took the first firm step toward bringing the country, and her leadership of it, under control: she declared a national emergency. According to Gwatkin (1979),

> In 1975 and 1976, India tired of serving as the epitome of the "soft state." Beggars, cows and shantytowns disappeared from India's cities; smugglers, criminals, and political wrong-thinkers were jailed; the clandestine, illegal "black money" economy was effectively controlled; labor unrest was contained; inflation was curbed; and the government of India got serious about family planning . . .

Under emergency rule, development controls by individual states were suspended along with many civil liberties. Labor strikes were declared illegal. The free and critical Indian press was muzzled. Oppositionists were swept into jail. The prime minister's younger son, Sanjay Gandhi, was given virtual control over the Union Territory of Delhi; rumors about his position as heir apparent to his mother's political power came to be regarded as accepted fact. It also became accepted fact that Prime Minister Gandhi intended to stay in power indefinitely.

The drive to reduce the nation's high birth rate, which had been conspicuously absent from Indira Gandhi's program for economic development announced at the beginning of the emergency, rolled over other developmental concerns as Sanjay's political star ascended. Sanjay's zeal for fertility control became so great that of his own five-point program, which included adult literacy, dowry abolition, reforestation, equality among castes, and family planning, only population control received active promotion.

As Sanjay's power grew, more and more political and ministerial heads rolled; Delhi was swept clean of slums, and the civil service was swept free of tax evaders. As the nation was whipped into a frenzy of meeting rising sterilization targets, often at Sanjay's insistence, coercion crept into the program.

Fortunately for Indira Gandhi, as the aggressive fertility-control program gathered steam, the monsoon rains were beneficial in 1975-76, and significant economic gains were made despite an almost exclusive concentration of development energies on the sterilization campaign. As agricultural production rose, prices declined. The imposition of tough labor policies resulted in a doubling of industrial output over 1975-76. Meanwhile, a marked rise in external financial assistance eased the nation's foreign exchange situation.

Apparently lulled by these gains into a false sense of
security, Indira Gandhi appeared blind to Sanjay's political
abuses and deaf to reports of coercive terror in the countryside and indignation among members of her own party. On
January 18, 1977, Prime Minister Gandhi startled both India
and the rest of the world by abruptly relaxing the emergency
and calling for open elections.

Despite economic improvements during the 19-month emergency, the aggressive and sometimes coercive efforts to curb
population growth had turned the electorate sour; many in the
prime minister's own party had deserted her. The elections
of March 1977 were a debacle for Indira Gandhi. In a dramatic
reaction to what many characterized as Sanjay's "fascist control" over both his mother and the country, the electorate
not only hurled the prime minister from power, but heaped
insult upon insult by installing in her stead a hastily formed
coalition of her opponents known as the Janata (People's) Party.
Morarji Desai, the man ousted from his position as Finance
Minister by Indira Gandhi in 1969 and now head of the Janata
Party, became prime minister.

Although he was politically savvy and a strong supporter
of family planning as a vital component of social and economic
development aimed at the common people, Desai was, at 80, the
leader of a party of old men.

Desai emptied the jails of political prisoners and lowered
tensions by relaxing emergency restrictions on civil liberties.
Press censorship, too, was eventually lifted, although state
control of the television and radio industries continues. Although the threat of Indira Gandhi was enough to hold the
Janata Party together, it was not enough to keep the party in
power. In the January 1980 elections, the steadily weakening
Janata government failed to recapture the electorate's imagination. Once again, Indira Gandhi became prime minister of India.

Fate and frustrations, however, have combined to keep
Gandhi's power base wobbly. The death of Sanjay Gandhi in the
crash of a small airplane in June 1980 left the prime minister
both personally and politically bereft.

With both India and Pakistan approaching nuclear capability,
the old concept of saber-rattling takes on a new and infinitely
more sinister connotation. And India's leap into the space age
has done nothing to dispel Pakistan's worst fears regarding
India's ultimate intentions.

Despite the fact that India is the world's 15th poorest
country, it has spent $664.5 million since 1963 on a space
program designed to turn the developing nation into a modern
state. By the end of 1981, four Indian communication satellites were circling the earth; two were still working, while
the others had been deactivated when no longer needed. Three
of the satellites were launched on rockets supplied by the
Soviet Union; one was launched on a rocket provided by France.
Two additional communication satellites now being built by a

United States company for India will be launched by the U.S. National Aeronautics and Space Administration (NASA).

India's satellites are not the last word in technological sophistication. But they make India the seventh nation in the world to launch its own satellite into orbit, behind the Soviet Union, the United States, England, France, China, and Japan. Although the communication satellites are generally agreed to have little use beyond their intended spread of educational and technological information throughout the country, at least part of India's space program is viewed as threatening by Pakistan. When India launched a tiny Rohini satellite from a rocket of its own manufacture in mid-1980, Pakistan protested.

THE ECONOMY

At the time of independence, the majority of India's population was enduring what Mahatma Gandhi called "an eternal compulsory fast." The partition of the subcontinent into India and Pakistan had deprived India of one-half of its well-irrigated land. A million refugees were pushed across the border from Pakistan to stretch India's limited resources even further. Moreover, vast portions of the country's rural regions were isolated during the monsoon season by a severe lack of all-purpose roads. Only one adult in seven could read and write; in the words of India's Nobel Prize-winning Bengali poet, Rabindranath Tagore, "a few 'educated' lived in the upper storey of a house and the vast illiterate millions below--with no staircase in between."

As Nehru saw it, the country's development could be undertaken in one of two ways. Society could be transformed on the model of the Soviet Union and China; people could be forced into a nearly static living standard so that funds could be freed to build factories and develop farmland. This, of course, would require strict regimentation; human values would have to be sacrificed for material gains. Or development could be achieved through a series of five-year plans aimed at preserving Indian spirituality while raising living standards.

Nehru opted for the latter. His brand of socialism, as set forth in the preface Nehru wrote to the Third Five-Year Plan, was designed to "secure rapid economic growth and expansion of employment, reduction of disparities in income and wealth and prevention of concentration of economic power." This was to be achieved through a vigorous program of industrialization to be set on a social base of "democracy and public participation."

But Nehru the idealist neglected to lend enthusiasm to the country's fledgling attempts at fertility control. If he did not exactly subscribe to the Marxist idea of increasing labor as the source of increasing capital, he was nevertheless ambiguous in his reaction to overpopulation and its effect on both economic and social development, as his successors have been until only recently.

India's economic growth since independence has been steady but unspectacular. The annual compound growth rate of real national income between 1950-51 and 1980-81 was 3.5 percent; agricultural and industrial production have grown at 2.7 percent and 6.1 percent, respectively. By 1982, inflation had dropped to 8-9 percent. The nation's population growth rate between 1950-51 and 1980-81, however, has been distressingly spectacular, at an average of nearly 2.2 percent per year. Thus, with overpopulation eating up economic gains, per capita gross national product (GNP) growth over this period was only 1.2 percent per year. As of 1981, per capita income was $190, and over half (51 percent) of the population was still living below the poverty line.

Energy, Forestry, and Conservation

Unlike neighboring Bangladesh, for example, India's vast and geographically diverse territory harbors an abundance of natural resources. The country is self-sufficient in coal, although it must be hauled over great distances by road and rail. About one-fourth of the nation's 80 billion tons of coal lies in proven reserves, 62 percent of which are concentrated in West Bengal, Bihar, and northern Madhya Pradesh; lignite deposits totaling nearly 2 billion tons are situated largely in Tamil Nadu. The nation's hydroelectric potential is estimated at 41 million kilowatts. Nearly 30 percent of this, however, is located in northeastern states in the Brahmputra basin and neighboring drainage areas, where the possibility of exploitation is remote. In southern states, with nearly 20 percent of the total hydroelectricity potential, 38 percent of the potential has been harnassed.

Known land-based petroleum reserves are concentrated in Assam and Gujarat. Henderson (1975) projected, on the basis of the 1969-74 annual production rate of 7.0 million tons of crude oil, that these reserves would last only about 17 years. During 1970-73, 71 percent of all crude oil and petroleum products consumed by India were imported.

Since the mid-1970s, offshore drilling in the Bombay High area off the Cambay basin has uncovered a considerable quantity of oil (estimated by Soviet geologist Kalanin to be as much as 1 billion tons) at reasonably shallow depths. Despite what is viewed as an offshore bonanza, India's need for imported oil is still on the increase.

Nuclear-generated electricity was introduced to India with the country's first nuclear power station at Tarapur near Bombay in October 1969. With a capacity of 420 megawatts, the station quickly became an important source of power for industries in both Gujarat and Maharashtra. And two more power

stations of the same size have since been constructed in
Rajasthan and Tamil Nadu.

However, international reaction to India's diversion of
nuclear technology and materials for its 1974 atomic test,
which violated international testing standards, and its continuing refusal to sign the Nuclear Non-Proliferation Treaty
have isolated India from the mainstream of world technology.
Left on its own, India's nuclear program is flagging. Nevertheless, domestic reserves of uranium, available in Bihar and
Rajasthan, eventually will be used to fuel heavy-water reactors under construction since the mid-1970s. The development
of fast-breeder reactors would increase the feasibility (and
the inherent dangers) of nuclear power and eventually cut its
cost, as does the presence of very large reserves of thorium.
Most of the thorium is in the monazite sands of Kerala and in
the Ranchi plateau on the border of West Bengal and Bihar.

Apart from coal and thorium, India is richly endowed with
high-quality iron ore reserves estimated by Henderson (1975)
at over 10 billion tons. In 1973, over 34 million tons of
iron ore were produced from deposits in northern Orissa,
Madhya Pradesh, Bihar, Goa, Karnataka, and Tamil Nadu; 60 percent of this ore was exported to Japan and Western and Eastern
Europe. India's mineral wealth also includes an estimated 108
million tons of manganese ore, ferroalloys, and chromite
reserves. There are large reserves of copper (estimated at
243 million tons in 1975) and bauxite (estimated at 249 million
tons in 1975) in Bihar, Madhya Pradesh, Orissa, and Tamil Nadu.

The growing energy demands of India's burgeoning population have brought the nation's acute forestry and environmental
problems to a point of crisis. As has been pointed out by
USAID (1983):

> Agricultural land, firewood, fodder, small timber
> for housing, agricultural implements and bullock
> carts and other forest products (fruits, herbs,
> etc.) are in increasingly short supply. In a coun-
> try where 80% of the population lives in villages,
> increasing demand has resulted in depletion of much
> of the communal and privately owned forest land.
> Similarly, severe encroachment and widespread deg-
> radation have occurred to government reserves. The
> [Government of India's] need for revenue from com-
> mercial sales has also placed enormous pressure on
> forests. . . .
> It is estimated that 4.2 million hectares [the
> equivalent of 420 million acres, at one hectare to
> 100 acres] of the forest land base have been lost
> since 1952. Nearly 37 million hectares, as Pro-
> tected Forest, received no systematic management.
> Hence out of the 75 million hectares officially
> classed as forest, many hectares are not producing

*anywhere near their potential either in terms of
revenue or for rural needs. Land stabilization
needs in the Himalayan foothills and associated
drainage systems in the central uplands also present
pressing problems. The combination of steep slopes,
high intensity monsoon rainfall and depletion of
vegetative cover from overgrazing and poor agricultural conservation have been devastating in some
areas. Land and water management problems are
serious now and will become more critical by 2000.
    On a national scale, the magnitude of the natural
resource problem described above is massive. Government action programs in reforestation and erosion
control on this scale can succeed but will require
many years and funding levels substantially above
those provided in the past. . . .*

The Economy Begins to Build

India's First Five-Year Plan for economic development
(1951-56) started, in Nehru's words, from the "cow dung stage"
(cow dung is a major source of fuel for India's poor). Its
formulation was simple: the government simply lumped together
all development projects under way at the time and called it
a plan. In a nation that almost totally lacked an industrial
infrastructure, where more than half the population was living
on the brink of starvation, and the average annual per capita
income was less than $52, the economy had nowhere to go but
up.

The monsoon (still a basic determinant of India's annual
food prospects) was good, the Korean War generated a demand
for Indian exports, and post-World War II relief and development activities of the United States had been extended to much
of South Asia in general and to India in particular.

On June 15, 1951, the U.S. Congress approved the Indian
Emergency Food Aid Act to ward off hunger in India. In 1952,
while presenting the case for economic aid and technical
assistance for India and the rest of South Asia during Senate
hearings on the Mutual Security Act, Secretary of State Dean
Acheson said:

*Poverty, disease, illiteracy, and resentments
against former colonial exploitations are our
enemies. . . . They represent turbulent forces
which the Communist exploits at every opportunity.
To achieve our objective of helping the people of
this area maintain independent governments friendly
to us, we must understand these forces at work in
Asia, and we must assure that the forces of nationalism and of the drive for economic improvement are*

*associated with the rest of the free world instead
of with Communism.*

Congress was convinced and, in fact, India's needs were
given priority when, during 1953-54, the amount of U.S. aid to
India increased by more than 20 percent, while assistance to
other South Asian countries was proportionately reduced. Between 1951 and 1956, India received $259 million in development
loans from the United States, plus $63.9 million of free PL 480
food and $5.5 million of other relief commodities. A wheat
loan of $189.7 million was also made in 1951.

During the first plan, India not only laid the beginnings
of an economic base, but experienced an economic growth rate
that exceeded 7.0 percent. Thus encouraged, the Indian government more than doubled the financial outlay for the Second
Five-Year Plan (1956-61) from Rs. 19.6 billion (an equivalent
of about $4.1 billion at the exchange rate of 4.75 rupees for
$1, which prevailed until mid-1966) to Rs. 46.7 billion ($9.8
billion).

The industry-based second plan soon ran into trouble.
Aside from the long gestation period required by industrial
development, investment capital began to dry up. On top of
this, the monsoon turned sour and food supplies again ran
short. Once again, the United States rushed to India's rescue
with a five-year total of $1.4 billion in development loan
funds; commodity aid was expanded to include fertilizers, steel,
and railway equipment in addition to food grains.

The United States also contributed $245 million during this
period to Export-Import Bank loans to India and cost-free PL 480
food equivalent to $84.6 million. In addition, $2.3 billion of
PL 480 food was "sold" to India under the U.S. Title I plan.
Since Title I food is sold by the U.S. government on the basis
of loans in local currency, and the money accumulated in the
recipient country is used primarily for development reinvest-
ment, Title I PL 480 food constitutes, in effect, a double
investment in the recipient country. (In 1958, for example,
the rupee equivalent of $18.4 million was withdrawn from PL 480
funds deposited in the Reserve Bank of India to help finance
the Orissa Iron Ore Project.)

By the late 1950s, however, the heavy industrial thrust of
the second plan was forcing the government of India to dig deep
into the foreign exchange reserves built up during World War II
as payment for India's assistance to England. At the time,
India was in the midst of setting up three steel plants at
Rourkela in Orissa, Bhilai in Madhya Pradesh, and Durgapur in
West Bengal with the assistance of West Germany, the Soviet
Union, and England, respectively. Another major steel plant
was on the drawing board for Bokaro, Bhihar; the United States
rejected India's request for financial assistance on this
project because of India's refusal to turn the plant over to
the private sector, and the Soviet Union stepped in again with

funding. Also under construction with Soviet assistance was
a heavy engineering plant (then the world's largest) at Ranchi
for the manufacture of steel plant equipment and other industrial machinery.

Prompted by the fear that communism might win its race
against democracy in India and, as a consequence, throughout
South Asia, the West jumped in with more development capital.
Under the leadership of the World Bank, a consortium of inter-
national donors was formed in 1958. Dubbed the "Aid for India
Club," the donor countries included the United States, England,
West Germany, France, Canada, and Japan and, later, Austria,
Belgium, Italy, and the Netherlands. The first order of busi-
ness was to raise $2.5 billion in assistance for India.

Thus, financially revitalized and reoriented by a new concentration on "core projects" (irrigation and power, essential
railway schemes, and the new basic industries), the economy
began to swing upward again. By the end of the Second Five-
Year Plan, steel production had doubled from 1.7 million to
3.5 million tons, aluminum production had nearly trebled from
7,300 to 18,500 tons, and the output of machine tools had more
than quadrupled. Petroleum products had risen from zero to
5.7 million tons in a decade, and overall industrial production
during this period climbed by 94 percent. By the time the
Third Five-Year Plan (1961-66) got under way, however, the
political and economic climate had turned decidedly cooler.

Caught up as it was in an industrial fervor, the government of India failed to foresee the extent to which development
via heavy industry would encourage the demand for agricultural
products and consumer goods. The increased expenditures on
industrialization forced the government into heavy deficit
financing: Rs. 9.4 billion (nearly $2 billion) had been added
to annual budgets during the second plan simply by printing
more currency. People accustomed to living on the brink of
starvation suddenly had money in their hands; it was a sellers'
market.

Prices skyrocketed and the competition for increasingly
scarce goods grew by leaps and bounds. There was no way production could keep up with demand, particularly in the food
market. Production targets for food grains, cotton, jute,
sugar cane, oil seeds, and other agricultural commodities were
revised upward in the late 1950s, but it was too late. Performance in the long-neglected agricultural sector was already
far from adequate. Inflated targets resulted in progress only
on paper. Meanwhile, India's relations with its heaviest
financial backer, the United States, had run into several snags.

U.S. food and commodity and development assistance, for
which 1962 commitments totaled $620.4 million, was abruptly cut
off when the Chinese attacked in October 1962. Between 1947
and 1962, the West had provided a total of $8.5 billion in
grants and loans, of which nearly $6 billion had come from the
United States. Foreign aid had come to mean U.S. aid; when it

was withdrawn, the effects on India's economy were immediate and severe.

Following India's defeat at the hands of the Chinese, the United States rushed military aid to India and reopened trade and loan agreements. Nonmilitary financial and commodity aid, however, was reduced sharply.

Between 1961 and 1964, the cost of Indian domestic commodities rose by almost 17 percent. The cost of food, which accounted for two-thirds to three-quarters of the family budget of about 70 percent of the population, climbed by 35 percent. Although Shastri tried one scheme after another to reduce prices when he took over as prime minister in June 1964, food prices rose by another 18 percent during the first year of his regime. Shastri had always been wary of the outcome of India's rush toward industrialization, when more than 80 percent of its people depended on the land for sustenance.

Convinced that agriculture was the key to solving India's problems, Shastri reoriented the third plan accordingly. But the Chinese aggression in 1962 had thrown India's development out of gear; the nation's industrial base had gotten it through the disastrous war, but now defense expenditures assumed first claim on Indian revenues.

The Soviet Union continued to supply aid in the form of trade credits and easy-term loans. But the reduction in Western assistance meant that the level of foreign aid, which had grown from 5.0 percent of the total investment in the first plan to 23 percent in the third, fell to about 17 percent in the Fourth Five-Year Plan (1966-72). Meanwhile, India's trade deficit had grown from Rs. 3.6 billion in 1961 to Rs. 6.6 billion in 1966, and poor weather turned Shastri's agricultural push into a mere shove. In 1967, with crops having failed for the second successive year, food grain production fell below the 1959 level, to 74 million tons. Only massive food shipments from the United States and Canada averted widespread starvation.

The costly Indian-Pakistani War of 1965 caused further difficulties: the West (particularly the United States, which had sided with Pakistan in the conflict) suspended all aid to India. The pinch was severe: in the absence of imported raw materials and spare parts, industrial growth fell from 8-10 percent per year to 4.3 percent. Between 1961 and 1968, when the population was growing at an annual rate of 2.2 percent, overall economic growth averaged only about 3.5 percent. With 15 million people already unemployed, nearly 4.0 million people were entering the labor force each year, while only 2.5 million new jobs were being created.

Unemployment hit the educated especially hard. For the first time since 1964, growing numbers of mining engineers remained unemployed; swelling numbers of civil engineers were also lining up at employment exchanges. The government's response was to cut back sharply on engineering institute enrollments, but by 1970, some 100,000 engineers were out of work. Meanwhile, the bureaucracy dumped more and more "non-essential" or inefficient, retired industry officials into the public sector. As industry became clogged by overstaffing, more taxes were levied to feed the unemployed.

With the economy plummeting, Prime Minister Gandhi turned again to the West. The World Bank, then New Delhi's major source of foreign loans, specified that further aid would be contingent upon India's consolidation of its industrial base and the concentration of development funds on the expansion and modernization of the agricultural sector. The World Bank also firmly recommended--and the United States insisted--that the highly inflated rupee be devalued. The Soviet Union, on the other hand, viewed the Indian economy as playing into the hands of capitalism. The Soviet Union was particularly concerned about the Bhilai steel plant, which it had been instrumental in funding. While Tatas and Indian Iron and Steel, the two private ventures in the field, were able to market their entire outputs, the public-sector Bhilai plant could not, even though production was kept at a relatively low level. The Soviet Union suggested that the prime minister nationalize the entire steel industry, and that she by no means devalue the rupee from the exchange rate specified in India's economic dealings with the Soviet Union.

In June 1966, however, after prolonged debate and a 47.5 percent increase in the prices of Soviet exports to India, the rupee was devalued from 4.75 per U.S. dollar to 7.40. With devaluation came World Bank assurances, a renewed PL 480 contract, and other Western aid and technical assistance. In July 1968, the United States informed India that its aid would have to be reduced again due to the U.S. shift in emphasis from international affairs to domestic problems.

In late 1972 and early 1973, with India's resounding victory over Pakistan, and the liberation of Bangladesh in 1971, Indira Gandhi's place in government was secure, and India pre-emptorily stopped receiving U.S. financial aid. Although many development programs (most notably in agriculture, public health, and family planning) came to a virtual halt and a series of social and political upheavals occurred, the economy managed to hang on. During the latter half of the 1970s, in fact, it began to experience marked gains.

Unfortunately, however, the nation's population was growing, too, even faster than anyone realized. By 1972, 82 million Indians were homeless.

From Emergency to Emergence

Between the imposition of a national emergency in mid-1975 and 1979, the rate of agricultural and industrial output accelerated to 6.1 and 6.6 percent, respectively, employment grew, and real income growth rose to 5.8 percent each year. India's

industrial capacity came to be second only to Japan's in Asia.
By 1977, the country had reached its goal of grain self-sufficiency, although inadequate food distribution patterns meant then,
as now, that the benefit of increased agricultural production
failed to be distributed to the impoverished masses.

During 1978-79, grain production, spurred by a favorable
monsoon and expanded use of modern fertilizers and high-yield
wheat varieties, reached a record level of 132 million tons,
compared to the annual average of 120 million tons. The nation
had grain reserves—a razor-thin edge against famine—of 20
million tons, and industrial output was also recovering.

Then, in 1979-80, the combination of a severe monsoon
failure and increasing strains on power and transport caused
a sharp economic reversal. Shortages of coal, steel, and
cement; an overabundance of bureaucratic controls; a reliance
on capital-intensive methods rather than on abundant manual
labor; and labor unrest blocked continued development of industry. While grain production fell by 17 percent, real income
fell by 5-6 percent, implying a 7-8 percent decline in per
capita real income.

During the same period, however, USAID returned to India,
and development assistance from foreign donors totaled approximately $1.9 billion in disbursements and $2.3 billion in new
commitments. Millions of poor people living in rural drought
areas received food in exchange for work under the National
Rural Employment Program.

The Sixth Five-Year Plan

With Indira Gandhi's comeback in January 1980, the Janata
Party's Sixth Five-Year Plan (1978-83) was dropped in favor of
a new sixth plan (1980-85). The new plan upholds the government's 15-year trend toward increasingly strong commitments to
rapid agricultural growth supported by favorable pricing policies and high expenditure levels for production inputs and
agriculture. Most importantly, the new plan focuses on the
nationwide expansion of rural development programs aimed at
small farmers and burgeoning numbers of landless laborers.

The government's administration of the plan, however, soon
came under fire when, in July 1981, Gandhi decided to import
1.5 million tons of U.S. wheat to fill India's dwindling reserve
stocks. The drought of 1979 and weak monsoon in 1980 had forced
the nation to draw heavily on its rice and wheat reserves despite assurances from Indian officials and the World Bank that
India had at last freed itself from the vagaries of weather and
the need to import grain. In May 1981, there were only 3.0
million tons of wheat in government warehouses. Although 1980-
81 monsoon was good, and the Indian wheat crop was estimated to
be in the range of 34-36 million tons, Gandhi decided to buy
the wheat as an anti-inflationary measure to fight the market
machinations of traders and hoarders.

To counteract India's vulnerability to weather conditions and to raise the proportion of higher-yield irrigated land to lower-yield rain-fed land, the new Sixth Five-Year Plan put a major emphasis on irrigation projects. A twin effort is under way to improve the utilization of existing irrigation facilities and to expand the area under irrigation from 57 million to 72 million hectares.

The 1983-87 funding proposals by USAID for surface irrigation and groundwater and land development are designed to irrigate approximately 1.2 million hectares of land and increase annual grain production by an estimated 1.6 million metric tons. Some 375,000 farm families, 50 to 60 percent of whom are now below the poverty level, would benefit directly; the income of 150,000 farm households would be raised above the poverty level. Jobs also would be created: 1.6 million worker-years of construction employment and an additional 600,000 worker-years of permanent agricultural employment would be provided. If undertaken, these projects will markedly expand the benefits of major irrigation projects now under way with the assistance of the World Bank and World Food Program and groundwater exploration projects undertaken in Maharashtra with the assistance of West Germany.

Although such vital inputs as cement, fertilizer, and electricity for pump operation continue to be in short supply, irrigation facilities are critical to the use of modern agricultural technologies such as fertilizer-responsive high-yield grain varieties. Moreover, irrigation stimulates increased seasonal cropping intensity and enables farmers to employ multiple cropping techniques and shifts in cropping patterns from low- to high-value crops. It is vital, however, that irrigation projects are technically appropriate in both design and operation; poor drainage from faulty systems raises soil salinity to a level where the soil is unable to support plant life. But through the proper intensification of technology and multiple cropping, farm employment as well as food production can be increased.

The government's fertilizer production, import, and distribution system works well in more developed areas with irrigation, power, and transport facilities. The government is now developing new distribution systems aimed at remote areas that lack wholesale and retail infrastructure and where transportation costs are high and storage facilities inadequate. The contribution of fertilizer to India's recent input-induced agricultural growth is estimated by USAID to be 70 percent. USAID-proposed expenditure levels shown in the following table include a five year total of $360 million for fertilizer promotion and importation. According to USAID, the increased use and proper application of fertilizer should increase grain production by an estimated 150,000 metric tons per year by 1987.

TABLE 1.2 *USAID/India: Funding Proposals, 1983–87*

Program Area	Planning Levels ($ million)					
	1983	1984	1985	1986	1987	Total
Food Supply and Rural Employment						
Surface Irrigation	120	135	165	175	225	820
Groundwater Irrigation	40	65	100	120	170	495
Agricultural Research & Education	10	10	15	25	25	85
Fertilizer Promotion	55	70	70	75	90	360
Food for Rural Works, Title II	(50)	(60)	(70)	(80)	(90)	(350)
Food for Vegetable–Oil Cooperatives, Title II	(30)	(30)	(40)	(50)	(50)	(250)
Fertility and Mortality Reduction						
Rural Health & Family Planning Systems[a]	15	40	45	65	90	255
Other Population Activities	5	20	30	40	50	145
Nutrition Interventions	10	10	25	30	30	105
Food for Maternal Child Health, Title II	(85)	(95)	(110)	(115)	(125)	(530)
Primary School Feeding, Title II	(70)	(55)	(40)	(35)	(35)	(235)
Energy, Forestry and Conservation						
Forestry and Conservation	20	40	50	60	70	240
Energy	–	10	–	10	–	20
TOTAL Development	275	400	500	600	750	2,525
TOTAL PL 480 Title II[b]	(235)	(240)	(260)	(280)	(300)	(1,315)

[a]Funding split 33/67 between Population and Health programs.

[b]Title II amounts shown are non–additive.

Source: USAID, *Country Development Strategy Statement, FY 83,* p. 33.

India has a continuing need to import U.S. vegetable oil to generate local currency. The government has an interest in developing the nation's forestry potential and management, in developing alternative energy sources (geothermal, wind, and solar), and in expanding the nation's rural health and now extremely low-key family planning programs. The PL 480 Title II funds referred to are for Food for Work programs implemented by voluntary U.S. agencies (CARE and Catholic Relief Services) in the areas of small irrigation projects and land development works plus the construction of rural feeder roads and some low-cost rural housing. This is in addition to food for schools and maternal and child health programs.

Employment and Land Reform

India's labor unions have been successful in regulating employment and pushing up wages in organized industries, particularly in public-sector enterprises. But they have had no effect at all on the 90 percent of India's workers—including virtually all rural workers—who remain unorganized. In 1970, 3.7 million Indians were registered as unemployed, and half a million people were being added to the unemployment rolls each year. In 1981, according to the International Labor Organization (ILO), registered unemployment reached the 16.3 million mark at mid-year and was growing at the rate of 2.0 million a year.

Employment figures for India are misleading at best, however. The extent of full-time, year-round unemployment is quite small in rural India, but there is widespread and severe underemployment.

India has been struggling with the implementation of land reform measures since the abolition of the *zamindari* (large landlord) system following independence. Although he has been stripped of his feudal rights, however, the zamindar still has power. His money translates into political power; he is able to control votes in his village and support like-minded candidates who, when elected to the state assembly, will throw their weight against drastic land-reform legislation and implementation. Consequently, about one-fourth of the rural population remains landless.

In the early 1950s, a ceiling of 30 acres per person was imposed on agricultural land holdings. But many landowners simple made paper transfers of their excess land to their children; some made transfers to fictitious persons. Even when land reform worked there were abuses: since there was no law to force landowners to till their land, even some peasants, who were given land by the government, became absentee landlords. The land picture is further confused by the fact that statistics on landholdings don't distinguish between arable land and land that is merely held or used for housing.

In the absence of effective land reforms, benefits from modern "green revolution" farming have similarly eluded the rural poor. While gains from modern agricultural technology and high-yield farming have primarily benefited the zamindars, economic inequalities have sharpened and class tensions have heightened.

In July 1970, a land grab movement was organized separately by the pro-Chinese Communist Party of India, the Samyukta Socialist Party, and the Praja Socialist Party. Although the movement was opposed by the Marxists on the grounds that it was anti-revolutionary, there was a rash of symbolic land occupations in Assam, Bihar, Kerala, Rajasthan, Uttar Pradesh, and West Bengal. As planned, the movement grabbed more headlines than land. But it did manage to embarrass several high-ranking government ministers as well as Gandhi herself, who owned a four-acre plot of land near Delhi.

One result of the movement was the government's convening of an urgent meeting of the state ministers to consider land reform in September 1970. The issue's urgency, however, was lost as each proposal was voted down. This, the twentieth such meeting since independence, ended without result.

By 1981, nearly 1.5 million hectares of land had been distributed to 1.2 million landless laborers. The consolidation of fragmented holdings has been more successful, having been completed on 46 million hectares by 1979. But the landless legions are growing and becoming increasingly restless. In 1961, an estimated 40 percent of India's farms were below the 2.5-acre minimum necessary to support a family. In 1971, 51 percent were below this minimum and, in 1972, an estimated two-thirds (63 percent) of rural households owned no land or less than 2.5 acres.

Land reform is delayed while small landholdings are divided over and over again among sons, contributing to a rapidly worsening situation. And, since desperately poor farmers tend to have large families to circumvent the need to hire outside help, the even more desperate landless laborers find that fewer jobs are available.

In a male-dominated society it is not surprising that employment opportunities for women are in critically short supply. The government's plans to promote cottage industries could go a long way in eliminating this job deficit. Unless women's employment is keyed to becoming a substitute for, rather than an addition to domestic chores, including the bearing and raising of children, one of the prime benefits of such work, fertility reduction, will be lost.

India's labor force of 300 million is growing at the rate of about 2.1 percent per year, almost the same rate at which the population is growing. In order to absorb more than 6.0 million new job-seekers a year and reduce the backlog of unemployment, the original Sixth Five-Year Plan projected the creation of a total of 46 million jobs during the period 1978-83. Since it was obvious that the stagnating industrial sector will not impact on unemployment in the foreseeable future, it

was assumed that over 80 percent of these new jobs would have
to be created in rural areas. Nonplantation crop production
would create only about 10 percent of the jobs needed. Other
employment opportunities would have to be found in rural enterprises, rural works, and allied agricultural activities (animal
husbandry, especially of dairy animals; horticulture; fisheries;
and forestry).

Work abroad offers an important, although increasingly
limited, opportunity for Indians seeking alternative employment opportunities. According to the *Financial Times* of London
(1981), "Several jumbo-loads fly every day to the Middle East,
Europe and the U.S. Such is the exodus, that remittances from
Indians working abroad are the single largest foreign exchange
earner for the country."

Vital as this emigration is to India's balance of payments,
the numbers involved are insignificant when it comes to either
unemployment or population growth in India. Visaria and
Visaria (1981) estimate that "the number [of Indian citizens
living and working abroad] in 1981 is only about one and a
half million, including some children born abroad to Indian
parents." Moreover, racial discrimination and declining
opportunities in other financially pinched countries have
resulted in a marked decrease in migratory enthusiasm.

The Visarias go on to point out that emigration is, in
fact, probably far outweighed by the continuing migration of
Bangladeshis into Assam. This migratory flow is at the bottom
of student-led protests which cut off exports of vital crude
oil, bamboo, and jute from Assam to the rest of the country
and blocked attempts by officials to carry out the 1981 census
in Assam.

Although the new Sixth Five-Year Plan's objectives differ
little from the old sixth plan, it is interesting to note that
the only broad objectives quantified are the overall economic
growth rate of 5.0-5.3 percent during the sixth plan and 6.0
percent during the seventh plan, and the annual growth rates
for agriculture (4.0 percent), industry (8-9 percent), and
export volume (10 percent). While the new sixth plan empha-
sizes energy conservation, ecological balance, and improved
efficiency throughout the economy, it states that the "removal
of poverty and unemployment will be the major thrust of all
plan programs." Featured in this respect are a new Integrated
Rural Development Program (IRDP), which will redirect programs
by channeling resources to the poorest village households,
identified by village councils, and a National Rural Employment Program (NREP), which provides all able-bodied job seekers
with employment on public works at about 90 percent of the
wages prevailing during the slack season.

In 1978-79, rural development programs launched in the
1970s began to pay off. Such programs as the Small Farmer
Development Agency, the Antyodaya program, dairy development,
Maharashtra's Employment Guarantee Scheme, and the government's

Food for Work Program generated an estimated 3.7 million worker-years of employment. This was the equivalent of more than 50 percent of the total annual labor force growth of roughly six million.

According to USAID (1981), "India now has the means to increase incomes on a substantial scale for the landless, who are the poorest and have been the most difficult to reach." The government has made significant progress in providing access to agricultural inputs, infrastructure, and productive assets other than land (primarily livestock). Rural electrification as of 1979-80 had reached 44 percent of the nation's villages, compared to 8.0 percent in 1965-66. Fertilizer consumption during the same period increased from 0.8 million to 5.3 million tons (or from 5 to 30 kilograms per hectare), use of improved varieties from 2.0 to 40 percent of the area planted with cereals, gross irrigated area from 33 million to 52 million hectares, and institutional credit for agriculture from about $1 billion to $8.8 billion in loans outstanding.

Markets and institutions are now generally effective in providing access to infrastructure and inputs regardless of landholding size. But many obstacles, not the least of which are a repressive class system and a grossly swollen and lethargic bureaucracy, stand between the landless millions and even minimal prosperity. Time will tell if the nation can muster the money and the will to translate economic potential into economic growth where it counts--in the nation's rural areas, where 76 percent of the population lives in abject poverty and ignorance. The nation's programs for rural development are ambitious and, for now at least, reasonably well funded. But even if food production and distribution systems advance to the point where equitable and adequate food supplies are made available to even the remotest of India's villages, there is no assurance that India's underemployed and poverty-stricken rural poor will have the means to buy the food.

Development takes time. And given the potentially disastrous effect of India's persistently high population growth rate on the nation's precarious economy and food production capacity, time is not on India's side.

Balance of Payments Picture*

The Indian economy has the potential for achieving higher growth and making major inroads into poverty, hunger, and poor health. Realization of this potential (particularly in light of the 1981 census count, which pushed the nation's population

---

*Much of the material in this section is drawn from USAID (1981).

at least 12 million beyond the expected number) will depend on
a commitment to equitable growth and success in mobilizing both
domestic and external resources. Above all, it will depend on
the adoption of an effective and acceptable program to reduce
rapidly the nation's birth rate.

Vigorous efforts to raise agricultural production have
paid off in recent years in grain self-sufficiency. But the
food-population balance is extremely precarious. Moreover,
both water and fertilizer are scarce. While the production
of wheat and rice has increased impressively during good monsoon years, the production of oil seeds and dietary stables
such as peas and beans have declined; many of the relatively
easy and rapid gains from the use of modern fertilizers and
high-yielding grain varieties are nearing their peak.

Resource availability is also critical to programs for
improved access to modern family planning, health, and nutrition services. Since the late 1970s, however, India's overall
resources position has declined markedly. Total investment
requirements for the Sixth Five-Year Plan are projected at
$212 billion; $113 billion of this will be needed for public
sector outlays alone. The Planning Commission estimates that
public sector resources available at 1979-80 rates of taxation
are on the order of $78 billion, including $5 billion in
deficit financing. The additional $35 billion needed to meet
plan objectives will have to come from increased taxation,
external assistance, reduced budget subsidies, and better
performance of public-sector enterprises. This is a big order
for a country as diverse as India and for a fiscal system that
does not adequately compensate for inflation.

If the government is successful in mobilizing adequate
domestic resources, external resource assistance is likely to
remain extremely precarious during the plan period. On the
credits side of the economic ledger are remittances from
Indians working abroad and export promotion efforts which have
given a significant boost to the export growth rate (7.0 percent per year by volume in the 1970s, compared to roughly 0.3
percent a year in the 1950s and 4.0 percent in the 1960s).

Inflation has leveled off at 8-9 percent, although supply
constraints and a rapid rise in petroleum prices contributed
to double-digit inflation in 1979-80 after four years of
relative price stability. The wholesale price index, which
rose by about 17 percent in 1979-80, was projected to increase
by 18 percent in 1980-81. But India's balance of payments has
been hit very hard by oil-price increases.

The cost of importing petroleum and petroleum products
(POL), which had risen from $265 million in 1972-73 to $1.45
billion in 1974-75, increased fairly slowly thereafter to
slightly over $2 billion by 1978-79. In 1979-80, however, the
POL import bill doubled to nearly $4.2 billion and, depending
on the level at which oil prices stabilize following the oil
"glut" of 1981-82, imports--needed partly to offset the dis-

ruption of domestic production and refining operations related
to political disturbances in Assam--are projected to cost as
much as $7.3 billion.

At this level, POL will account for over one-half of
India's imports by value and absorb over 80 percent of India's
export earnings. Meanwhile, the trade deficit was expected to
increase from $3.2 billion in 1979-80 to over $6 billion in
1980-81. Reserves including gold are likely to decline to $6
billion, or less than the equivalent of six months of imports
by the end of the Indian fiscal year.

A decline in reserves to a critical level of less than
three months of imports by 1982-83 is projected from current
trends. A real possibility exists, however, for a sharp
improvement in export performance, a breakthrough in reduction
of imports of products where India is already a low-cost producer (oil seeds, steel, cements, etc.), or a significant
shift in energy consumption patterns away from petroleum.

The government's overall economic planning is based on the
assumption that foreign aid will remain fairly constant. But
to achieve the kind of economic progress that will significantly reduce unemployment, underemployment, and poverty, the
country will need access to increasing levels of both public
and private external support for some time. By 1982, a number
of major donors were reducing the assistance levels necessary
to avert a balance-of-payments crisis and the attendant threat
of declining economic growth.

THE CRISIS

In late 1971, Indira Gandhi astonished foreign population
observers and knowledgeable Indian analysts alike by declaring
during a speech in Brussels that "the population problem no
longer is the dark cloud hanging over us which it once was."
Ten years later, the prime minister's thinking appeared to
have swung around 180 degrees when, during an address in late
1981 to the annual Conference of Central Councils for Health
and Family Welfare in New Delhi, she stated: "The time has
come to treat this [overpopulation] as a problem of our survival." Emphasizing the Indian population's need for better
nutrition, clothing, shelter, employment, and basic services,
the prime minister added, "If our dreams and our programs for
a better life for our people are to be realized, the birth
rate must be brought down."

What happened during those ten years to so radically
change Gandhi's perception of India's population growth?
First, there was a creeping awareness of the fact that, despite
two decades of massive financial and technical inputs, poverty
and malnutrition were as much the problems they had always been.
Added to this were unmistakable signs of growing social unrest
and a less fully realized awareness of the fact that just one

bad crop year could destroy India's grain self-sufficiency.
Then, in mid-March 1981, the release of India's 1981 census
figures shocked Indian politicians and economic planners
alike--the already drastically overpopulated country had at
least 12 million more people than the experts had projected.

India's mid-1981 population of 688.6 million had grown by
24.75 percent over the 1971 midyear level of 548.2 million
and was increasing at the annual rate of 2.23 percent instead
of the 1.9 percent expected. In other words, as Table 1.3
shows, the rate of population growth in India has remained
virtually unchanged since 1951, despite 30 years of family
planning programs and a total of $875 million spent on them
over the past 10 years.

In the 34 years between independence and mid-1981, India's
population doubled. At its current rate of growth, the population will double again in less than 31 years. The implications of such rapid and unrestrained growth for the nation's
economic prospects and the survival of its democratic institutions are indeed grim. Furthermore, they are a severe indict-
ment of the world's oldest and much-heralded family planning
program.

Speaking to the Asian Conference of Parliamentarians on
Population and Development in Peking in November 1981, Jordan's
Minister of Labor reminded the delegates of the economic consequences of overpopulation. Labor Minister Jawad Al-Anani
was quoted in *Popline* (1981) as saying that "Population growth
enhances consumption and decreases savings required to create
employment opportunities." Al-Anani noted that "A high birth
rate biases population distribution in favor of the age group
below 15, raises the dependency ratio, and applies pressures
on governments' budgets to direct more resources to meet basic
demands. As a result continuous population growth generates
forces within the system which work in the opposite direction
of efforts aimed at alleviating the problem."

Forty-one percent of India's population is under 15 years
of age. This not only places a high dependency burden on the
country, but assures it of a continuing high fertility rate.
Over the past 20 years, the nation's annual birth rate has
only dropped from 41 to 36 per 1,000, and many demographers
believe that census undercounting means that the birth rate
is now as high as 37 per 1,000. Less than one-quarter (22.6
percent) of Indian couples of reproductive age (women from 15
to 49 years of age) practice any form of birth control. Yet,
by comparison, China's birth rate dropped from around 35 per
1,000 to fewer than 20 per 1,000 in the same amount of time.

India, of course, is not China; the participatory, democratic form of government India strives to maintain and the
civil liberties guaranteed under its constitution create a
totally different atmosphere from that under which China's
remarkable gains in fertility reduction have been made. But
the question remains: how could such a heavily financed and
generally well-received program as India's fail so miserably?

TABLE 1.3 *Population Statistics, 1901-81*

Census Year	Total population (millions)	Average annual inter-census growth rate (%)	Persons per square kilometer	Sex ratio (males to famales)	Crude birth rate[a]	Crude death rate[a]
1891-1901		0.30			--	--
1901	238.3		77	1.029		
		0.56			49.2	42.6
1911	252.0		32	1.038		
		-0.03[b]			48.1	47.2
1921	251.2		81	1.047		
		1.06			46.4	36.3
1931	278.9		90	1.053		
		1.34			45.2	31.2
1941	318.5		103	1.058		
		1.26			39.9	27.4
1951	361.0		117	1.057		
		1.98			40.9	22.8
1961	439.1		142	1.063		
		2.20			41.1	18.9
1971	548.2		178	1.075		
		2.23			36.0	15.0
1981	688.6		222	1.069		

[a]Annual births and deaths per 1,000 population; inter-census averages.

[b]The population decline between 1911 and 1921 and overall slow growth up to 1921 was caused by frequent epidemics of plague and cholera, famines, and the influenza epidemic of 1918-19. The sharp acceleration of the rate of population growth during 1951-61 ia generally attributed to the control of malaria and infectious diseases, including tuberculosis, during the 1950s.

Source: Visaria and Visaria 1981, p. 10, Table 2. Population Bulletin, vol. 36, no. 4.

Ashish Bose of Delhi University's Institute of Economic
Growth has provided part of the answer. Bose is quoted in the
New York Times (Marshall, 1981):

> *The bureaucracy has administered family planning*
> *as if it were brick production. Targets are targets.*
> *It's a public works department mentality devoid of*
> *flexibility, and it doesn't work. . . . Family plan-*
> *ning projects financed with foreign aid have been*
> *largely counterproductive in India because they are*
> *alien to the Indian culture.*

Bose goes on to argue that foreign assistance programs
"have done more harm than good," apparently on the premise that
the government has been overwhelmed by a technical approach to
family planning. Similarly, Marshall reports the concern of
V. A. Panandiker of the Planning Commission over "a technical,
lackadaisical approach by the government" which has often "left
local health care centers understaffed and without proper supplies."

On the positive side, however, there is the fact that,
without the efforts made over the past 30 years, today's population would be much larger. But it is indeed disappointing to
consider that, in the light of India's nearly constant population growth rate, the country had to expend so much time, money,
and energy just to stand still.

Building Family Planning Awareness

Enlightened Indian economists have been concerned about
the problem of population in relation to resources and the
adverse effect of overpopulation on employment and agriculture
since about 1919. Then as now, however, there were economists
and political and social leaders who believed that industrialization and agricultural development would solve India's population problem, or at least keep pace with population growth.
Some observers, in fact, put this view of the long-range effect
of population growth momentum at the very bottom of India's
family planning failures. Many Indian leaders today do not
think that both resource-intensive industrialization and rapid
agricultural development will eventually be limited by resource
capability, while unrestrained population growth will proceed
at the expense of overall developmental gains and political
stability, and be limited only by starvation.

In 1923, the first family planning clinic in India was
opened in Poona and, in 1930, the government of the state of
Mysore (now Karnataka) opened the first government clinic in
Bangalore. The All-India Women's Conference advocated the
adoption of voluntary birth control. Although these efforts
reached only a small section of the population, private inter-

est in spreading the message of family planning was gathering steam. And, in 1949, the Family Planning Association of India, a private and still highly influential organization, was formed.

From the beginning, the Indian leadership was ambivalent on the question of population control. On April 2, 1925, Mahatma Gandhi stated in *Young India*: "There can be no two opinions about the necessity of birth control. But the only method handed down from ages past is self-control." Gandhi, however, believed the country was capable of supporting twice its 1925 population with the help of "a proper land system, better agriculture and supplementary industry." Ten years later Gandhi remarked (*Harijan*, 1935), "I believe in no children." In the *Harijan* of March 31, 1946, he observed that the "propagation of the race rabbitwise must undoubtedly be stopped" but that "regulation or restriction by artificial methods" would be "a calamity of the first grade."

Gandhi viewed birth control as lying within the set of moral and ethical values that had governed Indian life from antiquity. Birth control, Gandhi thought, was akin to the savings accrued from spinning one's own yarn, restricting meals to one dish and abstaining from alcohol and other "artificial" pleasure-inducing substances. The *charkha* (spinning wheel) symbolized Gandhi's message of self-reliance based on the Hindu tenet that, in this world, no one is responsible for another's pain or pleasure; each man is wholly responsible for the quality of his own life on earth.

No discussion of Indian social action programs in general, and family planning programs in particular, can long avoid the part played by the fatalistic concepts of *karma*, *dharma*, and the distinctively Hindu self-reliance through self-deprivation. The traditional Hindu views life as being proscribed by his birth station and actions in a previous life, not by governmental decree.

Even among those who were fully aware of the consequences of India's population growth, there was no clear agreement on how the problem should be solved. In 1938, Subhas Chandra Bose, president of the Indian National Congress, appointed a National Planning Committee under the chairmanship of Prime Minister Nehru to prepare a national plan of development. Bose advocated an emphasis on a definite restriction of population numbers. The result was the "Shah Report," completed by the Planning Committee's subcommittee on population under the direction of K. T. Shah in 1940.* This report gave rise to a committee resolution that "while measures for the improvement of the quality of the population and limiting excessive population pressure are necessary, the basic solution of the present disparity between population and standard of living lies in

---

*The material on the Shah Report, as well as other material in this section, is drawn from Visaria and Jain (1976).

the economic progress of the country on a comprehensive and planned basis."

The report further recommended that "in the interests of social economy, family happiness and national planning, family planning and a limitation of children are essential, and the State should adopt a policy to encourage these." The policy should "lay stress on self-control, as well as to spread knowledge of cheap and safe methods of birth control," but, the committee pleaded, "birth control clinics should be established and other necessary measures taken in this behalf and to prevent the use or advertisement of harmful methods." The latter apparently referred to abortion which, according to the report, "is not uncommon in India, effected by crude methods which are highly dangerous and damaging." The committee further recommended "the gradual raising of the marriage age," "discouragement of polygamy," and a eugenic program including "the sterilization of persons suffering from transmissible diseases of a serious nature, such as insanity or epilepsy," but did not specifically endorse the subcommittee's suggestion of "propaganda amongst the masses . . . in favor of 2-4 years spacing of births and the limitation of the total family to 4 children."

The Health Survey and Development Committee, appointed by the government of India in 1943, reported in 1946 that health improvements plus disease and famine controls would cause a serious acceleration in population growth. While considering deliberate limitations on family size to be "advisable," the committee also observed that such limitations could not be gained via self-control "to any material extent." The committee finally agreed that, where childbearing was likely to result in injury to mother or infant, the government should provide contraception information and free contraceptive supplies in public institutions. The committee, however, remained divided on the issue of governmental involvement in family planning and suggested that state action be restricted to control over the manufacture and sale of contraceptives, public assistance in research for a safe and effective contraceptive, and continuous study of the population problem and related factors.

Policies During the 1950s

With independence came pressures to import food and devote a major portion of the nation's resources to economy building. Family planning was pushed to the back burner until an evaluation of the 1951 census showed that India's population had increased during 1941-51 by 43 million, or about 14 percent. Spurred by the implications of this growth, the Planning Commission, which was appointed in March 1950 to formulate a plan for the most effective and balanced use of natural resources, turned to its Panel on Health Programs for recommendations on population growth and family planning.

Thus, in the draft of the First Five-Year Plan (published in July 1951), the Planning Commission observed that "population policy is . . . essential to planning" and that family planning is an important factor in improving health, particularly that of mothers and children. It further endorsed the committee's recommendation that "facilities for sterilization" should not be withheld and that "advice on contraception" should be granted to those who "seek and need it on social and economic grounds" subject, however, to the "availability of personnel in hospitals and health agencies." An amount of Rs. 2.5 million ($0.52 million at the prevailing exchange rate) was allotted for information collecting and research promotion on all aspects of family limitation and the development of "inexpensive, safe and efficacious methods of birth control suitable for all classes of people."

During the early 1950s, Rajkumari Amrit Kaur, the health minister and a former associate of Mahatma Gandhi, advocated the use of "self-control" (withdrawal or abstinence) for family planning. And, in 1951, a Western advisor was invited to India under the auspices of WHO to oversee pilot studies of the rhythm method. The same year, the government of India undertook an intensive population survey with the assistance of the United Nations in Mysore (now Karnataka) State.

The final draft of the First Five-Year Plan, presented to Parliament in December 1952, referred to a program for "family limitation and population control" and revised the budgetary provision for it upward to Rs. 6.5 million (U.S. $1.35 million), 0.03 percent of total development outlays. Thus, India became the first nation to involve itself in a national family planning program. However, since family planning was considered to be a highly personal (and therefore, politically sensitive) matter, the first plan funds were channeled mainly into research on population growth dynamics, experiments and studies into the acceptability of the rhythm method, and research on various aspects of contraception and contraceptives. Since the nation's family planning program had no precedent to build on, it became a primarily academic exercise.

Evaluations of the family planning program and patterns of assistance to voluntary organizations in the field were undertaken by the Family Planning Research and Programs Committee established by the government in May 1953. Among the recommendations made by the committee was the provision for family planning centers for "sex education, marriage counseling, marriage hygiene," health and nutrition education, and antisterility counseling. The committee recognized, however, that in the early stages of "the family planning campaign," the centers "would concentrate mainly on the spread of contraceptive practice." Furthermore, the committee recommended that "the development of the family planning program should be . . . the primary responsibility of Governments and local health authorities" and that "as far as possible, new family

planning centers should be developed in association with
institutions for the health protection of mothers and children." This was the beginning of the national family planning
program's integration with maternal and child health services.

The Second Five-Year Plan allotted Rs. 50 million ($10.5
million), or about 1.0 percent of the total development budget, for family planning activities, and proposed the establishment of one clinic per 50,000 people in urban areas and
1,800 clinics in rural areas. Each rural clinic was to serve
about 80,000 people.

Following the plan's recommendation of a "more or less
autonomous . . . central board for family planning," the
Central Family Planning Board was formed in September 1956.
Family planning boards were soon set up in the various states
to act primarily in an advisory capacity.

As early as 1953, the Family Planning Research and Programs Committee noted the growing acceptance of tubectomy
(female sterilization) and the tendency of some family planning clinics to recommend it. This tendency, however, was
considered to be a result of distressing socioeconomic conditions; "wise family planning" was thought to be a greatly
preferred substitute. One of the committee's vasectomy (male
sterilization) supporters, however, later became chairman of
the Program Committee of the Family Planning Board in Madras
State (now Tamil Nadu). Under his leadership, attempts were
made to popularize vasectomy throughout the state. Cash
incentives of Rs. 25 (about $5.25) were given to selected
private medical practitioners in Madras City for each vasectomy performed on a low-income person.

Other incentive schemes included remunerations to "can-
vassers and tutors in family planning" who sent persons to
approved surgeons or government hospitals for sterilizations.
And, during 1959, the government of Madras began making a cash
grant of Rs. 30 ($6.25) to every "poor" person who was ster-
ilized in a government hospital in Madras City. Gradually,
the scheme was extended to other areas in the state. The
grant was considered to be compensation for transportation
costs and time lost from work; the services were limited to
persons with at least three living children.

The response to the scheme was so favorable that the
government came to accept sterilization as one of the recognized methods of family limitation. A number of sterilization
centers were set up, mainly in urban areas. In rural areas,
mobile units and special camps began to spread sterilization
services.

Policies During the 1960s

The family planning provisions of the First and Second
Five-Year Plans were drafted according to the expectation that

the population would continue to grow at the average 1941-51 rate of 1.26 percent. Thus, both plans were aimed at lowering the birth rate concurrently with the death rate. The 1961 census, however, showed that the population was growing at the annual rate of nearly 2.0 percent and gathering speed.

The Third Five-Year Plan was molded with a much stronger emphasis on family planning. Accepting "the objective of stabilizing the growth of the population over a reasonable period" as "at the very center of planned development," the plan recognized the "valuable contribution" of voluntary sterilization to the family planning program. The extension of family planning services to district hospitals, subdivisional hospitals, and primary health centers was envisaged; provisions were made for the use of mobile sterilization units in areas beyond the reach of hospitals.

Toward the end of 1961, rural "sterilization camps" were organized in Maharashtra State. The approach also began to spread to other states and, after 1965, camps focusing on IUD (Lippes loop) insertions also were organized. In the early 1960s, disillusionment with the role of clinics as family planning promoters had begun to set in.

It was proposed that the clinic approach be dropped in favor of a nationwide community extension program. The program was to be implemented by nurse-midwives (dais) attached to the nation's 5,400 primary health centers. Each dai would serve 10,000 people. The primary functions of the family planning program were to be "(1) educational work, which can produce the group support needed for adoption of family planning and provide specific information about contraception; and (2) supply of contraceptives through channels which pose the least possible psychological or physical barriers to obtaining them.

The main goal of the program was "to accelerate the rate of adoption of family planning so as to reduce the birth rate . . . to 25 per 1,000 . . . by 1973." To emphasize the link between family planning and family health and well-being, the family planning centers were redeisgnated as Family Welfare Planning Centers.

A United Nations Advisory Mission visited India in early 1965 at the request of the government of India. In its 1966 report, the U.N. mission optimistically concluded that it would be possible to reduce India's birth rate by about one-third in 10 years and that the annual rate of population growth would decline from the 1965 rate of 2.2 percent to 1.6 percent by 1975 and to 1.0 percent before 1985, provided the mission's recommendations were immediately and vigorously implemented. Among the recommendations were: concerted efforts to raise the age at marriage and promote other social changes that might reduce fertility (i.e., relax or abolish the dowry system, measurably increase female education and employment, instigate a governmental social security system, etc.); intensification of the sterilization program; exploitation of the IUD as an effective method of family planning; and expansion of the

domestic production of condoms and improvements in the distribution system to increase consumption.

In November 1966, with its basic organization in place,
the national family planning program adopted a symbol: the
inverted red triangle began to sprout outside of family planning service centers and appeared on billboards, construction-
site fences, buses, walls, buildings, trees, and trains.   They
flew through the air on kites, floated on boats, with the
symbols of smiling parents and two equally happy children.

Meanwhile, as the family planning slogan shifted from
"two or three children" to "we two, our two" and the ubiquitous
red triangle came to be recognized all over a country where a
wide diversity of languages and attitudes makes common messages
almost impossible to impart, other things were happening.   For
one, Dr. D. N. Pai, a dynamic Harvard-trained medical-school
professor, was made Bombay's Director of Family Planning and
Maternal and Child Health in 1967.   The results of his appointment were almost as remarkable as the man himself.

The British had steered clear of instigating family planning measures during their tenure of power in India on the
grounds that the problem was of an inviolable religious nature.
Pai, however, was convinced that resistance to family planning
was rooted in fear, ignorance, and indifference rather than in
religion.   He initiated a massive campaign to educate the
people of Bombay on the merits and methods of contraception.

Believing that male sterilization was the best answer to
the population problem, but realizing that people would not
seek out hospitals and health centers for family planning
services, Pai literally mobilized his resources and took the
services to the people.   Condom distribution centers were set
up on teeming railway platforms to serve people who were too
embarrassed to get contraceptives at a drugstore.   By 1971,
35,000 condoms were being distributed a day, as compared to 60
condoms per day three years before.   But that was only the
beginning.

Unlike most of his medical compatriots, Dr. Pai was fully
aware that poor people, who considered hospitals to be a place
to die, would not go to them for sterilizations.   So Pai took
sterilizations to them: vasectomy facilities joined condom
distribution points on the railway platforms.   Pai's "motiva-
tors," volunteers who had had vasectomies and came from the
same class as most of the people jamming the railway centers
on their way to and from work, found ready acceptors for the
simple 10-minute procedure.   In just five months, vasectomies
in Bombay shot up from 179 in April 1967 to 6,239 in September.
The sterilizations were performed by unpaid physicians, assisted by unpaid nurses.

But the indefatigable Pai was still not satisfied.   The
railway station wasn't the only crowded place; Bombay teemed
with humanity, about a half-million of whom were homeless
"sidewalk people."   Dr. Pai took his unique brand of clean,
safe vasectomy service to them, too--in discarded Bombay city
buses converted into mobile vasectomy clinics.   Each day, the

buses drove to particularly crowded city areas to serve people
who were eager to stop having more and more unwanted children
and to pocket the Rs. 20 offered after the operation.

Another thing that began happening during the late 1960s
was the highly innovative commercial distribution of domestically produced Nirodh condoms at subsidized prices. At the
same time, major industrialists and tea plantation managers
were building full-fledged programs for the distribution of
contraceptive information and supplies to their employees.
And the government was taking a hard new look at the high
prevalence of often fatal "folk" abortions performed in the
country.

Evidence of the practice of abortion in India, as in every
other part of the world, goes back to the beginning of recorded
time. As mentioned earlier, the Shah Report (1940) (Visaria
and Jain, 1976) had alerted the government to the dangers of
widespread crude abortions sought—but not always effected—
through the use of sometimes toxic herbal abortifascients or
sharp sticks inserted into the womb. During the enlightened
1960s, however, definite steps were taken to correct a situation that caused so many women so much pain and often death,
and, when abortions were unsuccessful, led to so many mal-
formed infants.

In a report to the Minister of Health and Family Planning
in 1966, the National Planning Committee's subcommittee on
population denounced the existing abortion law, which limited
legal abortion to those cases in which the mother's life would
be threatened by childbirth, as being "too restrictive." In
November 1969, a bill to liberalize the law was introduced in
Parliament. The Medical Termination of Pregnancy Act provides
for abortion on three grounds: when a woman's life or physical or mental health is threatened; on humanitarian grounds,
when pregnancy results from a crime such as rape; and on
eugenic grounds, when there is substantial risk that the child,
if born, would suffer from severe physical or mental abnormali-
ties. The act specifies that a pregnancy resulting from contraceptive failure "may be presumed to constitute a grave
injury to the mental health of the woman."

Hooked on Rigidity

Despite its long buildup, India's national population
program really got going only in 1966, with the disbursement
of central budgetary funds to state ministries of health.
Although foreign contributions to the program at the time
appeared sizeable from the perspective of the leading donor,
USAID, they contributed only $20 million to the program, less
than 5.0 percent of the total federal budget for family planning.

As the program gathered momentum during the late 1960s,
both enthusiasm and expectations ran high. The clinical

approach, adopted initially in deference to the technical
skill and sanitary conditions required for sterilizations and
IUD insertions, eventually gave way to the "community extension" approach facilitated by outreach workers and mobile
family planning units. The search was on for the one method
best suited for general acceptance.

In early 1965, the introduction of the IUD (Lippes loop)
was met with excitement. Mass IUD camps shot up to provide
easy access to the contraceptive that encouraged even United
Nations observers to predict that population growth could be
reduced to 1.0 percent by 1985. By the end of 1967, more
than 1.7 million IUDs had been inserted.

By 1968, however, IUD acceptance levels began to fall off.
Some observers think that the squatting defecation habits of
most IUD wearers, particularly those who have given birth to
many children, led to a high IUD expulsion rate. But it was
most likely side effects that tarnished the reputation of
IUDs. The lack of hygiene in many insertion centers led to
infection; the monthly cramping experienced by some women
kept them from their work, and those who experienced increased,
prolonged, and more profuse menstrual periods lost even more
time from their work since, in the traditional Hindu household,
menstruation is thought to be an expellation of "toxic substances," and menstruating women are considered to be unfit
for performing such duties as food preparation and serving.

Moreover, the family planning leadership became concerned
about the fact that, after two years or so, only about 60
percent of the women who had received IUDs were still using
them and, after three years, the rate had dropped to about 50
percent. Alarmed over this less-than-perfect continuation
rate (and regarding the glass as being half empty rather than
half full), the government virtually abandoned its IUD campaign. It began to concentrate on the promotion of male
sterilization as the best, easiest, and cheapest method of
family planning.

It is, in fact, this almost slavish devotion to a rigid
system that has held India's family planning efforts back and
set the stage for the sterilization campaign excesses of 1976-
77.

During the late 1960s, a Ford Foundation medical advisor
in India spread the word that oral contraceptives had dire
side effects and were, therefore, too dangerous to be introduced to the country. Despite the fact that the relative risks
of repeated pregnancies in a malnourished woman--not to mention
the dangers of overpopulation itself on an already overcrowded
and poverty-stricken country--render the possible side effects
of pills negligible in terms of overall public health, oral
contraceptives are still practically unavailable through the
government's health system. Indian scientists and clinic
officials continue to show more concern over possible side
effects than over the Indian woman's difficulty in keeping

track of her daily dosage, a situation that could be alleviated by careful instructions from pill dispensers.

The injectible depo-provera^R, used since 1975 in nearby Thailand and many other countries, has still not been added to the list of contraceptive choices, probably simply because it has never been used in India. On a somewhat different scale, but also affecting overall contraceptive acceptivity, is the absence of modern lubricated condoms from the highly imaginative and large-scale commercial distribution scheme that sells condoms at nominal prices through the marketing facilities of established firms selling such products as tobacco, soap, and cooking oil.

Ironically, it is India's very size, the legacy of decades of general indifference to or outright rejection of population growth as being the major obstacle to economic development, that confuses the family planning picture. By 1970, just when financial support was beginning to roll in and results were becoming obvious, it became equally obvious to knowledgeable and concerned Indians that the national program was heading for a fall. The momentum built up over four years of active promotion of family planning could not be maintained in the face of the far greater momentum achieved over four decades of virtually unrestrained population growth.

The efforts by states to meet fertility reduction timetables continue to be frustrated by the rigidity of targets set for the nation as a whole, without sufficient consideration of regional differences in both attitudes and resources. Efforts to allocate resources appropriate in a regional sense are frustrated by the government's strict adherence to democratic principles: by granting equal assistance to all states for training, purchase of contraceptive commodities, reimbursement for sterilization services, etc., the government avoids charges of discrimination.

Such states as Kerala, Haryana, Maharashtra, Punjab, and Karnataka, which have relatively developed infrastructures and are comparatively socially progressive, are able to make optimum use of available resources, and are indeed managing to bring their birth rates down significantly. In other states—particularly those that lack an organization conducive to the delivery of any kind of service—the task is infinitely more difficult. And it is even harder to promote family planning education and provide access to contraceptive services in those states where the leadership is as backward as the economy is depressed.

The Turbulent Seventies

Despite disappointments over the declining acceptance of IUDs, the nation's sterilization drive started out with a bang. In the Fourth Five-Year Plan (April 1969–March 1974), the family planning program was highlighted as being "amongst items of the highest national priority." The integration of family planning efforts with maternal and child health care was accepted along with the program's new targets of an annual birth rate of 32 per 1,000 by 1979-81. The "right approach" to providing mass access to sterilization facilities was, however, still being pondered.

Then in the fall of 1970, the young, dedicated, and forward-looking collector of Ernakulam district in Kerala came up with an idea that revolutionized the family planning "establishment." Despairing of government policies that failed to deliver and of targets that were constantly being set and then pushed ever further into an increasingly grim future, District Collector S. Krishnakumar decided to take action.

In 1971, India's population problem found its most acute expression in Kerala, one of the most densely populated regions of the world. In this narrow strip of land running along the southwestern tip of India, a population of 21.3 million was crowded into an area of 15,002 square miles. Eighty-five percent of the population was dependent on agriculture, primarily the low-return production of *coir* (coconut fiber) and cashew nuts. The high ratio of population to land had bound the state to low per capita income from agriculture, and the economy was further depressed by a very low rate of industrialization. With more than a million persons unemployed and 67 percent of the population consisting of non-wage-earning dependents, the state's population had grown by 26.3 percent and that of Ernakulam by 27.4 percent since 1961, as compared to a growth of 24.8 percent for India as a whole.

The state of Kerala did, however, have some important things going for it. Thanks to educational reforms initiated by the Communist Party of India, which first came to power in Kerala in 1956, the state's literacy rate of 60.4 percent (66 percent of males and 54.3 percent of females) in 1971 was second only to that of Chandigarh (61.6 percent). The state's strong educational system--a result of Kerala's refusal to subsidize education for small elites at the expense of broad majorities--and the high proportion of women benefiting from it has also resulted in a higher age at the time of marriage. While the average age of women at marriage is 17 for India as a whole, it is now about 21 for women (26 for men) in Kerala. Over the past two decades, more and more of Kerala's women have chosen careers over marriage and childbearing; a major portion of Indian nurses are Keralites. But Kerala was only able to produce about half of its food needs.

The average Indian has no basis for understanding the relationship between his or her family size and national poverty. Krishnakumar recognized the fact that the idea of limiting one's family size is viewed by deprived Indians as just one more area of deprivation, even though many of those same Indians despair at the number of unplanned children born

to them. He decided that the way to get Keralites to accept
voluntary sterilization was to promote community participation and make the experience of having a vasectomy immediately
rewarding. The incentives used would be geared to the population's needs.

A pilot one-day vasectomy camp at Kalamassery proved that
Krishnakumar was on the right track: incentives for vasectomy
candidates rolled in from such agencies as Premier Tyres, Ltd.,
and the Lions Club of Alwaye; about 746 vasectomies were performed. And Krishnakumar set about the business of organizing
a massive vasectomy camp to last for an entire month at Ernakulam's capital city, Cochin; a concurrent subcamp would be
operated for one week at Thodupazha for the convenience of
people living in panchayats in the district's easternmost hilly
areas.

Everyone got into the act. Two hundred doctors, nurses,
paramedics, and administrators offered their services for pay
and allowances averaging Rs. 500 (about $67) for a month's
work. Local radio stations and newspapers made constant and
prominent references to the event; posters, banners, and red
triangles were plastered throughout the district, and local
volunteers spread the word door to door. Public meetings were
held to advertise the event, local movie houses showed family
planning slides, and variety shows and other cultural enter-
tainments added dramatic flair to the family planning theme.
Incentives were requested and received, and funds were gathered
from the central and state governments as well as from panchayats or municipalities and private sources to cover the costs
of cash incentives and medicines.

By the time the camp opened for business in November 1970,
the district was primed. Inside the Ernakulam town hall, 40
curtained booths, fitted with operating tables and sterilized
equipment were waiting. And so were the first clients, who
had been driven to the site free of charge in government trucks
and private buses; many of them had brought their entire families. Later, groups of men would also arrive on foot, chant-
ing in Malayalam:

> Hear the voice of the Indian masses
> Who sweat and toil on their sacred land;
> Hear this patriotic clarion call,
> Two (parents) we are, and two (children only) for us!

Upon their arrival, acceptors were immediately registered
at booths prepared for each panchayat, and then given a free
medical checkup. Those pronounced medically fit were prepared
for surgery and ushered into the operating booths for the ten-
minute procedure. From there, the men were directed to the
medical section for medical instructions, an antibiotic injec-
tion and supplies of medicated ointment, vitamins donated by
pharmaceutical firms, and condoms for use over a three-month

period, after which their sperm would be tested for proof of
sterilization. For those who wanted to rest, beds were provided in another area.

The next stop was at the cash section, where each volunteer
received Rs. 21 (almost $3.00) in cash plus a certificate worth
a week's ration of food from his home shop. From there, pa-
tients were led to one of several long tables for a hearty--
and, by local standards, lavish--sit-down meal. Then, at the
end of the meal, they were taken to the gift section to draw
for prizes ranging from *dhothis* (the draped-cotton pants worn
by men in the area) to wristwatches, transistor radios, and
bicycles, as well as stoves, cooking utensils, stainless-steel
vessels, suitcases, flashlights, and petromax, all donated by
local business firms. At the CARE food section, each man
received a marketing bag decorated with a red triangle, 16
lbs. of bulgar wheat, 4 lbs. of corn soya meal and 1-1/2 lbs.
of vegetable oil with printed instructions (in the local dia-
lect, Malayalam) on the proper cooking of the donated food.

In an average of just one hour, each volunteer had closed
the door forever on the begetting of more unwanted children,
had been dignified by his treatment as a valuable human being,
fed well, showered with gifts and considerable attention and
care, and sent on his way, again, via free truck or bus.

In just 31 days, from November 20 through December 20,
1970, 13,950 men received vasectomies at the Ernakulam town
hall, and an additional 1,050 accepted sterilization at
Thodupuzha town hall, for a total of 15,000 vasectomies. Furthermore, under these camp conditions, vasectomies were performed at the total cost of Rs. 113 per patient (Rs. 74 of
which was provided by the government), far less than the Rs.
200-300 cost of a vasectomy under usual conditions through the
district's family planning program. And one-third of these
costs were borne by public contribution.

Buoyed by the results of the 1970 vasectomy camp, Krishnakumar decided to launch an even bigger effort from July 1 to
July 31, 1971. However, since sterilization was limited to
persons having two or more children, Krishnakumar decided to
provide services for couples interested in spacing births as
well as terminating them.

This time the camp conducted at the banner-draped and
electric-light-festooned Ernakulam town hall would provide
facilities for Nirodh (condom) distribution and vasectomies
and tubectomies to be performed in a total of 50 wood-parti-
tioned cubicles. Those who wanted to have IUDs inserted or
previous vasectomies reversed would be directed to district
hospitals for free procedures. Arrangements would be made for
the family members of all acceptors to have free medical check-
ups at the camp, for baby contests, dance performances and
other cultural programs, and an audiovisual family planning
show. A sterility clinic would provide services to infertile
couples via a series of medical tests, medication, and advice.

The camp was conceived to symbolize not only family limitation, but the total concept of family welfare in a fun-filled holiday atmosphere. In both name and concept, it would be a massive Family Welfare Festival.

Publicity efforts were stepped up to include organized *jathas* (parades) of marching, dancing, and singing volunteers; special promotional efforts were directed toward communities of Harijans and fishermen as well as city slums, labor unions, plantation laborers, and office workers. The government recognized the camp as a potential model for similar efforts in other parts of the country, and agreed to provide Rs. 20 (Rs. 15 for each volunteer, with the remainder going toward other camp expenses). CARE agreed to increase its contribution from the Rs. 25 of food the agency provided for each patient during the previous camp to Rs. 54. Included in the CARE gift packet given to each sterilization volunteer were a zippered shopping bag or plastic pail, a dhothi, a saree, a black umbrella (a status symbol among India's poor), and three kgs. (a little more than 6.6 lbs.) of rice. Part of CARE's contribution also went toward a Rs. 10 fee presented to each sterilization "motivator." Volunteers also received a lottery ticket, a certificate for a week's food rations, free coffee and snacks before treatment, and a banquet enlivened by a colorful stage show afterwards.

The publicity for this camp was so effective and widespread that the camp attracted many more people than expected, particularly from outside Ernakulam District. Incentive supplies were constantly in need of updating as the numbers of acceptors swelled.

By the time the camp closed its doors, the original goal of 20,000 vasectomies had been exceeded by nearly 200 percent. A total of 62,903 vasectomies had been performed at the main camp (59,367), a 10-day subcamp at Thodupuzha (2,540), a mini-camp at the Cochin Naval Base (611), and auxiliary mobile units (385). Hospital tubectomies totaled 505, and an additional 10 tubectomies were performed at the naval base. Recanalizations (vasectomy reversals) were performed on 117 men, and 879 couples registered for the treatment of infertility. More than 8,000 gross of condoms were distributed at the camp sites and by medical institutions throughout the district. Although only a negligible number of IUD insertions were performed during the festival itself, it was expected that the publicity given to the method would promote its later acceptance.

An outstanding feature of the landmark family planning festival was the participation by people outside of the district; of the 63,418 procedures performed during the festival, 43,600 were performed on people from other districts in Kerala; five vasectomies were performed on men from outside the state. Eighty-five percent of the males receiving vasectomies were between the ages of 30 and 49; 42 percent of the men had three or less living children, while 46.3 percent had from four to six living children.

Gujarat State followed Ernakulam's lead by conducting vasectomy camps in all 19 state districts from November 15, 1971 to January 15, 1972. A total of 223,060 vasectomies were performed in these camps, exceeding the original target of 150,000 by about 49 percent. By April 1, 1972, similar camps had also been conducted in 32 districts of another seven states and, during 1972 and 1973, the camp approach had spread to 210 districts in 16 of the nation's 31 states and union territories.

The success of the camp approach stemmed from topflight organization, strong community participation, and a genuine sense of dedication to the well-being of the people served. Acceptors were attracted as much by the camps' atmosphere of comradery that served to relax the intense embarrassment usually felt by Indians when confronted by matters pertaining to sex as by the incentives that averaged Rs. 100 ($12) per volunteer in cash and goods, more than six times the compensation usually paid. And the camp approach to voluntary sterilization paid off in impressive gains in the volunteer rate. Between 1971 and 1973, a total of 5.3 million Indians accepted sterilization, more than half the number of sterilization acceptors (8.7 million) recorded for the entire period 1956-71.

During 1973-74, however, the camp approach to family planning began to falter. A number of cases of tetanus and infection-related deaths were reported to have occurred in one of the camps; others were plagued by administrative problems. Of at least equal concern to the government were the declining numbers of vasectomies being performed throughout the country. Funds allocated to the overall family planning program were cut drastically, and the camp approach was discontinued.

The Emergency Drive*

Against the background of emergency rule declared by Indira Gandhi on June 25, 1975, an aggressive fertility control drive was launched. Although the prime minister's primary concerns at the time were the nation's acute economic and political problems, Sanjay Gandhi added political will to governmental funding for birth control. Nearly Rs. 5 billion ($66 million), representing nearly 2.0 percent of total development funds, had been budgeted for family planning by the Fifth Five-Year Plan. And family planning became the central theme of the development program formulated by the Indian Youth Congress, the wing of the ruling Congress-I Party under Sanjay's domination.

---

*This section is drawn from Gwatkin (1979) and from Visaria and Visaria (1981).

The new family planning drive adopted many of the features, including cash incentives, that had made previous camps so successful. In addition, however, a number of states added a variety of "negative incentives" to their program thrust. As the sterilization movement gained momentum, the threatening and sometimes brutal negative incentives came to outweigh the program's positive aspects.

Some Indian states had begun to experiment with negative incentives to limit fertility as early as the mid-1960s. Most notable among these was the decision by the government of Maharashtra State in June 1967 that "any concession, loan, subsidy, relief, grant or any other benefit, as specified below, would, hereafter, not be available to those families which do not restrict their size to three living children, if they have less than three children, or to their present size, if they have more than three children." Among the benefits were free medical treatment for government officers and the general public, government quarters for civil servants and accommodations in public housing projects for the public, and most government scholarships.

The state of Uttar Pradesh similarly decided to provide educational benefits only to children whose parents limited the size of their families. Compulsory sterilization also had been proposed and widely discussed. In 1972, the government's Task Force on Family Planning proposed legislation to legalize enforced sterilization; the government of Haryana State expressed its interest in the enactment of such legislation, as did the state of Maharashtra in 1976. Although none of these proposals was adopted, and no coercive legislation was ever passed, the idea had attracted a significant number of adherents and, by 1975, was becoming increasingly respectable.

The message of family planning, which gained urgency during Sanjay Gandhi's frequent public addresses, was given prominent space in the emergency-controlled press. On March 25, 1976, the *Statesman* reported Sanjay's exhortation that the family planning program must be given "the utmost attention and importance because all our industrial, economic, and agricultural progress will be of no use if the population continues to rise at the present rate." Similar but stronger was the declaration of the Indian Youth Congress, led by Sanjay Gandhi, as reported by the *Times of India* on November 21, 1976:

> *There should be no more delay in checking the*
> *growth of population since the demographic deluge*
> *is already fast closing in on us, threatening to*
> *throw all our socio-economic efforts off balance.*

There can be no doubt that Sanjay Gandhi truly understood the seriousness and scope of India's population problem and was deeply and genuinely concerned over it. But what the heavily

censored press did not report were the extremes to which
fertility control efforts would be taken.

Those in command were fully aware of the government's
firm new commitment to swift measures to reduce the nation's
growth rate. They knew that results had to be produced even
at the expense of arousing public animosity.

The first result was an extraordinary outburst of frantic
activity as various governmental groups grappled with the
problem of translating the general directive to do something
into action. Family planning proclamations flooded the
country; a bewildering array of incentive and disincentive
schemes were proposed, debated, approved, and promoted. At
the same time, as Gwatkin (1979) reports, there was "the
quieter mobilization of the government's administrative
machinery. The word was passed to all governmental agencies
that everybody would be held responsible for assuring the
family planning program's success."

In April 1976, the Central Health and Family Planning
Ministry's national population statement opened with a recognition of the relationship between population and development.

> *Our real enemy is poverty, . . . in the ultimate
> analysis it is only when the underlying causes of
> poverty and disease are eliminated that the nation
> will be able to move forward to its desired goals.*

Sixteen population-related measures were given prominence.
These included increasing the minimum legal age of marriage;
making 8.0 percent of central government assistance to state
governments dependent on family planning performance; asking
state governments to accord higher priority to female literacy;
increasing cash incentives for sterilization by 50 percent, to
Rs. 150 ($19), for volunteers having two or less children, and
providing cash payments of Rs. 100 for those having three
children and Rs. 70 for those families with more than three
children; changing civil service regulations to ensure that
central government employees adopt a small family norm; and
permitting state governments to enact and implement compulsory
sterilization legislation for couples with more than three
children.

State and local bodies, too, were caught up in the frenzy
of proposing and adopting hundreds of measures. Some incentive
plans were of a positive nature (Andhra Pradesh's announcement
that government employees accepting sterilization would get a
raise, for example); a great many were negative (Himachal
Pradesh's withdrawal of maternity leave for female employees
who already had two children). Some negative incentives were
quite mild (West Bengal's decision to cover government employees' leave travel costs for no more than two children, for
example); some were exceptionally harsh (Bihar's denial of
public food rations to families with three children).

Orissa decided to grant government loans only to sterilized persons or to those with small families. Rajasthan ruled that no one with more than three children would be accepted for government employment unless they were sterilized. Madhya Pradesh granted irrigation water at subsidized rates to all persons from villages meeting a specified sterilization quota. Some states ordered government employees to get sterilized on the threat of losing certain employee benefits if they refused. Uttar Pradesh ordered teachers to consent to sterilization or forfeit a month's salary; the state also withheld the pay of family planning workers who failed to meet their quota of sterilization volunteers.

Many of the measures adopted during the emergency were passed primarily to emphasize the government's dedication to fertility control. The harshest measures, in fact, were never implemented at all. Maharashtra's highly publicized proposal calling for the compulsory sterilization of couples with eight or more children, for example, died in New Delhi. But, while Maharashtra's family planning efforts turned out to be much less aggressive than others in the South, nothing could match the ferocity with which the program was pushed in the North--in the states of Haryana, Himachal Pradesh, and Uttar Pradesh and the union territory of Delhi, where Sanjay and his colleagues were particularly active. As it turned out, legislation was not at all a requirement for compulsory sterilization to take place.

In the years prior to the emergency, national contraception target rates had been divided among the states according to their population size, social and economic situation, and level of family planning performance. In 1976-77, sterilization targets allocated among the states by the Central Ministry of Health and Family Planning totaled 4.3 million volunteers. But now, in an atmosphere in which family planning officials were given to believe they had more to lose than to win, unilaterally raised targets came in waves as one state after another declared they could better their targets. All but three of India's major states (the exceptions were Assam, Kerala, and Jammu and Kashmir) raised their targets as much as three to six times for a total national goal of 8.6 million volunteers. It was alleged that the raising of targets in Delhi (from 2,000 to 200,000), Uttar Pradesh (from 400,000 to 1.5 million), Haryana, and other states came at Sanjay's personal command. The official Ministry of Health and Family Planning was largely bypassed.

Directives issued by state governments were both terse and intimidating. "Inform everybody," Uttar Pradesh's chief secretary telegraphed to field officials, "that failure to achieve monthly targets will not only result in the stoppage of salaries but also suspension and severest penalites. Galvanize entire administrative machinery forthwith--repeat, forthwith--and continue to report daily progress by crash wireless to me. . . ." As intended, the directives were taken seriously; mobile sterilization units roared into action all over India. As before, monetary incentives were paid to volunteers and sanctions were placed against those who failed to comply with the government's orders. But unlike before, sterilization was not always extended on a voluntary basis.

The central government never legislated compulsory measures. But coercion was widespread except in the three non-Congress-Party-governed states mentioned previously: Kerala, with its highly respected Communist leadership and dislike of Sanjay's rabid anti-Communist views; Jammu and Kashmir, with its two-thirds Muslim majority; and oil-rich Assam. Tamil Nadu, which had long resisted domination from the North, also dragged its feet on program implementation.

Coercive actions ranged from harassment to outright brutality. Among Gwatkin's (1979) illustrations of harassment were the sudden crackdown on India's time-honored ticketless railway travelers, who were now given the choice of heavy fines or sterilization, and the imposition of sterilization as a condition of employment for road-building laborers, who were given the choice of accepting sterilization and a cash incentive equal to four to six weeks' pay, or going without work. School teachers were instructed to spread the government's concern with family well-being to their students' parents by informing them of the financial benefits of sterilization acceptance and of the governmental decree that children from large families may be denied school entrance unless a parent undergoes sterilization. The teacher's failure to meet a five or six person sterilization quota was tantamount to forfeiting a month's salary.

Similarly, a family head presenting his ration card at a government "fair price shop" for subsidized food discovered that, because his card indicated he had six children, his family's weekly rations would be withheld until he was sterilized. It is a well-known fact that some rural families invent fictitious children to receive higher ration allotments. But even if the family head confessed to, say, having only two children instead of the six indicated on his card, the shopkeeper was under greater pressure to produce sterilization volunteers than to conserve food grain. He was unlikely to hand over even the adjusted amount of food. And the various disreputable characters living on the fringes of Indian society also found their former police friends were far less likely to overlook, in Gwatkins' words, "deviations from the straight and narrow for old times' or a few rupees' sake."

Sometimes, the pressure to produce sterilization volunteers led to direct coercion, as in Uttawar, a Haryana Muslim village near Delhi, whose town council had formerly led the area's strong resistance to the sterilization drive. The *Indian Express* of March 8, 1977, recalled:

> *At 3 a.m. on November 6 the villagers of Uttawar*
> *were shaken from their sleep by loudspeakers*
> *ordering the menfolk--all above 15--to assemble at*
> *the bus-stop on the main Nuh-Hodol road. When they*
> *emerged, they found the whole village surrounded by*
> *the police. With the menfolk on the road, the*
> *police went into the village to see if anyone was*
> *hiding. . . . As the villagers tell it, the men on*
> *the road were sorted out into eligible cases . . .*
> *and about 400 were taken to various thanas, most to*
> *Palwal. Many had cases registered against them--a*
> *large number for alleged possession of illicit arms*
> *but most on the suspicion of the threat of violence*
> *--and they were taken from there to clinics to be*
> *sterilized.*

No one knows how many Uttawars were taken during the emergency, but as the fear of coercive sterilization swept the country, large numbers of men took to hiding out in the fields, sometimes for weeks at a time. Attendance at the November 1976 camel fair in Rajasthan, an annual religious and commercial event that normally attracts huge crowds, was down by one-third to one-half. In the absence of a free press, reports of anti-sterilization demonstrators, particularly in the Muslim areas, and the deaths--probably in the hundreds--of volunteers from infections were passed along city and village grapevines.

It is believed that only a relatively small portion of India's population actually suffered from extreme brutality during the emergency sterilization drive. But many thousands experienced harassment at the hands of police and other government authorities, and millions more were subjected to strong indirect social pressures. And the fear of coercion was nearly ubiquitous.

On May 7, 1981, the *Times of India* quoted Indira Gandhi as denying to the World Health Organization that India had ever practiced "forcible sterilization as a matter of policy." She further claimed that "an entirely erroneous picture had been created by wrong reporting." Policy, no; but coercion nevertheless.

In such a nation, where voluntary measures to curb fertility are neither vigorous nor rapid enough to bring about the kind of setting conducive to economic development and social and political stability, coercion may very well be almost inevitable. One equally grim alternative to significant fertility reduction is starvation, already a growing possibility in India. Another that has been proposed by some developmentalists is a "triage-life-boat" system of splitting the massive and culturally diverse nation into regions worthy of saving and those to be cut loose to procreate themselves into oblivion. It could just be that the line between brutality and humanity comes down to a blurred point of semantics defined by culturally acceptable expedience.

Philosophy aside, the sterilization drive did produce
results: 8.3 million sterilizations were performed during
1976-77--over three times the 2.7 million performed in 1975-76,
and nearly 200 percent of the official target of 4.3 million.
Although IUD insertions declined and condom acceptors increased
only slightly, Table 1.4 shows that the estimated proportion of
married couples of reproductive age protected by modern contraceptive methods rose by more than a third from 17.2 percent in
March 1976 to 23.9 percent a year later.

Shockwaves and Retreat

The aggressive and often abusive sterilization drive that
pushed Indira Gandhi from office also produced a severe and
widespread family planning backlash. The Janata Party, which
assumed control of the central government in March 1977,
espoused the cause of "the little man" over big business
interests; the same developmental trend was extended to the
field of family planning.

In the Population Policy Statement issued by the Janata
Party in June 1977, family planning was to be promoted "without any compulsion, coercion or pressures of any sort." To
emphasize the program's reorientation toward "the total welfare
of the family and the community," the Ministry of Health and
Family Planning was renamed the Ministry of Health and Family
Welfare. The policy statement also announced that the government's family planning efforts would be concentrated on the
underserved rural areas. The former practice of setting hard
targets was at first rejected and then later replaced by
"expectations of achievement" in terms of the acceptance rates
of various contraceptive methods.

Monetary incentives for sterilization and IUD acceptors
were retained, although the rates paid by the central government for sterilization were revised to an across-the-board
payment of Rs. 100 ($11 at the current rate of exchange) per
vasectomy and Rs. 120 ($13) per tubectomy, regardless of how
many children an acceptor had. Of these amounts, Rs. 30 for
a vasectomy and Rs. 50 for a tubectomy were to be kept by the
state to cover surgical costs.

Program achievements for 1977-78 dropped almost to the
1973-74 level. This time, the particularly populous but
emergency-battered northern states of Uttar Pradesh, Bihar,
Rajasthan, Madhya Pradesh, Punjab, and Haryana, which together
comprised 42 percent of the nation's total population, contributed less than 12 percent of total acceptors. Such legislation
as the act that finally raised the minimum legal age at marriage from 15 to 18 years for women and from 18 to 21 years for
men in 1978 became mere tokens in a token program.

Upon regaining her seat at the head of government in January 1980, Indira Gandhi noted that family planning programs had

TABLE 1.4 *Family Planning Program Acceptor Targets and Achievements, 1974-75 to 1980-81*

Methods	1974-75			1975-76		
	Target	Achievement	Achievement as % of target	Target	Achievement	Achievement as % of target
Sterilizations	2.00	1.35	67.5	2.49	2.67	108.1
Vasectomies	--	0.61	--	--	1.44	--
Tubectomies	--	0.74	--	--	1.23	--
IUD insertions	0.60	0.43	71.7	0.91	0.61	67.0
Equivalent conventional contraceptive users[a]	3.50	2.52	72.0	4.26	3.53	81.0
Total	6.10	4.30	70.5	7.76	6.81	87.8
MACRAs effectively protected	--	15.1%	--	--	17.2%	--

Methods	1976-77			1977-78		
	Target	Achievement	Achievement as % of target	Target	Achievement	Achievement as % of target
Sterilizations	4.30	8.26	192.1	--	0.95	--
Vasectomies	--	6.20	--	--	0.19	--
Tubectomies	--	2.06	--	--	0.76	--
IUD insertions	1.14	0.58	50.9	1.00	0.33	33.0
Equivalent conventional contraceptive users[a]	4.69	3.47	86.8	5.00	3.25	65.0
Total	10.13	12.53	123.7	--	4.53	--
MACRAs effectively protected	--	23.9%	--	--	22.8%	--

Methods	1978-79			1979-80		
	Target	Achievement	Achievement as % of target	Target	Achievement	Achievement as % of target
Sterilizations	3.97	1.48	37.3	3.05	1.77	58.0
Vasectomies	--	0.39	--	--	0.47	--
Tubectomies	--	1.09	--	--	1.30	--

Table 1.4 (continued)

	1978-79 (cont'd)			1979-80 (cont'd)		
	Target	Achievement	Achievement as % of target	Target	Achievement	Achievement as % of target
IUD insertions	0.60	0.55	91.7	1.15	0.63	54.8
Equivalent conventional contraceptive users[a]	4.00	3.47	78.9	5.00	3.04	60.8
Total	8.57	5.51	64.3	9.20	5.44	59.1
MACRAs effectively protected	—	22.8%	—	—	22.5%	—
				1980-81		
Sterilizations				2.90	1.99	68.6
Vasectomies				—	0.42	—
Tubectomies				—	1.55	—
IUD insertions				0.79	0.60	76.2
Equivalent conventional contraceptive users[a]				5.54	3.74	67.5
Total				9.23	6.34	68.7
MACRAs effectively protected				—	22.6%	—

MACRAs, Married couples of reproductive age.

[a] Mainly condoms, but also a few users of foam tablets, jelly, and diaphragms.

Source: Visaria and Visaria 1981, pp. 40–41, Table 13.

79

"lost the momentum built up in earlier years," called for a
reversal of this "dismal trend," and increased the budget.

In the new Sixth Five-Year Plan (1980-85), family planning
was allocated Rs. 10.1 billion ($1.1 billion). Although the
current budgetary allotment is more than one and a half times
greater than that made in the fifth plan, the proportion of
total development funds it represents (1.04 percent) is considerably less than the fifth plan's 1.26 percent, and a far
cry from the nearly 2.0 percent of development funds budgeted
for family planning in the fourth plan (1969-74).

Family planning programs, even massive ones, are extremely
cost-efficient; between mid-1951 and mid-1974, the government
spent only nine-tenths of the modest total budgeted for family
planning, and many states spent a considerably smaller portion
of their allotments. The missing component is not money. What
is missing from the national family planning program is, apparently, the energy and general imagination of a Pai or Krishnakumar. Rather than being geared to the individual and regional
needs of the population, India's family planning program has
been locked into a rigid structure based on the one best
approach to the one best contraceptive.

To promote family planning awareness on a national scale,
an Indian Association of Parliamentarians for Problems of
Population and Development was formed in 1981. During a
national conference in May of that year, the association officially adopted a firm commitment to a vigorous family planning
program. The association's future plans include conferences
in various states plus a series of workshops aimed at involving
legislators at all levels and in all geographical locations.

Although the Indian leadership now views family planning
as a necessary component of development, it still appears to
both underestimate the problem and lack a true understanding
of it. The bulk of physicians in charge of the program continue to treat family planning as a clinical, medical problem
despite the awareness of such outstanding demographers as
S. N. Agarwala, Director of the International Institute for
Population Studies in Bombay. As long ago as 1971, Agarwala
asserted in the *Illustrated Weekly of India* that "family planning is not a medical problem, it is an integral part of the
process of social and economic development." Agarwala explained
the situation:

> *The rural people are still tradition bound and*
> *their level of literacy is very low. Many of them*
> *still think that a large number of children is a*
> *sign of their virility, that male children are a*
> *source of strength in the event of a quarrel, that*
> *more children mean more hands in the fields,*
> *specially when hired labour gets scarce at times*
> *of harvesting and higher wages are demanded. The*
> *cost of a child has not entered their calculations.*

> . . . A smaller population may be advantageous to
> the country and may hasten the process of develop-
> ment, but an average villager cannot visualize how
> a smaller family will be economically advantageous
> to him. This can be done through personal contacts
> and small group meetings by leaders and family
> planning workers. . . .
>   It should not be expected that if family planning
> clinics are opened, people will [necessarily] visit
> them for contraceptive service. . . . The doctors
> engaged in family planning work have to adopt an
> attitude of service, and take the role of social
> reformers in initiating and convincing people to
> use contraceptives.

Part of the problem is that no one really knows how big
the problem is. Despite the country's strong statistical
performance, it is impossible to keep track of such vital demographic information as babies delivered in rural homes and
deaths which may go unreported due either to ignorance on the
part of the survivors or to a family's reluctance to lose the
subsidized food rations allotted to the deceased person.

There is also widespread agreement among the nation's
demographers that the optimism generated by the nation's
strong family planning policies during the 1970s led to the
shocking surprise uncovered by the 1981 census. And on top
of the 12 million "unexpected" people who showed up on the
1981 count, allowances must always be made for the possibility
of an undercount. Visaria and Visaria set the 1981 Indian
undercount at about 1.0 to 2.0 percent, which would push the
actual population count as of March 1, 1981, to 690 or 697
million.

Important as they are—particularly to an awareness of the
scope of the population problem—numbers take a back seat to
the need for strong family planning efforts aimed at people
rather than at statistics. India's rich and poor alike know
the country is overcrowded. The poor are becoming increasingly
aware that life is not as good as it should be; such current
and widespread practices as abortion and the nutritional neglect of females indicate an awareness—albeit a noninternalized
one—of the adverse economic impact of having too many children. But India's rural poor lead lives proscribed by a variety
of social and economic constraints. What mobility there is is
seldom upward.

For India's program to succeed, family planning education
and services must be released from clinic and conference boundaries and directed toward the doorstep; but first, they need
to get moving. The government's family planning program suffers from ennui. Those responsible for it appear to have
become overwhelmed by the problem, disillusioned by the range
and severity of obstacles in the way to its solution, and

resigned to both. Having been stung by the emergency experience and deflated by program shortfalls, India's leadership
is looking for new and creative ways of addressing itself to
the population problem.

The Role of Incentives

The part played by incentives in the Indian family planning program has had mixed reviews. In Gujarat, where the use
of state funds to augment central government allowances for
sterilization payments has raised the compensation to Rs. 125
($14), cash incentives have probably played a major role in the
economically backward state's high level of contraceptive use.
During a "Family Planning Month" designated in the Gujarati
capital, Ahmedabad, during September 1981, sterilization payments were raised to Rs. 200 (about $23) for men and Rs. 175
(about $20) for women, plus Rs. 25 for each sterilization
"motivator."

The system of paying large cash incentives on an individual
basis in a country as poor and overpopulated as India, however,
is bound to be fraught with difficulties. Prompted by severe
financial need, men and women are sometimes drawn to sterilizations they later regret. Also, Visaria and Visaria (1981)
point out, "Lengthy, complex checking and auditing are necessary, and bogus claims, misappropriation of funds, and cheating
are possible."

Nothing, of course, is perfect. But incentives granted
within a community setting, where peer pressure encourages
contraceptive acceptibility, could go a long way toward solving
India's population problem.

J. R. D. Tata, India's leading industrialist and president
of the Family Planning Foundation, has long been a critic of
the government's approach to family planning. In a speech in
April 1981, Tata reported that, in conjunction with the contraceptive education and services offered to his employees, incentive payments of Rs. 200 ($23) had been made to sterilization
volunteers at one of his steel mills since 1978. The result:
a drop in the birth rate among his employees from 40 to 24 per
1,000 in just three years.

Although Tata believes that "a much larger figure [for
incentives] would produce spectacular results," it must be
remembered that his success was experienced within the framework of a captive audience. While large cash incentives may
have adverse side effects where a sense of community action
and participation is absent, similar industry-promoted programs
can certainly have a significant impact on population growth
and serve as models for village incentive programs.

To combat the potential inflationary effect of the incentive payments, the Working Group on Population Policy is
researching a scheme to combine the concept of social security

with installment-plan incentives. The idea is that incentives would be turned into savings, and thus become substitutes for children as a form of old-age security. A small study carried out in rural Maharashtra in 1975-76 by Viassoff and Viassoff (1980), however, casts a shadow over the widespread prospects for such a scheme. This study showed that the majority of 25- to 59-year-old men surveyed had never thought about their old age; of those who had, only slightly more than half had thought about the need for economic support.

Nevertheless, a form of old-age insurance as part of complete health and family planning care has been extended to resident tea plantation workers in southern India. Beginning in 1971, a savings account was opened in the name of each female leaf picker. This company-provided nest egg, which was to be drawn on only at the end of the woman's childbearing years, mounted by Rs. 5 a month and 5 percent interest a year. However, the account was decreased by Rs. 50 to Rs. 100 if a woman gave birth to a third child, by Rs. 250 on the birth of a fourth child, and was closed entirely if she had a fifth child, although a new account would be opened for her if she were sterilized.

Since the experiment proved to be impractical, it has since been abandoned. However, the birth rate among those enrolled in the scheme dropped to 22 per 1,000 by 1977 compared to 28 and 34 among female pickers in two neighboring tea es-estates. Although inflation would erode incentive payments delayed in this manner, it still appears to be a viable option. In fact, a similar scheme is currently being implemented in three villages in Kerala. There, a "Family Prosperity Fund" has been set up to provide "inheritances" of 1,200-rupee bank accounts for each woman who has a six-month-old baby and does not become pregnant again over the next 36 months.

The manner in which incentives and disincentives were set and imposed during the emergency sterilization drive has caused a negative reaction to the entire concept of family planning incentives in India. Salary increases and reduced housing loan interest rates are now offered by the central government to employees who accept sterilization after having two or three children.

Experience has shown that meaningful incentive schemes take careful and appropriate planning, energetic and dedicated implementation, and strong bureaucratic follow-through.

The Role of Foreign Assistance*

Although all major foreign financial and technical assistance to developing nations is predicated on the request for it,

---

*Much of the material in this section is drawn from Minkler (1977)'.

the role of the foreign advisor has long been debated, on both
sides of the fence. In India, which boasts an exceptionally
high level of developmental expertise, foreign family planning
advisors are viewed by many in the country's scientific community as intrusive, even disruptive. The technical advisors
themselves, meanwhile, are often confused as to their own
roles, particularly in a sometimes hostile atmosphere.

Many foreign agencies have played major roles in the
development of India's family planning program. Since the
Ford Foundation and USAID have been the most prominent of
these agencies, they have been the primary targets of such
critics of foreign involvement as Ashish Bose of Delhi University's Institute of Economic Growth. As mentioned previously,
Bose views external advisors as being at the very root of
India's family planning failures.

It is, of course, never easy to be in the position of
having to ask for assistance; what is less obvious, however,
are the difficulties under which assistance must often be
rendered. The matter comes down to an issue of both personal
and national interest on the parts of both the donor agency
and the recipient country.

USAID entered the Indian population arena in 1966. Between
1966 and 1973, it disbursed Rs. 225 million ($30 million) to
the national family planning program for contraceptive supplies,
vehicles, and other service and training equipment. USAID also
provided wide-ranging technical assistance in such areas as
program implementation, maternal and child health care, nurse-
midwife training, external and internal voluntary organization
coordination, and family planning promotion. Most of the support was in the form of direct grants to the Indian government,
and costs for USAID staff advisors and contract consultants
were paid from the U.S.-owned rupee funds accumulated from the
sale of PL 480 food to India.

USAID personnel performed a variety of functions. Population program officers processed documents, approved loans,
oversaw monetary and commodity dispersals, and maintained a
close liaison with Indian family planning officials and appropriate cabinet ministers. Other advisors were attached to
such national programs as the USAID-initiated commercial condom
distribution program and various research, training, and communications projects around the country.

Some USAID consultants were also attached to government
ministries or Indian institutes; others were assigned to Indian
organizations outside of New Delhi, such as the Demographic
Training and Research Center in Bombay, or to specific state-
level programs. Wherever they were located, USAID advisors
were expected to act both as representatives of the official
U.S. aid agency and as collaborators with their Indian counterparts and colleagues.

India's attitude toward foreign advisors progressed from
congeniality in the mid-1950s to suspicion in the late 1960s

to outright hostility in the early]970s. Meanwhile, India
itself had developed enough sophisticated expertise in family
planning to prompt it to want to go it alone. It became clear
that whatever aid was accepted would be in the form of multi-
lateral assistance from such international agencies as the
World Health Organization, whose assistance comes without real
or imagined political strings.

The contributions made by the Ford Foundation and USAID
population advisors were generally appreciated by most officials
of the Indian family planning program. But by 1973, India had
reached a new stage of family planning development. From then
on, any innovations it might incorporate or directions it might
take would be purely Indian.

Since 1973, India has experienced the devastating aftermath
of the emergency and a jolting realization that all of their
expertise and program experimentation have resulted in little
more than a family planning holding pattern. The atmosphere
has changed, and so has USAID. The U.S. agency, which was
reinstated as one of the nation's major donors in 1980, has
become as cautious as India's prime minister. Its program of
population assistance is gearing up slowly, with a firm commitment to appropriateness and acceptability.

About $40 million of USAID's current (1980-85) $60 million
assistance package will provide nearly two-thirds of the
financing for a model village health project in the states of
Maharashtra, Gujarat, Haryana, Punjab, and Himachal Pradesh.
The remaining $20 million is being directed toward India's
commercial condom distribution scheme and a fund to be drawn
on by the government of India for the strengthening of private
rural institutions.

USAID is no longer India's largest external donor, however;
the United Nations Fund for Population Activities (UNFPA) has
taken over that role. The UNFPA's five-year funding total of
$100 million is being used to improve the maternal and child
health-family planning staff, facilities, and program development. In addition, the U.N. agency will help support an
intensive effort to develop a total health care program in
areas of Bihar and Rajasthan where the literacy rate is particularly low and economic conditions are especially poor.
Under the UNFPA umbrella, the ILO is working on projects relat-
ing to Indian laborers and labor unions, while UNESCO is carrying out a program aimed at installing population education in
the school system.

The World Bank remains active in India, too. Between 1973
and 1980, the World Bank cooperated with the Swedish International Development Authority in a $31.8 million assistance
package for experimental programs in Uttar Pradesh and Karnataka. World Bank assistance to these programs consisted of
building construction, the provision of vehicles, ambulances,
training facilities, and equipment and a system for evaluating
the programs. The World Bank's current project, which began

in 1980, extends a $46 million credit as part of a $96 million program in six districts of Uttar Pradesh to lower infant mortality, increase health care for mothers and children, and reduce fertility.

In addition to the United States, several other countries have committed assistance to India's integrated health and family planning program. The Norwegian Agency for International Development is spending $32.8 million on the establishment of postpartum centers which will also offer family planning services. The British Overseas Development Administration spent $6 million between 1975 and 1971 on building and equipping subdistrict hospitals for primary health centers for female sterilization. In 1979, it committed $22.8 million for a five-year program in Orissa State to build up a rural health and family welfare system. Smaller projects have also been undertaken by the Swedish and Danish governments, as well as by a number of nongovernmental international organizations.

Family Planning International Assistance (FPIA) has supplied 333 Indian institutions with family planning commodities, while Church World Service has supported hospitals and health care centers in India since 1968. The International Planned Parenthood Federation has supported numerous projects through its Indian affiliate, FPAI. The organization's financial assistance to FPAI totaled $1.9 million in 1979, $2.3 million in 1980, and about $2.6 million in 1981.

The Population Council of New York has made a number of small grants to Indian institutions involved in the training of rural medical workers. These workers are being trained to give instructions on general health care and to promote and give instructions on the use of IUDs. The Rockefeller Foundation, meanwhile, has made small grants to Indian institutions for conferences on family planning and contraceptive development and for the study of rural health problems. Very small grants have been made by World Neighbors since 1955 to family planning and health clinics and for the training of village health workers. Clinical reproductive health care services for women have been supported by the International Women's Health Coalition via the private Jan Mangal Sanstha.

Appropriateness and acceptability are the key words for assistance from all these agencies and organizations. The problem, however, is that what might be appropriate and acceptable to the Indian government may have only a minor impact on India's number one problem, overpopulation. The question is: can the government of India mold its resources and expertise into a program of fertility control that will be equally appropriate for and acceptable to all elements of its radically nonhomogeneous population? And can it do it fast enough and yet humanely enough to create the necessary social atmosphere for development?

Obstacles to Gaining Acceptance

Between 1978 and 1982, India's family planning program returned to levels of acceptance accomplished in 1974 and 1975. The Janata government's Sixth Five-Year Plan for 1978-83 set a national goal of replacement-level fertility by the year 1996. In a reversal of the Gandhi closeout, the welcome mat was extended to foreign donors, who came through with nearly $300 million--about 12 percent of the Indian government's combined allocations for family planning and health--for the five years 1980-85. The bulk of this aid is being channeled toward the nation's integrated family planning, maternal, and child health care program in particularly backward districts of 12 states.

Between mid-1978 and mid-1980 the number of sterilizations performed throughout India exceeded the pre-emergency level of 1974-75, and the numbers of people accepting conventional contraceptives (condoms, mainly) almost reached the emergency drive's peak level. Overall achievements, however, were less than two-thirds of expectations during the same period. Furthermore, because of the backlash from vasectomies pushed during the emergency, the majority of sterilizations done were tubectomies. The number of tubectomies done in 1981 of 2.3 million were the same as done during the height of the emergency campaign.

To keep the support that had given her an overwhelming victory in the January 1980 elections, Indira Gandhi adopted a very low profile on family planning. During 1980-81, the 1.99 million sterilizations performed represented only a 12 percent increase over the 1.77 million performed in 1979-80. Meanwhile, IUD insertions fell from 634,000 to 602,000, while the numbers of condom users, who formed the vast majority of the 3.7 million "equivalent conventional contraceptive users" for 1980-81 shown in Table 1.5, reached an all-time high. (Other "conventional" methods include diaphragms, spermicidal foams and jellies and, since 1976, pills.) The relatively low effectiveness of condoms, however, means that the overall 22.6 percent of protected couples recorded at the end of March 1981 was lower than the 23.9 percent level of March 1977.

The continuing success of the commercial distribution of domestically manufactured Nirodh condoms at subsidized prices seems assured. Launched in 1968, the program started at outlets of the country's six largest consumer goods companies. By 1980, condoms were being distributed by 12 companies and carried by 380,000 retail shops throughout the country and by government "fair price" shops in some states. The volume of condom sales grew from some 16 million in 1968-69 to 110 million in 1977-78. With the relaxation of family planning efforts in 1979-80, however, condom sales fell off to 78 million. But with condom sales having reached a record level in 1980-81, the outlook for that method seems favorable.

Also showing some promise is the All-India Hospital Postpartum Program, launched in 1969. The aim of this program is

TABLE 1.5 *Family Planning Acceptors by Method, 1956-81*

Year	Sterilizations	IUD insertions	Equivalent conventional contraceptives	Total acceptors	Equivalent sterilizations[a]
1956	7	--	--	7	7
1957	14	--	--	14	14
1958	25	--	--	25	25
1959	42	--	--	42	42
1960	64	--	--	64	64
1961	105	--	--	105	105
1962	158	--	--	158	158
1963	170	--	298	468	187
1964	270	--	439	708	294
Jan 1965-Mar 1966	671	813	582	2,066	974
1966-67	887	910	465	2,262	1,216
1967-68	1,840	669	475	2,984	2,089
1968-69	1,665	479	961	3,104	1,878
1969-70	1,422	459	1,509	3,390	1,659
1970-71	1,330	476	1,962	3,768	1,598
1971-72	2,187	488	2,354	5,030	2,481
1972-73	3,122	355	2,398	5,874	3,373
1973-74	942	372	3,010	4,324	1,233
1974-75	1,354	43	2,521	4,307	1,638
1975-76	2,669	607	3,528	6,803	3,069

Table 1.5 *(continued)*

Year	Sterilizations	IUD insertions	Equivalent conventional contraceptives	Total acceptors	Equivalent sterilizations[a]
1976–77	8,261	581	3,692	12,534	8,663
1977–78	948	326	3,253	4,527	1,242
1978–79	1,483	552	3,469	5,505	1,865
1979–80[b]	1,773	634	3,036	5,443	2,158
1980–81[b]	1,994	602	3,742	6,338	2,407
Total thru Mar 1981[c]	33,403	8,366	37,694	79,850	38,439

Numbers in thousands.

[a] Equivalent sterilizations are calculated by adding the number of sterilizations, one-third of IUD insertions, one-ninth of equivalent pill users, and one-eighteenth of equivalent conventional contraceptive users.

[b] Provisional.

[c] Cumulative figures for IUD insertions and users of conventional contraceptives indicate only acceptors within the government program.

Source: Visaria and Visaria 1981, p. 37, Table 12.

89

the promotion of contraceptive acceptance among women who use
government hospitals and medical colleges for deliveries or
abortions. A total of 509 medical institutions were participating in this program by March 1981. Between the program's
inception in 1969 and 1980, 385 participating institutions
with a total obstetric and abortion case load of 5.6 million
had persuaded 53 percent, or 2.96 million, of the women or
their husbands to adopt contraception.

In a speech to the World Health Organization in May 1981,
Prime Minister Gandhi called for "a new, dynamic and better
coordinated program of research in contraception." Her plea
is not new: the world's search for a better (safe, easy, and
above all, foolproof) contraceptive has been quite protracted.
But the fact is, the variety of contraceptives now in use
around the world can be used safely, easily, and effectively
if they are made available, and follow-up services are provided along with explicit information concerning their use and
possible side effects. Contraceptives all too often are blamed
for human or system failures.

Nevertheless, illiterate women do have a particularly hard
time remembering to take the pill; the small volume of pills
available in India are used almost exclusively by more educated,
urban women. The use of condoms is constrained by the lack of
running water and disposal facilities in rural homes. IUDs,
which lost their initial popularity due to inadequate medical
follow-up and information regarding possible pain and extra
bleeding, probably will never make a comeback in India. Vasectomy, which is still suffering from its overzealous promotion
during the emergency, is also widely believed to inhibit both
sexual performance and physical strength. Men refusing to
undergo vasectomies, not surprisingly, will often agree to a
wife's tubectomy. Consequently, tubectomies performed by
laparoscopy accounted for 74 to 80 percent of all sterilizations performed between April 1977 and March 1981. In 1983,
the number of sterilizations rose to 5 million, about one half
of which were female. The cost of medical equipment and training required for laparoscopies, however, have just about limited
the procedure to urban areas.

Rather than indicating a need for the "one best" contraceptive method and approach, the folk constraints placed on the
general acceptance of the various contraceptives points up the
need for a widespread availability of a full range of contraceptive methods. Yet the Indian medical community refuses even
to experiment with the injectible contraceptive so widely used
in neighboring Thailand, and ignorance continues to beget ignorance in the Indian countryside. The only contraceptive measures
known to the majority of rural women are coitus interruptus,
rhythm, and abstinence. Hindus have an exceptionally low rate
of sexual intercourse, due in part to the large number of men
who are absent for long periods of time while working in the
countryside or in cities, as well as ritualistic abstinence

during frequent religious holidays. Abstinence, therefore, is already built into the Indian system. Neither rhythm nor withdrawal, however, are effective enough to keep people who know they cannot afford to feed and clothe the children they already have from having still more children.

Even during delivery, the forces of ignorance and fatalism come into play. In some villages around Delhi, for example, a woman counts the beams of the room's ceiling at the time of delivery. If she counts three beams, she believes her next child will be born after three years. If she counts only two beams, the period between her current delivery and the birth of her next child will be only two years.

Some women also believe that if the room where the child was born is plastered after childbirth, the next child will be born after an interval of one year. But if both the floor and the walls are plastered, the interval will be between two and three years. Such superstitions may seem humorous to Westerners, but to the village woman they are as reasonable as any other facet of a life over which she has only minimal control.

Meanwhile, the nation's rural health system continues to fail to meet the health and family planning needs of uneducated and neglected rural women and infants during the critical period between birth and the age of 3-5 years. According to USAID/India (980),

> Doctors in PHCs [public health centers], ANMs
> [auxiliary nurse-midwives], MPWs [multi-purpose
> workers] and CHVs [community health volunteers]
> do appear to reach the poor directly with services
> and address some important needs, while other
> important services could be considerably strengthened
> --e.g., treatment of diarrheal diseases and assessment
> or treatment of respiratory infections, the two
> principal causes of death in children under five.
> Concerted efforts at recognition and treatment of
> malnutrition are virtually lacking among all levels
> of workers. Promotion and use of non-permanent
> contraceptive methods--oral contraceptives, condoms,
> IUDs--receive only slight emphasis.
>
> The rural health system in India currently appears
> to be used heavily by older children and males, with
> the exception of childhood immunizations. The
> National Institute of Health and Family Welfare's
> comprehensive evaluation of the CHV scheme points
> out that 'pre-school children and women constitute
> a small percentage of the users of services of the
> CHVs.' A similar conclusion may hold for the PHC
> level, except in the case of sterilization, which
> large numbers of women receive in PHCs. Trained
> dais and ANMs provide antenatal, delivery and
> postnatal services--but otherwise women are not

frequent users of the system. Young children under
age five also appear to use the system infrequently.
This certainly diminishes the ability of the system
to affect young child mortality.

A Numbers Game

Although the achievements of India's family planning program are modest in terms of the country's gigantic population
size and density, the sheer numbers involved make a substantial
impact on both the positive and negative aspects of the family
planning program.

Between 1966-67, when the family planning program really
got under way, and March 1981, more than 31.9 million people
ended their reproductive lives permanently via sterilization,
and another 7.6 million were protected by IUD insertions within
the government program. Moreover, the proportion of women in
the reproductive age group effectively protected by modern
contraceptives as of March 1981 (22.6 percent) is disappointing
from the perspective of national targets.

In terms of global population (which in mid-1981 stood at
4.5 billion and is growing at an annual rate of 1.7 percent),
however, India's growth drastically diminishes the numerically
impressive contribution made by its family planning program.
Its relatively small but equally overcrowded neighbor, Pakistan,
adds 2.5 million people to the world per year; Bangladesh, which
is growing at the rate of 2.6 percent a year, adds 2.4 million
people annually. Sri Lanka, meanwhile, which is growing at the
same annual rate of 2.2 percent as India is, has a much smaller
population (15.3 million in mid-1981) plus a much higher age
at marriage and, therefore, adds only 336,600 people per year--
less than the 457,248 people the Indian state of Kerala alone
adds at its remarkably low population growth rate of 1.8 percent
a year.

Even China, currently the world's most populous nation,
with a mid-1981 population of some 985 million but an annual
growth rate of only 1.2 percent, adds less people than India
does--11.8 million, compared to the more than 15 million people
that India adds each year to this vastly overpopulated, resource
depleted, politically insecure world. And India adds this many
people in spite of an annual death rate of 15 per 1,000, compared to only 6 per 1,000 for China.

Neither India's family planning successes nor the extreme
difficulties any population program would encounter in a diverse
and scattered society should be underestimated. But the magni-
tude of the country's population problem should not be underestimated, either. India is staggering beneath a crushing load
of malnourished, uneducated, impoverished people. Overpopulation has a stranglehold on development programs aimed at alleviating the suffering of hundreds of millions of people unwittingly

perpetuating and deepening their misery at the rate of 41,095 more people per day.

Despite Indira Gandhi's expressed determination to deal firmly and swiftly with India's population problem, her exhibited caution in the matter seems to be interpreted by the bureaucracy as indifference. Even in the upper reaches of government, the family welfare section of the Ministry of Health and Family Welfare is given short shrift and low status. The important post of Secretary for Family Welfare was left vacant between August and December 1981 upon the transfer of the previous secretary; the new secretary has had no experience in the population field.

A lack of cooperation among the many ministries involved one way or another in family planning promotion and infrastructure development finds particularly hostile expression between the women's division of the Social Welfare Ministry and the Department of Family Welfare. The low regard with which everyone connected with family planning is viewed also presents stumbling blocks at the village and district levels.

In addition to general discord and laxity and the resulting denigration, the nation's family planning program has run into structural lapses ranging from inadequate training of dais, rakshaks, and auxiliary nurse-midwives to a severe shortage of vehicles necessary for supervision. The distribution of contraceptives is also severely inadequate, particularly in the case of pills and IUDs. While the government insists that only domestically produced versions of these contraceptives be used in the government program, quantities fluctuate and quality is often unsatisfactory. While some parts of the country go for long periods without adequate supplies, those available in other areas are often underutilized.

A population the size of India's does not exist in a vacuum; India's problem is the world's problem. Humanitarian considerations aside, the free world can no longer afford to close its eyes to the fact that India's economic and political stability --or lack of it--is critical to the ultimate trade and security interests of every free nation on earth. The country is unable to provide even a humane level of nutrition, housing, education, and health care for its current population of over 700 million. Yet it has already exploded at least one nuclear device, and will no doubt complete the manufacture of a rocket-launching system in the near future.

Situated as it is with China, Pakistan, and the Soviet Union nearby, India is well aware of its extreme vulnerability to the possible geopolitical pressures. Its position as the Third World's democratic leader also is tenuous; political instability in India would surely push the nation from that seat.

Desperate people make desperate enemies; India itself found that out during the emergency. To what extremes might an even more desperate India go to find some measure of security--or just plain survival--in ten years, when its population exceeds 870 million, or in 20 years, when it passes the 1 billion mark? India's runaway birth rate is viewed by most other national leaders as well as most of the Indian family planning establishment as a uniquely Indian problem requiring a uniquely Indian solution. High-level Indian family planning officials join the nation's rigid, self-serving bureaucracy in a continuing resistance to innovation and flexibility in a program that must be extended rapidly to a poor, illiterate, socially backward, and culturally fragmented population. The notion that sophisticated technology will solve India's problems is gaining ground while the people are losing theirs.

Since independence, the Indian leadership has been struggling to graft modern technology onto self-conscious "Indianness" which, apparently, includes the inevitability of caste, male domination, and a distinct, Hindu view of life as a period to be endured. Graham (1978) quotes a poet from Bombay as saying "Everything in India needs to be changed. The issue is to know where to start."

REFERENCES

Agarwal, Anil. 1978. "Preparing for the Second India." *People* (London: International Planned Parenthood Federation) 5, no. 4.

Agarwala, S.N. 1971. "Three or Two or One or None." *Illustrated Weekly of India* (Bombay), February 7, 1971.

Aggarwal, Partap C. 1974. "Green Revolution and Employment in Ludhiana, Punjab, India." *Employment in Developing Nations*, edited by Edger O. Edwards. New York: Columbia University Press.

Auerbach, Stuart. 1981a. "Indian Census Spurs Call for Birth Control Plan." *Washington Post*, May 12, 1981.

---. 1981b. "Dwindling Reserves Force India to Buy Wheat from U.S." *Washington Post*, July 22, 1981.

---. 1981c. "India Hitches Its Future Development to a Homemade Satellite." *Washington Post*, December 4, 1981.

---. 1981d. "Peaceful Indian Program Has Military Potential." *Washington Post*, December 4, 1981.

---. 1981e. "An Anxious India Cultivates Its Neighbors." *Washington Post*, December 10, 1981.

---. 1981f. "Gandhi's Splintered Opposition Groups Join Unified Challenge." *Washington Post*, December 28, 1981.

---. 1982a. "Untouchables Still India's Outcastes." *Washington Post*, January 3, 1982.

---. 1982b. "World Bank Cuts India's Share of No-Interest Loans." *Washington Post*, January 23, 1982.

Cain, Mead. 1981. *Landlessness in India and Bangladesh: A Critical Review of Data Sources*. Center for Policy Studies, Working Paper no. 71. New York: The Population Council.

Cassen, Robert. 1978. "The Future of Indian Society." *People* (London: International Planned Parenthood Federation) 5, no. 4.

Chandrasekhar, S. 1965. *American Aid and India's Economic Development*. New York: Frederick A. Praeger.

Crowley, H. Thomas. 1969. "Role of Advisory Services." In *Population Control: Implications, Trends, and Prospects*, edited by N. Sadik et al. Islamabad: Pakistan Family Planning Council.

Encyclopaedia Britannica. 1977.

Finkle, Jason L. 1972. "The Political Environment of Population Control in India and Pakistan." In *Political Science in Population Studies*, edited by Richard L. Clinton. Lexington, Massachusetts: D.C. Heath and Co.

Frankel, Francine. 1978. *India's Political Economy*. Princeton, New Jersey: Princeton University Press.

Fullam, Maryellen. 1978. "The Family Planning Factor." *People* (London: International Planned Parenthood Foundation) 5, no. 4.

Graham, Otis L., Jr. 1978. "India's Dilemma." *World Issues* (Santa Barbara, California: Center for the Study of Democratic Institutions) June/July.

Grawe, Roger. 1980. *Human Development in South Asia*. Washington, D.C.: World Bank.

Gulhati, Ravi and Kaval Gulhati. 1978. "India—Forging a Strategy for Development." *People* (London: International Planned Parenthood Foundation) 5, no. 4.

Gupta, Dharam. 1978. "A Campaign for Revival." *People* (London: International Planned Parenthood Foundation) 5, no. 4.

Gwatkin, Davidson R. 1979. "Political Will and Family Planning: The Implications of India's Emergency Experience."

Population and Development Review (New York: The Population Council) 5 (March).

"Harijans at Work." *Illustrated Weekly of India* (Bombay). October 3, 1971.

Henderson, P.D. 1975. *India: The Energy Sector*. Washington, D.C.: World Bank.

Hürlimann, Martin. 1967. *India*. London: Thames and Hudson.

"India's Fastest Growing Export--Indians." *Financial Times* (London). April 23, 1981.

International Labour Organization. 1983. *Bulletin of Labour Statistics, 1981-83*. Geneva: ILO.

International Planned Parenthood Federation. 1978. "An Interview with Avabai Wasia." *People* (London: International Planned Parenthood Federation) 5, no. 4.

Jha, Saroj S. 1978. "Doctors for India's Real Needs." *People* (London: International Planned Parenthood Foundation) 5, no. 4.

Kangas, Georgia Lee. 1972a. "Bargain Hunting with History." *News Circle Magazine* (New Delhi) 17, (January).

---. 1972b. "Art with a Difference." *News Circle Magazine* (New Delhi) 18 (December).

Krishnakumar, S. 1971. *The Story of the Ernakulam Experiment in Family Planning*. Cochin, Kerala: S.T. Reddiar & Sons.

Lewis, John P. 1972. "Population Control in India." In *Are Our Descendents Doomed?* edited by H. Brown and E. Hutchings, Jr. New York: Viking.

Marshall, Tyler. 1981. "Family Planning Stalls in India." *New York Times*, May 7, 1981.

Minkler, Meredith. 1977. "Consultants or Colleagues: The Role of U.S. Population Advisors in India." *Population and Development Review* (New York: The Population Council) 3, no. 4.

Montero, John. 1976. *Corruption*. Bombay: Bombay Press.

Myrdal, Gunnar. 1968. *Asian Drama: An Inquiry into the Poverty of Nations*. New York: Pantheon.

Nagarajan, T.S. 1971. "Bapu's Bhangi Colony Today." *Illustrated Weekly of India* (Bombay), October 3, 1971.

Nayar, Kuldip. 1971. *India: The Critical Years*. London: Weidenfeld & Nicolson.

Population Action Council. 1981a. "A Problem of Our Very Survival." *Popline* (Washington, D.C.: Population Action Council) 3, no. 11.

---. 1981b. "Population Growth Greatest Constraint on Full Employment." *Popline* (Washington, D.C.: Population Action Council) 3, no. 11.

Population Crisis Committee. 1981. *Status Report on Population Problems and Programs of India*. Washington, D.C.

Population Reference Bureau. 1980. *Family Planning and Marriage, 1970-1980: A Data Sheet*. Washington, D.C.

---. 1981. *1981 World Population Data Sheet*. Washington, D.C.

Purandare, B.N. 1971. "Abortion is Safe." *Illustrated Weekly of India* (Bombay), August 29, 1971.

Rajabhoj, P.N. 1971. "Harijans." *Illustrated Weekly of India* (Bombay), October 3, 1971.

Ram, N.V. Raghu. 1971. *Health Administration and Policy Development*. Hyderabad, India: Ramalakshmi.

Rao, Elizabeth. 1971. Interviews with family planning leaders and acceptors. *Illustrated Weekly of India* (Bombay), February 7, 1971.

Ratcliffe, John. 1978. "Kerala: Testbed for Transition Theory." *Populi* (New York: United Nations Fund for Population Activities) 5, no. 2.

Robinson, Leonard H., Jr. 1981. *India Trip Report*. Washington, D.C.: Battell.

Rudolph, Susanna and Lloyd Rudolph. 1980. "The Centrist Future of Indian Politics." *Asian Survey* (June).

Saxena, Badri N. and Shanta S. Rao. 1978. "Can Technology Help?" *People* (London: International Planned Parenthood Foundation) 5, no. 4.

Siamwalla, Ammar and Alberto Valdes. 1980. "Food Insecurity

in Developing Countries." *Food Policy* (Washington, D.C.: International Food Policy Research Institute) 5, no. 4.

Singh, Khushwant. 1972. "The Prime Minister Speaks." *Illustrated Weekly of India* (Bombay), August 13, 1972.

U.S. Agency for International Development. 1978. *Asia Regional Conference of Health, Population and Nutrition Staffs—Conference Report.* Manila.

———. 1980. *Integrated Rural Health and Population Project.* New Delhi.

———. 1981. *India—Country Development Strategy Statement, FY 83.* Washington, D.C.: U.S. International Development Cooperation Agency.

U.S. Bureau of the Census. 1978. *Country Demographic Profiles—India.* Washington, D.C.: Department of Commerce.

Viassoff, M. and Carol Viassoff. 1980. "Old Age Security and the Utility of Children in Rural India." *Population Studies* 34, no. 3.

Visaria, Pravin and Anrudh K. Jain. 1976. *Country Profiles—India.* New York: The Population Council.

Visaria, Pravin and Leela Visaria. 1981. *India's Population: Second and Growing.* 1981 World Population Data Sheet, vol. 36, no. 4. Washington, D.C.: Population Reference Bureau.

Wray, J.D. 1981. Report on a consultation to the USAID/India Integrated Rural Health and Population Project during February 3–14, 1980. Washington, D.C.: American Public Health Association.

Chapter 2

The Philippines:
Testing the Limits of Paradise

The Republic of the Philippines is a land of scenic ex-
tremity, an extravaganza of the senses. From pagan north to
Islamic south, the nation is bathed in vibrant green and
daubed with pink bougainvillaea and red hibiscus. High in the
mountains running north to south through the islands, one can
catch the scent of pine; in the lowlands, plumeria sweetens the
evening breeze.

There is a sense of pageantry that melds this luxurious
environment with fact and legendary fiction, animism and Christianity, East and West. If the Philippines' national character
could be summed up in one word, it would be flamboyance. A
constant round of fiestas spells show time for Spanish traditions grafted onto Philippine customs. Whether the celebration
honors a Christian or Islamic saint or the deities of isolated
tribes that make offerings of food on hallowed stones, it is
an occasion for merrymaking, a time for lavish feasting and new
clothes.

It is impossible, however, for anyone to overlook the fact
of overpopulation in the Philippines. The nation's cities
have become teeming urban-industrial sprawls; *barong-barongs*--
one- or two-room shanties, usually about six by nine feet constructed of cardboard or plywood and roofed with galvanized
iron sheets from World War II--are heaped into every available
space. Contrasting life styles--rich and poor, urban and rural,
traditional and modern--are startling. Suspicion is the legacy
of centuries of political oppression and decades of socially
uneven development.

Although this basically agrarian nation finally achieved
rice self-sufficiency in the late 1970s, a major portion of the
country's population still suffers from severe malnutrition.
Poor food distribution patterns, rampant deforestation and
resultant decreases in soil quality, and a young population,

placing a high burden of consumer dependency on an underdeveloped economy, point to increasing hunger and growing social,
economic, and political instability.

Forty-three percent of the nation's population of 49 million is under]5 years of age, a fact that guarantees high
population growth for the next several decades. At its current
population growth rate of 2.4 percent each year, the population
will double in just 29 years. Metropolitan Manila, a conglom-
erate of four cities and thirteen townships, is expected to
grow from 9 million in 1984 to almost 11 million by 1990. The
patience of the ordinarily adaptable Filipino, with an increasingly poor life lived on promises from the government, next to
the opulence of the country's own and foreign elite, is wearing
thin.

A national program of fertility control has reduced the
population growth rate from an average of 3.01 percent per
year between 1960 and 1970 to the current rate of 2.4 percent
a year. And it has achieved this in the face of a Catholic
majority and a cultural predisposition toward large families.
But unless the country's high birth rate of 34 per thousand
per year is further reduced significantly, and soon, the mush-
rooming realities of hunger, overcrowding, unemployment,
underemployment, housing shortages, and inflation are bound
to push the country into social and economic turmoil.

The country's population effort is problematic but working. The questions now are: Can the nation achieve population
stabilization at a level consistent with its resources and
capacity to provide for the well-being of all its citizens?
And can it do it in time?

HISTORICAL AND CULTURAL BACKGROUND

The Filipino character has been forged by adversity and
colored by mysticism. The entire archipelago lies astride the
western Pacific typhoon belt; hurricane-force winds and rains
sweep through the island from late April to mid-November,
flattening farmlands and palm trees in their wake. The easternmost islands straddle a geologic fault lying above one of
the deepest sections of the ocean. Earthquakes frequently
rock the islands and destruction in the form of fiery molten
lava occasionally explodes from a number of active volcanoes.
The violence of nature and a succession of colonial invaders
form the bases of folk legends passed from generation to generation and of historical dramatizations marking religious
holidays.

According to Philippines folklore, the archipelago was a
solid strip of long, narrow land until one day long, long ago,
a couple named Angalo and Angarab fought over a collection of
pearls they had found in giant clams at the northern end of
the land. In their rage, they stamped their feet and hurled

stones and great clods of dirt at each other, causing the
earth to crack open. Water rushed in, and the newly separated
pieces of land plus the stones and clods that had been hurled
in all directions became islands. Thus, the archipelago was
born. Geologists, however, indicate that the islands are
actually the tips of a great submerged mountain chain. The
question of their earliest inhabitants' origin is unsettled,
although legends concerning Malakas (the Strong One) and
Maganda (the Beautiful One), who sailed to the islands and
founded the family that was to become the Filipino people, are
probably not far from fact. Whatever their origins, a visual
melee of physical features, a diversity of ethnic orientations,
and the presence of about 85 mutually unintelligible languages
attest to a wealth of migratory infusion.

Around 4,000 B.C., after the land bridges had been inundated by glacial melting, people began to arrive by sea.
These fishermen, hunters, farmers, metalworkers, traders, and
pirates came from what are now known as Indochina, China,
Indonesia, Malaysia, Borneo, Melanasia, Polynesia, and even
India and the Arab world. The first seafaring immigrants, the
New Stone Age Indonesians, employed dry agriculture for the
cultivation of millet and yams. Between 800 and 500 B.C., the
introduction of irrigation facilitated the cultivation of taro,
new varieties of yams and the present food staple, rice. The
world renowned rice terraces, which are still farmed by the
tribal Ifugaos, were carved into the rugged mountains of north-
central Luzon during this period. The domestication of animals
was introduced as were central Asian techniques of copper
mining and smelting. The manufacture of metal ornaments and
glass beads began.

In the eighth or ninth century A.D., the islands began to
experience contact with some of the world's most highly developed cultures. Arab traders from the Middle East were followed
by Indians and Hindu Malayans from the Shri Visayan Empire.
During the thirteenth century, increasing numbers of Chinese
traders and goldsmiths reached the islands. And in 1521, the
Spanish arrived with Portuguese explorer Ferdinand Magellan at
the helm of an expedition of five ships and 200 men. Within
six weeks, Magellan lay dead at the hand of Lapu Lapu of Mactan,
a feat that insured the native chieftain's place in history as
the first Filipino folk hero. Forty-four more years would pass
before the Spanish would gain a firm foothold in the islands.
But even before their first settlement, the Hispanicization of
the archipelago had begun: in 1554 the Spanish navigator Ruy
Lopez de Villalobos named the archipelago Filipinias (Philippines) as a tribute to Philip, Prince of Asturias and later
Philip II of Spain.

The Spanish Period

In February 1565, Miguel Lopez Legazpi landed in the
Visayas, made peace with the local chieftains, and set about
Spain's primary business in the Philippines, the spread of
Catholicism. The nation's first church was built in the
nation's first Spanish city, Cebu, a flurry of baptisms and
Christian weddings was performed, and Legazpi and his men--
the expedition was composed of more Flemish, Italians, Greeks,
and French than Spaniards--moved north to spread the word of
God under the flag of Spain.

On Mindoro, Legazpi's forces skirmished with the Chinese
before moving on to Manila Bay in 1570 to defeat the Muslim
forces of Tondo and Manil, villages on opposite sides of the
Pasig River at the point where it empties into the bay. With
the resisting Muslims having been pushed south into Mindanao
and other islands in the Sulu and Celebes Seas, where they
remain today, Legazpi began to build Manila in Spain's image.

The Muslim fort at Manila was rebuilt and renamed Fort
Santiago. Churches, government buildings, schools, and an
eventual total of 600 Spanish residences sprouted within a
fortresslike walled city, Spanish Intramuros. The Christian
era had arrived.

Before the Philippines came under Spanish rule, most of
the islands' natives lived in small communities called *barangays*, the word used by the Malayans for the dugouts that carried
them to the islands. (A nationalistic movement during the
mid-1970s reinstated the term *barangay* to apply to townships
which, since Spanish days, had been known as *barrios*.) Most
of the archipelago was covered by forests which had to be cut
back to provide room for agricultural products to supplement
a diet of fish caught in the seas, rivers, and lakes bordering
these primitive communities. Social organization in the
barangays then as now was based on kinship. To preserve the
family unit, marriages were arranged by parents, and elders
were revered. What religious beliefs the people held were
based on ancestor worship and animism.

Although a large number of mountain tribes and the southern-
based Muslims remained apart from the Spaniards' influence, the
accessible lowland populations were quickly conquered and
Christianized. It was not, however, so much a matter of the
Filipino becoming Christianized as Christianity in the islands
becoming Filipinized. Even today, with about 83 percent of the
population having embraced Catholicism, Filipinos' primary
alliances are to their families, followed by loyalty to their
ethnolinguistic groups.

The insular Philippine society is broken up by mountains
and water. Ethnic differences tend to merge into regional
solidarity in the shade of steep mountains separating people.
Filipinos with common ethnic roots often "face" in different
directions and adopt a mutual language and culture with Fili-

pinos across a bay or inland sea. The Spanish may have brought
a sense of religious and social structure to the islands, but
they did little to change the Filipino's basic values. Not, at
least, in the beginning.

The Spanish built roads and set up a central administrative
framework and municipal and provincial governments. As more
people moved into towns, regional differences began to disap-
pear. Filipinos began to adapt to Westernization, but at the
expense of becoming second-class citizens in their own country.

Things didn't work out quite as the Spanish had hoped,
either. Although they seem to have had little or no interest
in the Philippines' natural resources, the Spanish were eager
to establish the islands as a point of control for Spanish
grading interests. King Philip II viewed them as his stepping-
stone to a glory on the order of that surrounding his predeces-
sors, Ferdinand and Isabella. To that end, he sent waves of
priests to put a Spanish face on the Philippines.

It was the secular government's policy to promote the
teaching of the Spanish language. What happened, however, was
that upon being assigned to a village, a priest--often the only
foreigner in the village--would discover that he could gain
control only by learning the native languages. Many of these
priests were, in effect, the mayors of their communities. As
their powers grew, so did their desire to maintain the relative
autonomy that a drive toward the general use of the Spanish
language would disrupt. Thus, Spanish was learned only by
Filipino intellectuals in Manila and by those wealthy enough
to go to Spain for university educations. It became the language of the nation's elite. Meanwhile, the native languages
were preserved and today, most Filipinos speak one of three
major languages: Cebuano (spoken in the Visayas), Tagalog
(Manila area), and Ilocano (northern Luzon).

The various mixed-blood groups also began to emerge during
the early Spanish days. The term *Filipino* was applied only to
people of pure Spanish stock born in the Philippines; natives
of Malayan ancestry were called *Indios*. A new *mestizo* emerged
from the union of a Spaniard and an Indio. Unions between
Chinese and anyone else produced Chinese mestizos, and other
unions down the colonial road would result in American mestizos. Today, of course, the terms *Filipino* and *Filipina* (the
feminine form) apply to anybody born in the Philippines.

The Chinese, who came as traders and goldsmiths and settled
in as commercial leaders, remained in a class by themselves.
Because their business acumen has always threatened the establishment, the Chinese have been subject to discrimination and
a period of outright persecution throughout their history in
the Philippines. In 1603, the Spaniards' fear of the Chinese
who were settling outside the walled city in ever increasing
numbers erupted and resulted in the massacre of more than
23,000 Chinese. In retaliation, the Chinese burned the settlements of Tondo and Quiapo outside Intramuros. The Indios

rushed to the aid of the Spanish, and a cultural pattern of an alliance of Spanish and Filipinos against the Chinese was set. For this reason, many Chinese have adopted Spanish surnames and it is not uncommon among Chinese families for one son to be known by his family's surname and another to go by a Spanish surname.

Muslims, too, who make up about five percent of the population, have remained separate and relatively isolated, although raids and retaliations between the Christian Spanish and Islamic Moros flared often during the Spanish period. A war for Muslim autonomy continues to exist today.

By the seventeenth century, the port of Manila had become the center of trade between East and West. Fearing that Oriental goods might replace Spanish goods in North American colonial markets, Spain slapped a monopoly on Pacific trade that lasted from 1593 to 1815. For over 200 years—even during the brief occupation of Manila by the British from 1762 to 1764 —the Spanish-owned Galleon Company monopolized trade between the Orient, California, and Acapulco, Mexico. Although the trade was enormously lucrative for the Spanish crown, Filipinos gained little from their geographic importance.

During the early part of the nineteenth century, an economic upper class emerged. Well-to-do Spanish and mestizos became landlords, farmers, lawyers, doctors, teachers, and governmental heads. They had the advantage of education, something denied the vast majority of Filipinos who remained uneducated even after the establishment of the first system of public schools in 1863. By 1989, when the population of the Philippines was more than 7 million, only 200,000 students were enrolled in the islands' 2,160 schools.

Filipinos began to chafe at their lack of educational and clerical opportunities, at their lack of representation in the Spanish *cortes* (legislature), and at blatant discrimination symbolized by the enforced wearing of the *barong tagalog*, the light, often elaborately embroidered overshirt worn with pride by Filipino men today for all dress occasions. The wearing of this garment was imposed for two reasons: it readily identified the wearer as Filipino rather than Spanish and, since it was transparent and without pockets, it prevented the wearer from carrying concealed weapons. Another rule required Filipinos to vacate sidewalks when approached by Spaniards.

By 1872, Filipino nationalism had begun to rise and revolution was in the air. In 1896, the brilliant physician-poet-historian Jose P. Rizal, who was a mestizo of Spanish, Chinese, Japanese, Malayan, Tagalog, and Ilocano ancestry, was executed for his political writings by the Spanish. The revolutionary forces had gained a hero, while frequent and bloody uprisings against the Spanish in the Philippines and economic problems at home weakened Spain's hold on the islands.

The American Period

By 1897 the United States had begun to spread its net over
the Pacific. It had already taken over the harbor of Pago Pago
and the islands of Midway, and held a 40-year-old lease on
Pearl Harbor in the Hawaiian Islands. Alaska had been purchased
in 1869. And when the Chinese empire broke up at the end of
the Sino-Japanese War in 1895, the United States joined Germany,
Great Britain, France, and Japan in a rush to plant their flags
in the Pacific.

Americans were producing more than they could consume; they
were clamoring for new markets. President William McKinley's
assistant secretary of the navy, Theodore Roosevelt, viewed a
war with Spain as conducive to the nation's trade interests.
A base in the Philippines, he reasoned, would provide the means
for Asian trade without threatening China's sovereignty. War
would be launched on three fronts: Cuba, Spain, and the
Philippines. For this purpose Roosevelt secured the appointment of George Dewey, who was a student of Oriental affairs,
as well as a naval officer of distinction as commander of the
Asiatic fleet.

Following the sinking of the U.S. battleship *Maine* in
Havana's harbor, the subsequent U.S. declaration of Cuban
independence would put the Philippines up for grabs by other
nations eager to stake out territorial claims in the Pacific.
It was an accidental exchange of gunfire between a Filipino
guard and an American soldier that settled the matter. The
Philippine-American war erupted, and two years and 70,000
American troops later, the Filipinos knew that independence
was not theirs. A writer of the time reported, "A short time
after the hostilities were over we had 10,000 young American
schoolmarms and experts on sanitation, nutrition, tropical
medicine and agriculture in the islands sent there to improve
living conditions and wipe out disease."

Working against rising charges of imperialism at home,
President McKinley went about the business of setting up a
"predemocratic" form of government in the Philippines. The
idea was to turn the Philippines into a showcase of American
democracy in Asia. While referring to Filipinos as "our
little brown brothers," the U.S. government maintained law
and order through a liberal use of gunpowder.

On July 4, 1901, William Howard Taft was installed as the
first civil governor-general of the Philippines. His motto of
"The Philippines for the Filipinos" became the rationale for
U.S. control "during a period of training in the art of self-
government." The feeling was not entirely mutual, however,
as was indicated in the 1920s by future Philippine Commonwealth
President Manuel L. Quezon, who declared, "I prefer a government run like hell by Filipinos to a government run like heaven
by Americans."

During Taft's administration, the government purchased the
enormous estates owned by the Catholic Church and sold them to

Filipinos. As might be expected, most of the land ended up in the hands of the rich elite. Taft justified this by remarking that it was the only class with the education and wealth necessary to manage the lands.

The next step was to set up an educational system patterned after the U.S. model and based on the English language. In the summer of 1901 some 1,100 U.S. teachers arrived in the Philippines. By 1930, the level of literacy in the country was higher than in any other Asian colony—a remarkable feat, considering literacy was achieved in a new language. Today, about one-half of the population speaks at least some English—albeit creatively accented American English—although the recently proclaimed national language, Pilipino (a Tagalog derivation), has not surplanted English in the country's schools. And, since 1903, when Filipino *pensionados* were sent by the Philippine government to study in U.S. colleges, the United States has remained the land of first choice for Filipinos who go abroad for their college educations.

In August 1916, the U.S. Congress passed the Jones Law providing for the general election of a Philippine congress and the U.S. governor-general's appointment of representatives from the Islamic and tribal minorities. Freedom for the Philippines was set for 1921, but pressure from the American Catholic Church erased the independence date from the law.

It was not until March 1934 that Congress passed the Tydings-McDuffie Act providing for Philippine independence in 1946. The bill was viewed as a relief measure by those U.S. farmers who saw tax-free trade between the United States and its colonies as a major contributor to the depression. And the Filipinos believed that, at long last, they were beginning to see a light at the end of the tunnel to independence. In June 1944, however, the act was amended to provide for Philippine independence with the stipulation that U.S. control over the installations at Subic Bay and Clark Field, Pampanga, would continue. The gigantic naval and air bases have been subjects of contention ever since.

Seven hours after the Japanese attacked Pearl Harbor on December 7, 1941, they attacked the Philippines. Most of the planes at Clark Field were destroyed. Corregidor was isolated; U.S. and Filipino soldiers there lacked both food and arms, commodities the United States was either unable or disinclined to supply. On January 2, 1942, the Japanese occupied Manila; resident U.S. citizens were interned at the University of Santo Tomas. On May 6, 1942, the war in the Philippines was over as far as the United States was concerned. The Filipinos, however, continued the struggle against the Japanese until the end of the war, which was marked by the dramatic return of General Douglas MacArthur and Philippines President-in-Exile Sergio Osmena to Leyte in October, 1944.

Independence

On July 4, 1946, the Philippines received its promised
freedom from the United States. Independence, however, did
not bring peace to the beleaguered nation. About 80 percent
of Manila lay in ruins. The Japanese had plundered the
nation's industries, office buildings, and mines. Transportation was at a standstill; people were starving throughout the
country. Charges of Japanese collaboration as a means of
survival by members of Manila's Spanish elite turned the gap
between the upper and lower classes into a chasm. The army
was powerless against the Hukbalahap (Huks), nationalist
guerrillas banded together to fight the Japanese with "seques-
tered" American weaponry. The Huks, who rallied now under a
communist line, were taking over villages and even levying
taxes on them. By 1950, the Huk forces, which were said to
be 20,000 strong and backed by a million peasants, controlled
central Luzon.

By 1953, a vigorous government resettlement program had
pushed the Huks underground, but the nation's general population was still armed to the teeth. Over the next two decades,
murder, robbery, and corruption kept the nation in a state of
internal siege that outdid the North American wild West. A
joke of the period referred to the wealthy who "bulged both
front and back." They bulged in front at the expense of the
starving poor and in back at the cost of private armies that
followed them everywhere.

Although the postwar Philippines was nominally a democracy
with a constitution based on that of the United States, political and economic power continued to rest in the hands of the
wealthy oligarchs. New schools were built, a system of rural
banks was established to facilitate farm credit, and industrial
expansion was encouraged. The nation's food deficit was eased
by huge exports of U.S. grain surpluses on a soft-loan basis
under U.S. Public Law 480 (PL 480). But the rural sector's
burgeoning population was becoming increasingly hungry and
disenchanted with politicians who bribed and/or coerced their
way into power, promising much and delivering little other
than more of the same.

Ferdinand E. Marcos was elected to the presidency in 1965
on a platform of social reform and economic development. But
by 1972 the economy had come to a halt. Devastating typhoon
floods had wiped out 34 percent of that year's rice harvest.
Every port was a smuggler's haven and gangs of thugs roamed the
streets of Manila; police records for murder, robbery, and bur-
glary were overflowing.

During this period, the secessionist movement in the South
had gained momentum and the Maoist New People's Army (NPA), an
outgrowth of the old Hukbalahap organization, had filled its
ranks with anti-U.S. student dissidents from Manila's universities and was staging ambushes from bases in the mountains of

Luzon. Manilans lived in constant fear of dissidents' bombs.
The country was in a state of virtual anarchy.

History had created a colorful and richly complicated
culture and people bent on self-determinism, which was a matter
of individual and family interest. The ingrained system of
cronyism stemming from and perpetuated by large families, the
streak of violence underlying the Filipino's copability, and
a marked class system and dualist economy favoring urban
industrialization and flashy monuments to modernity over life-
sustaining agricultural advancement proved to be incompatible
with the precepts of democracy.

Centuries of foreign domination had fostered a sense of
national inferiority on one hand, and a dependence on heavy-
handed, paternalistic leadership on the other. But neither
President Marcos' stature as a World War II hero nor his
personal charisma and nationalistic resolve could pull the
country together under a blanket of Western-oriented idealism.
Internal strife was in the way of national development.

On September 21, 1972, Marcos took the only path he saw
open to him and his country's development: with a character-
istic flourish, he issued Proclamation 1081. The Philippines
had been placed under martial law. Private armies were dis-
mantled. Thousands of political opponents, journalists, and
student activists were thrown into jail. The free press was
muzzled and a number of feudalistic oligarchal landholdings
were broken up. The U.S.-style presidential system was
replaced by a Westminster-style parliamentary system, and
Marcos became both president under the old constitution and
prime minister under the new. The "New Society," Marcos
declared, would be marked by long overdue land reform, improved
social services, a drive against corruption, and a better life
for all Filipinos. The New Society appeared to be on the move.

Marcos loaded the government with family and friends, many
of whom turned out to be capable and energetic. Marcos'
responsibilities included industrial and agricultural development, internal security, and foreign affairs. Imelda Romualdez
Marcos, President Marcos' wife, had the responsibilities for
social welfare and cultural programs to advance the arts.

The authority relegated to the first lady had a two-fold
impact. By lumping population, nutrition, health, and human
resettlement concerns with the relative fluff of the performing
arts, Marcos diverted heat from sensitive social issues away
from himself. And, by putting social welfare in the hands of
his wife and then appointing another woman, Dr. Estefania
Aldaba-Lim, to head the Department of Social Welfare, he made
it obvious that this area was not to receive top priority in
the New Society. But Imelda Marcos, a politically astute and
highly ambitious person herself, took her job seriously. Her
enthusiastic endorsement of a string of social action projects,
and the high degree of prestige and visibility she brought to
them, got the programs off the ground and her into the lime-
light.

Filipinas are considered by the rest of the world to be among the most liberated women on the face of the earth. In the villages and urban slum areas they hold the family purse strings. In the cities they sit on corporate boards and are evident in the professional ranks of doctors and lawyers. Inheritance laws distribute wealth equally among male and female heirs, and women are the stabilizing force that holds the all-important family unit together.

To many, Imelda Marcos' governmental influence in her positions as governor of metropolitan Manila and minister of human settlements might seem to epitomize the Filipino concept of female liberation. And indeed it does, but not entirely in the way it appears. The village woman who manages the family money often controls only the income that she and her children are able to command; her husband the jeepney driver or construction worker is free to spend his earnings in bars and on *masamang babae* (prostitutes). Similarly, even the most prestigious and professional Filipina is likely to be kept in the dark when it comes to her husband's income and extracurricular activities. The Catholic church has managed to keep divorce out of the Philippines, except in the South, where the right to divorce has been granted to Muslims as part of their religiously endowed freedom. Separations between married couples throughout the rest of the country are common, but the double standard persists: many Filipinos (excluding the wives of the men who have one) consider it perfectly acceptable for a man to keep a mistress on the side, but the woman must not risk besmirching the family name by straying from the straight and narrow. Children secure their mother's place in the family.

Imelda Marcos is no exception to the rule of the woman's place; her family situation has, however, given her the opportunity to use her femininity to win extraordinary power. Although she has been severely criticized both at home and abroad for her extravagance and a coquettish arrogance that has led Western journalists to dub her "the Iron Butterfly," she has accomplished much. As the Philippines' ambassador-at-large (Foreign Secretary Carlos Romulo has even called her the nation's "de facto vice-president"), Imelda Marcos has charmed goodwill and diplomatic concessions from the divers likes of Mao Tse-tung, Fidel Castro, Muammar Qaddafi, Jose Lopez-Portillo and U.S. Presidents Nixon, Johnson, and Reagan.

At home, her accomplishments are more concrete. The gracefully modern cultural center of the Philippines, which opened in 1969, provides the country's upper and middle classes with international entertainment and supports the world-renowned Filipino ballet troupe, the CCP Dance Company. The accompanying folk arts theatre serves as a pavilion for cultural presentations geared to the masses, and the convention center of the Philippines serves as a luxuriously appointed backdrop for international conferences. The 1976 International

Monetary Fund-World Bank Conference in Manila was preceded by a building blitz that set the city on its ear. When the dust cleared, fourteen new first-class hotels commissioned by the first lady stood ready to receive the conference delegates.

The resettlement of tens of thousands of Manilan squatters to two new towns constructed by the Department of Social Welfare with help from USAID has garnered mixed reviews. A precarious water supply and lack of local employment have hindered the progress of these towns built 20 miles from Manila in the hills above San Pedro. Children in the resettlement areas have benefited, however, from playground space, a diet augmented by U.S. PL 480 food, and Peace Corps involvement in setting up schools and teaching the basics of animal husbandry.

A nationally sponsored nutrition program was launched by the first lady in the early 1970s with funding and technical assistance from USAID, CARE, and UNICEF. Under this program, the elements of nutrition were taught in the country's rural areas and PL 480 food was distributed--much of it in the form of innovative and well-received "nutri-buns" for school children--in the areas where malnutrition is the most severe.

It was Imelda Marcos' support of a national family planning effort that enabled it to get off to a fast start. Although the program came late in the nation's history of a high birth rate, and has a long way to go before the population is stabilized at a point of resource sustainability, the fact that it got started at all in the face of years of Catholic influence and a cultural predisposition toward large families is commendable. In fact, when the program was announced in 1970, its acceptance came as a huge surprise to Secretary of Health Clemente Gatmaitan. A political survivalist with 43 years of public health experience under his belt and an exhibited disinterest in fertility control, Gatmaitan remarked, "I didn't believe [the program's acceptance] would be that favorable."

A Mystical Way of Life

When the Spanish arrived, they found that the Indios already believed in an active spirit world which included an underworld, an afterlife, and a supreme being, Bathala, who ruled over all. Catholic proselytizing was a simple matter: the friars merely substituted Dios (God) for Bathala, added new rituals to old, introduced saints around whom fiestas revolved, and chalked up any slippage in the system to native primitivism.

Although about 83 percent of the population today claim Catholicism as their formal religion, animist traditions still permeate the lives of all Filipinos. An exotic panoply of mythological animals and spirits is still believed to rule both man and nature, particularly in the rural areas. And among the country's jungle tribes, pure animism is the dominant feature of life.

The spirit world and animistic beliefs of the Igorots of Luzon's mountain province, former cannibals who practice head hunting only occasionally today, are among the richest in the world. The Ifugao tribe, which farms the rice terraces of Benawe, has a complicated spirit world consisting of the Downstream Region (*Lagud*), the Upstream Region (*Daya*), the Skyworld (*Kabunian* or *Angadal*), the Underworld (*Dalum*), and Earth (*Pugao*). The Thunderer and his subordinates dominate the Skyworld by controlling lightning, landslides, typhoons, wind, and rain. In the Underworld live the Earthquaker and his servants. In the Downstream and Upstream regions dwell the rice-culture deities as well as gods of reproduction, hunting, and weaving. The Igorots' (there are many Igorot tribes, including the Ifugaos) rice harvest is still insured by rituals revolving around carved figures of rice gods and granary guardians.

Similarly, Muslim Filipinos (Moros) practice a form of Islam that has been highly modified by infiltration through India, Sumatra, and Malaya. Many practices and beliefs of the Moros are charged with an animism which would never be tolerated by the strongly monotheistic orthodoxy of Middle Eastern Islam. While the representation of the human form is taboo to the Middle Easterner, it is found in abundance in Moro art. The Islamic ban on the eating of pork is enforced by Muslim Filipinos, who take their protein in the form of fish. Many northern Luzon tribal groups, on the other hand, consider fish to be unclean; they eat pork when it is available, although spit-roasted dog is their prime delicacy.

Although somewhat less dramatic in their manifestations, ancient myths still surround the life--particularly family matters--of the Filipino Christian.

The natural and uncomplicated sexuality that is the inheritance of Malayan culture is discussed without inhibitions by Filipinos. Jokes are frequently made, and they consider their sexuality and the children that come as a result of it as *biyaya ng Dyos*, a gift of God.

Marriage Begets Honor and Vice Versa

Among the upper and middle classes, the age at the time of marriage has been increasing as a result of urban migration and the greater opportunities for education and upward mobility that urbanization brings. The mean age of women at the time of marriage is now 24.4. Among the rural and urban slum populations, however, marriage among teenagers is not uncommon. Eleven percent of all 15- to 19-year-old females are married. In comparison with U.S., Latin American, and African populations, premarital sex is surprisingly uncommon.

Among the poorer segments of Philippine society, early marriage fulfills two functions. It assures the semblance of a virgin bride. It also serves to elevate the bride and groom to adulthood, a position in which their opinions are honored and their authority within the extended family structure is recognized.

To guard against premarital relations that could result in an "unsuitable" marriage, the Spanish elite still often employ the *duena* (chaperone) system to prevent young men and women from being alone together. Among the poorer classes, however, where everyone in the family except the very old or very young are apt to be working, young people can often manage to find time to be alone.

With marriage comes not only the stature of adulthood, but the responsibilities of a family provider. Income sharing is extended throughout the entire family, which embraces both spouses' families, distant cousins, servants, and close friends, as well as the more immediate family in which three or four generations may live under one roof. The family's social status is dependent on the preservation of each individual's honor and self-esteem.

Relationships are built and maintained according to the "four faces of honor." *Amor propio*, the concept of honor and self-esteem, involves a personal perception of one's social value and the Filipino's need to be treated as a person and not as an object. This encompasses a radical, vindictive reaction to real or imagined insult. The Filipino's fragile sense of personal worth makes criticism enormously painful and the admission of having made a mistake very difficult. The impulse to protect one's actions or integrity transcends the fear of retaliation, and fatal incidents, especially among young people, are often attributed to the protection of amor propio.

Closely related to amor propio is *hiva*, which carries a connotation of shame or embarrassment. This is a face-saving mechanism learned in the third to fifth year of life in the extended family setting. It involves a sense of inferiority and of potential rejection or alienation which is used to keep children in line and becomes acutely distressing in adulthood.

Pakikisama is the Filipino's method of getting along with people, of keeping relationships running smoothly. This involves a subtle form of manipulation, ranging from simple politeness to the deliberate yielding of one's own ideas or principles in favor of another's. Filipinos place such high value on good interpersonal feelings that they will sacrifice something as simple as clear communication. What Westerners view as evasiveness is pure coping behavior for the Filipino. Frankness is feared; people who are outspoken about their opinions are thought to be uncultured and are ostracized. Thus, Filipinos tend to agree with what another says, and keep their reservations to themselves. The expected rewards for pakikisama,

for giving in to another person's wishes, may be immediate, as
in the form of *lagay* (a gift, bribe, or tip), or in the form
of future concessions. The failure of Westerners to understand
and appreciate the concept of pakikisama and the necessity for
lagay has stood in the way of many a social action program
aimed at the Philippines' poor.

One of the most important sources of group cohesion is
utang na loob, literally "debt of the inside." This refers to
the feeling of obligation or indebtedness which develops when
one has done a favor for another. The asking for and receiving
of help is neither a neutral matter nor a matter of unselfish-
ness and gratitude on the part of donor and recipient. A Filipino who seeks a favor from someone outside her or his family
in the form of a loan, recommendation, or intercession with
someone in authority, places himself or herself in a situation
of obligation. The debt of gratitude can be repaid with a
different sort of favor, but it must be repaid. Utang na loob
has a great deal to do with the tremendous respect shown by
children to their mothers who gave them life--a debt that can
be only partially repaid later by providing for their mother's
comfort in her old age--and political favors doled out to a
politician's supporters.

These concepts make it possible for large, extended families
to live together in harmony and for upward mobility to proceed
without endangering the Filipino's sensitivity and extremely
fragile sense of self-worth. They also explain the pervasive
family-centered cronyism in Philippine politics and business
life. Only in a large family does one find the kind of social
security that has as much to do with self-esteem as with economic survival. And only through the act of parenting does the
Filipino find a true sense of self-worth and personal identification. The Filipino is extremely power conscious; children
are a manifestation of and means toward power.

Mythology Confronts Reality

There is a strong streak of fatalism in the Filipino
character that arises from a history of supernatural beliefs,
natural environmental disasters, and social upheaval and is
perpetuated by the security blanket of the large extended
family. Convinced that they have only limited control over
their destinies, Filipinos tend to react to trouble with "It
was my fate" or "Bahala na. May awa ang Dios" (What God wills
He will provide for). Success is considered to be more a matter of luck than effort. And children are thought to bring
buenna (good luck) in life.

A Filipino's children attest to his virility, serve as
proof of a husband's love for his wife, are sometimes believed
to be angels with mystical healing powers, and are often viewed
as economic necessities in areas where they can be put to work

at an early age. Since it is considered unlucky to have children of only one sex, parents will continue to produce children until at least one of each sex is born. As the saying goes, "Kung maari sa isa bakit hindi sa dalwa" (If it is possible for one, why not for two?). In the extended family, where sharing is a matter of honor as much as responsibility, there is always room for another child. Similar to this is the slum-dweller's likening of life to a blanket with which one can always keep warm by curling up and covering the legs. "Kung maikli ang kumot, matutong mamaluktot," they say (If the blanket is short, learn to crouch). In other words, by limiting individual needs, even the meagerest resources can be stretched.

In traditional households, however, the stretching of resources is not equal. The patriarchal structure of these households dictates that men be fed before women and children. This pattern contributes heavily to the high incidences of malnutrition among Filipino children.

Economic realities have intruded on family-centered mythology. Even before overpopulation and unemployment became recognized problems by the Philippine leadership, more and more Filipinos began to view large numbers of children as economic liabilities. It was often extremely difficult to follow the church's tenet that it was sinful to tamper with what God has given people--the ability to bear children. The desire for upward mobility is gradually supplanting the large-family norm. And abortion has long been a fact of Filipino life.

Traditional folk methods of abortion are painful and often life threatening. A common method is by *hilot*, or massage, in which the womb is twisted until the fetus is expelled. Another common method results in the puncturing of the fetus by a foot-long rubber catheter which is allowed to protrude about an inch from the vagina and is left in place overnight. Hemorrhaging is frequent with this method. Folk abortifacients are also used widely. These include overdoses of aspirin or drinks concocted from the boiled stems, barks, leaves, and roots of medicinal herbs purchased from vendors such as those around the Quiapo church in downtown Manila. Some of the plants used, however, are poisonous; overdoses sometimes prove fatal.

Until the early 1970s, the use of artificial contraceptives was unpopular among the vast majority of the nation's poor, and not for either moral or financial reasons. The use of condoms was frowned on by married women because they associated them with the precautionary methods taken against disease by men engaging in sexual relations with prostitutes. A fact that still dictates against the popularity of condoms is the nuisance of putting one on. Oral contraceptives, or pills, also have a negative connotation due in part to press reports and rumors about side effects and long-term health effects. The acceptance of the pill was often a response to urging by a lover rather than a voluntary decision. Vaginal spermicides were known

early to both married and single women, but their frequent
failure to live up to their advertised effectiveness turned
many of these women against contraceptives altogether. The
rhythm method, on the other hand, proved to be ineffective for
women with irregular menstrual cycles, which they attributed
to hard work in the fields or as pushcart vendors or city-dump
scavengers.

Although more and more women are opting for smaller families, the traditional care lavished on pregnant Filipinas is
a form of seduction in itself. Women often joke that they take
advantage of their husband's concern and generosity during
pregnancy because "It is only then that you get what you want
from your husband." An entire lexicon of superstitions surround
pregnancy and childbirth and, just as vinegar, salt, and garlic
(the major seasonings in present-day Filipino cooking) are
traditional protections against evil farm and household spirits,
newborn babies are protected against evil by amulets of grass
seeds or pendants of wrapped ginger or crocodile's teeth.
Whenever possible, however, mothers take the added precaution
of presenting their infants to health centers for innoculations
against polio, typhoid, cholera, and measles.

Venerated as large families are, such cultural anthropologists as F. Landa Jocano of the University of the Philippines
believe that the small family began to emerge as a socially
viable option during the early 1960s. Jocano points out that
by the early 1970s, about half of the families studied for his
work on Manila slum life wanted to limit their families to
about three children rather than leave the matter to fate.
Given the Filipino's fear of criticism, it is very possible that
many parents express the desire for six or more children as a
sort of preemptive strategy of rationalization for children that
may be born because they do not know how to limit their family
size in a physically and psychologically nonthreatening way.

A PROGRAM OF FERTILITY CONTROL IS BORN

Although President Marcos was one of the early signers of
the 1968 United Nations Declaration on Family Planning, the
Philippine government's stance on population was still essentially laissez-faire at the end of the 1960s. In the 12 years
between 1948 and 1960, the country's population growth rate
rose sharply from an average of 1.91 percent per year between
1939 and 1948 to about 3.06 percent. Most of this increase,
which caused the population size to leap from 19 million in
1948 to 27 million in 1960, was due to a postwar baby boom and
rapidly declining mortality rates. Despite volunteer efforts
in rural family planning under the aegis of the International
Planned Parenthood Federation, however, the growth rate fell
only to an average of 3.01 percent between 1960 and 1970. Overpopulation was rapidly becoming a problem that the government
could no longer ignore.

In 1969, with his country's population fast approaching
the 37 million mark and the economy stagnating, President
Marcos decided to follow the direction taken earlier by neighboring Taiwan, Korea, Indonesia, Thailand and Singapore.
Marcos named a Commission on Population (POPCOM) whose report,
at the end of 1969, provided the basis for the establishment
of a national population effort. The commission then continued,
in reduced form, as a coordinating body.

In 1970, having discovered from surveys that the people
were far ahead of their government in terms of open demands for
contraceptive services, the government moved more resolutely
toward making POPCOM a permanent body. Imelda Marcos recruited
the Harvard-trained obstetrician-gynecologist, Dr. Conrado
Lorenzo, for the post of POPCOM executive director. Dr. Lorenzo,
was young, aristocratic, politically well connected, and a go-
getter. His mission: to carry out Republic Act 6365 which
put into law a policy decision that "for the purpose of further-
ing the national development, increasing the share of each
Filipino in the fruits of economic progress and meeting the
grave social challenge of a high rate of population growth, a
national program of family planning involving both public and
private sectors which respects the religious beliefs and values
of the individual shall be undertaken."

Between 1971 and 1974 family planning centers were opened
at the dizzying rate of almost one per day; by 1975, contraceptive supplies and services were being provided at a nationwide
total of 2,049 clinics. At the same time, the government began
to seek foreign assistance for its fertility program with undis-
guised eagerness. USAID became heavily involved in both funding
and technical assistance, and the United Nations Fund for Population Activities (UNFPA) added its support. Thousands of
doctors, nurses, midwives, and fieldworkers were trained in
family planning servicing and the art of gentle persuasion.
The family planning word was spread among the people by virtually every agency of the government.

In 1974, contraceptive choice was expanded to include
voluntary sterilization for both men and women. Previously,
sterilization was available only through private agencies and
several university medical schools and teaching hospitals.
Acceptance, however, was very gradual and had little effect
for the first two or three years. Now all contraceptive
methods--with the exception of abortion--were legal and obtain-
able through the government-sponsored program. That same year,
contraceptive acceptance levels rose to roughly 35,000 per
month. In late 1974, an estimated 1.4 million couples (about
25 percent of all married couples of reproductive age) were
protected by some form of contraception, primarily pills, IUDs,
and condoms.

Following the permanent establishment of POPCOM in 1971,
an agreement was reached with USAID on sharing such basic costs
as salaries, transportation, and utilities over the next five

years. During the first year, USAID agreed to cover almost
100 percent of the operational costs. After that, USAID's
share dropped by 20 percent each succeeding year. Simultane-
ously, the government of the Philippines agreed to increase
its contribution by increments of 20 percent a year. To its
enormous credit, the government exceeded its required contribution each year, and this during a phase of rapid program
and budgetary expansion. From an initial 1972 budget of $1.2
million, the Philippine contribution rose to $8.7 million in
1975. That same year, USAID contributed $5.9 million and
UNFPA funded the effort to the extent of $2.0 million. Con-
tributions by other donors totaling $0.7 million brought the
year's funding total to $17.3 million. UNICEF became involved
in training teachers to integrate elementary school family
planning education.

During the period 1970-75, high growth continued, adding
an average of 1.0 million people annually as the country
increased in size from 36.8 to 42.1 million. The between-
census growth rate of 3.01 percent per year during 1960-70
showed only a modest decline to 2.78 percent during the period
1970-75. Other Asian countries such as Korea, Taiwan, and
Thailand, meanwhile, were reducing their growth rates by one-
tenth of one percent annually--more than twice as fast as the
Philippines.

In 1975, the Internal Revenue Code was revised to provide
tax exemptions for no more than four children per family. The
Labor Department jumped on the bandwagon by ruling that maternity leaves would be limited to the first four deliveries.
(This ruling, however, was later unilaterally overturned by
the powerful teachers' union, which insisted on a clause providing for unlimited maternity leave in all female teachers'
contracts.)

Service statistics data that year, however, clearly showed
that the family planning program had reached a plateau in the
numbers of new volunteers and the percentage of continuing
users. There were several reasons for this. The people who
wanted contraceptive services and were near enough to clinics
to get them easily had been serviced. The limited reach of
the relatively static, clinic-based family planning service
system had become a major obstacle. The post-World War II
baby-boom generation, meanwhile, was embarking on marriage and
its own spurt of child rearing. On top of these problems,
interagency competition and infighting, endemic since POPCOM
was first created, continued to debilitate POPCOM efforts.

In 1973, another of Imelda Marcos' institutional dreams
was realized: the Population Center Foundation (PCF) was
established. Soon afterwards, the organization set up house
in a magnificent new building of the same name built by equal
contributions from the government of the Philippines, USAID,
and the Rockefeller Foundation. POPCOM, the government's
population arm, became the PCF's tenant. The first lady's

idea was that the PCF would be devoted to program innovation and research, and would attract funding from private as well as international donors. POPCOM, on the other hand, would continue to carry out broad programs of contraceptive services and information. What happened, however, was that the private sector resisted the lure of population program investment and the two organizations became adversaries.

Initial heavy PCF funding by USAID gave way to primary support by the government of the Philippines and the UNFPA. But the nonbureaucratic nature of the PCF (as opposed to a billowing bureaucracy at POPCOM) and the new organization's capacity to pay comparatively high wages, led to disparities that rankled. The PCF was able to recruit the best and brightest from the nation's medical and academic ranks; it quickly assumed an aura of glamour. In 1974, Dr. Lorenzo shifted from POPCOM to become the PCF's executive director. The government appointed Dr. Rafael Esmundo to head POPCOM.

Esmundo, whose roots were firmly attached to the lower middle class, was the complete antithesis of the elite insider Lorenzo. His particular saving grace was his genuine and fervent concern for the masses. Population programs, he believed, should be developed on the barangay level and lumped together in a "Total Integrated Development Approach" (TIDA). As he said in defense of TIDA:

> *Necessarily, the new thrust seeks to shift the approach from what has been dominantly a contraceptive-oriented program to a concept-oriented program. This is based on the firm belief that when the program becomes conceptually understood and accepted as a way of life worth living, the people will seek on their own--in accordance with their moral and religious convictions--the services they can continuously avail of, except abortion.*

Esmundo was an ideologue, a man who envisioned development in the Philippines as a means of dignifying the human condition. His models were the communes of China and the kibbutzim of Israel. Speaking of TIDA on more than one occasion, he would say. "It's going to be either a kubbutz or a commune, I don't know which, but it will be like that."

TIDA placed the government-sponsored population effort squarely in the hands of the National Economic Development Authority (NEDA). At NEDA's head was a political insider and brilliant MIT-trained economist, Dr. Gerardo P. Sicat. A major ideological stumbling block among family planning leaders in the Philippines is their own general tendency toward large families; family-centered elitism is the name of the game at all levels of government. Unlike the family planning leaders, however, Sicat's priority remained economic development. Although Sicat was a strong supporter of foreign assistance for

family planning, he was highly ambivalent toward fertility
control efforts themselves. Under NEDA's influence, TIDA's
original focus on fertility control was pushed aside by the
more immediate concerns of "integrated development." Esmundo
also failed to gain favor with and energetic support from
President and Mme. Marcos.

In January 1977, Esmundo resigned under pressure. The
TIDA had been in deep trouble for at least a year prior to his
resignation and the POPCOM was in disarray. Failure of the
program was due primarily to two factors. First, Esmundo had
vigorously promoted TIDA to the neglect of the other programs.
Second, as happens in many family planning programs, a lack of
management and organization left development workers without
any forms of legitimizing authority.

Open support for the national population program from the
president and first lady seems to have peaked in 1974, at
least in terms of public announcements. Among the last of
President Marcos' strong statements on the subject was made
on May 6, 1974, during ceremonies commemorating the fall of
Corregidor: "Expanding populations can cause tremendous
stresses and tensions," he declared. "All nations should
devote all their resources, all their energies and all their
talents to defuse this possible source of conflict."

Imelda Marcos' decreasing public support for the fertility
control program may stem from her disappointing experience
with another of her own programs, Project Compassion. Following the Philippines' official recognition of the Peoples'
Republic of China, a brief flurry of activity occurred which
attempted to combine nutrition, population, rural health, and
backyard vegetable growing in one package, modeled on the
Chinese experience. Financial support for Project Compassion
was culled from a variety of sources including provincial
governments, the POPCOM budget, U.N. agencies, and USAID.
Funds were also raised by a series of musical events to which
multinational corporation executive and international agency
heads were invited.

By 1978, however, internal squabbling had become as
apparent as the lack of sustained support from the first lady,
who by that time had become mayor of metropolitan Manila and
was off setting up new projects. Project Compassion ran out
of steam and eventually fizzled out.

More important than public pronouncements and sustained
enthusiasm from the top, however, is the fact that the government has allocated increasingly larger amounts of budgetary
support to the family planning program. Today, approximately
80 percent of all costs are borne by the government—a complete reversal from 1972. The funding balance comes from USAID
and the UNFPA.

Support for fertility control and population policy from
the technocracy continues to be adequate, although far from
universal and often lacking in commitment. Important help has

been readily forthcoming from such quarters as the University
of the Philippines Population Institute and the social sciences
faculties of the Jesuit universities of Ateneo de Manil and
Xavier on Mindanao. Analytical, demographic, and social
science contributions have also been made by the University of
San Carlos in Cebu and by the Department of Economics at the
University of the Philippines. It is at the provincial level
that support has had to be carefully courted and where it still
remains uneven.

The Outlook from Outreach

    Against this muddled background of on-again, off-again
support and enthusiasm, it was decided in 1976 that a new and
more energetic approach to fertility control would be adopted.
The so-called Outreach program, designed by POPCOM and the
USAID/Philippines population staff, quickly gained the full
support of Secretary of Social Welfare Aldaba-Lim. The program
would accommodate the differing regional and personal characteristics of the country's heterogeneous population. And, as
Table 2.1 indicates, even while it was in its formative stages,
the Outreach program managed to give a significant downward
nudge to the country's growth rate.

TABLE 2.1 *Population and Growth Rate, 1898-1981*

Year	Population	Intercensus Growth Rate
1939	16,000,303	
1948	19,234,182	1.91%
1960	27,087,685	3.06%
1970	36,384,485	3.01%
1975	42,200,000[a]	2.78%
1981	54,000,000[b]	2.71%

[a]Non-census POPCOM estimate.

[b]Midyear estimate by the Population Reference Bureau. The
midyear population for 1983 was estimated at 52.0 million.

Source: POPCOM 1980.

    On August 31, 1977, the Outreach program was launched with
government backing of $15.8 million and a USAID grant of $13.7
million to cover three years. The national program not only

gained a new face, but a new acronym as well. Rather than
adopting the conventional mode of referring to program targets
as MWRAs (Married Women of Reproductive Age), the USAID/Philip-
pines Chief of Population introduced MCRAs (Married Couples of
Reproductive Age) to embrace the other half of the human race
as potential parents. In a business where acronyms not only
expedite discourse, but assume an almost mystical force in
themselves, this first official acceptance of the role of men
in reproductive behavior by a member of the international
population establishment was an event in itself.

The new program began operations on an essentially parallel
basis with the established public health service network. One
full-time Outreach worker (FTOW) was recruited and assigned for
every 1,800 MCRAs. A district supervisor was put in charge of
every six to eight FTOWs, and each district supervisor, in
turn, was managed on the provincial level by a population officer. A key feature of the program was the establishment of
supply points in all barangays having a volunteer to maintain
stocks of pills and condoms at the ratio of one supply point
for every 100 or so MCRAs. By the end of 1980, 43,000 barangay
service points had been established throughout the country.

What the Outreach approach addressed was the phenomenon
documented by the University of the Philippines Population
Institute in 1975 of a nearly 30 percent use of contraception
among MCRAs living within two or three kilometers of a rural
health unit. When contraceptive use at a five to ten kilometer
distance was measured, however, it was discovered that only 13
percent of the eligible couples at five kilometers and only
four percent at ten kilometers were regular contraceptive users.

In 1981, USAID pledged its continued financial and technical support to the Outreach Program at least through 1985. The
U.S. agency's major activity during this five-year program will
be the promotion of sterilization, with a goal of 20,000 USAID-
sponsored sterilizations a year by 1985. (The actual number
of sterilizations performed since 1981 has been approximately
100,000 per year.) USAID also will continue to provide contraceptive supplies, the cost of which is projected to comprise
about $26.9 million of the total new program loan of $56.7
million.

Related support can also be expected to continue from the
World Bank, which has provided loans for primary care, training, and organization; and UNFPA, which continues to provide
important supplementary assistance to population programs.
UNICEF and the World Health Organization, although minimally
involved in population, both provide assistance in the areas
of health and nutrition. For the national fertility control
program to develop the momentum necessary to bring the nation's
birth rate down from the rate of 34 per thousand per year in
1981 to the goal of below 20 per thousand by the year 2000,
however, the spotlight will have to focus on the Outreach workers.

The Method Is the Message

In a 1980 community Outreach survey, it was found that 45 percent of the FTOWs were unwilling to provide an initial supply of pills to women, even if there were no contraindications regarding their use and the woman could not get to a clinic to pick up supplies. A pill-dispensing course now in progress should make a marked improvement in this service. But further training in all aspects of contraception is needed: half of the FTOWs interviewed in 1980 were not even able to provide acceptable advice regarding the abstinence period required during a regular 28-day menstrual cycle for calendar rhythm effectiveness, and rhythm remains one of the more popular methods in the program.

The survey also pointed out that the family planning practices among the FTOWs and BSPOs themselves mirror contraceptive practices under the national program. Surveys have shown a growing preference among rural people for rhythm and withdrawal, probably due in great measure to widespread rumors concerning dire side effects from the use of artificial contraceptives. The feeling is that if more effective methods were used by Outreach workers, they would gain wider acceptance by the general public.

Nearly three-fourths of the married FTOWs and two-thirds of the married BSPOs were found to be contraceptive users. FTOW usage was evenly divided between more effective methods (pills, IUDs, sterilization) and less effective methods (rhythm, condoms, withdrawal, abstinence). Most of the FTOWs preferred a combination of rhythm and condoms; next in popularity were ligation (sterilization) and pills. Thirty percent of the BSPOs favored more effective methods while 36 percent were using less effective methods. The most favored method among BSPOs was ligation, followed by rhythm plus condoms, and pills and rhythm alone. Rhythm, either alone or in combination with other methods, was used by 30 percent of the FTOWs and 21 percent of the BSPOs, making it the single most popular method of all Outreach workers.

In addition to the predominant use of less effective contraceptive methods, one reason for the continuing high birth rate in the Philippines is the discontinuation of contraceptive use. This fact clearly points to the importance of the IUD (which is shown to provide an average of 27 couple-months of protection as compared to the pill, which is discontinued after an average use period of only 15 months) and sterilization to the success of the program.

Given the discontinuation rates and a relative effectiveness of various methods, a study estimates that the number of births averted (per couple) by pill use is 0.64; by an IUD, 1.2; by rhythm, 0.5; by condoms, 0.21; and by sterilization, 2.7. Breastfeeding, which causes an extension of postpartum amenorrhea, was found to avert an average of 0.15 births, and despite program problems (including unreliable survey data which, for example, report an impossible decline in the prevalence of sterilization between 1979 and 1980), scare rumors, and the Filipino's moral and religious resistance to family planning, unwanted pregnancies are being averted in growing numbers. However, the higher prevalence of less effective methods among contraceptive users points to a critical need for widespread and constantly available family planning education for both potential clients and service providers.

Although there is no current interest in the Philippines, the introduction of government and donor agency incentive and disincentive programs would increase contraceptive acceptance rates. However, according to Dr. Mercedes B. Concepcion, dean of the Population Institute, the introduction of such programs is not in the near future.

By 1978, the lack of interagency coordination presented a major stumbling block to family planning program implementation. POPCOM was rapidly losing its senior staff to both the private sector and the nonbureaucratic PCF. Symptomatic of POPCOM's management difficulties was the resignation of its third director, Primitivo De Guzman, which left behind a disorderly and demoralized POPCOM management.

Problems within the various population agencies and ministries were exacerbated by Imelda Marcos' declaration in 1978 of her view that family planning was really not a government responsibility, but one that should be taken over by the private sector. With inflation on the rise, questions also were being raised as to the government's ability to continue salary support for the network of Outreach workers and supervisors providing the backbone of the effort in rural areas.

A straightforward economic analysis of the impact of the Outreach system on contraceptive prevalence and reduced population growth rates would have shown that few other development investments have such a high cost-to-benefit ratio. Rather than examining it this way, however, critics and budget manipulators simply looked at the line item costs of salary schedules, and transportation and travel allowances when confronted with the need to reduce government expenditures. There is always the risk that this kind of thinking might prevail over a longer-range perspective with a superior economic payoff.

In 1981 relations improved between POPCOM and the FTOW, especially at the provincial level. The competition for contraceptive users plaguing the program in 1978 had virtually ended, probably because in the absence of a new executive director for POPCOM, Dr. Lorenzo had taken over the organization as well as the PCF.

The Outreach program has now become firmly institutionalized in the local government structure. Unlike neighboring Indonesia, however, no vigorous attempt has been made by the central administration in Manila to encourage provincial governors to play a more direct role in the management of

family planning activities in their areas. Consequently,
support from many of the country's 76 governors has been
enthusiastic and exceptionally well directed, while others
have remained either lukewarm or totally uninterested. Since
a major condition of the program is the extension of local
government salaries and support for Outreach workers, half-
hearted interest among the governors has resulted in limited
program success.

The interagency fence mending accomplished recently, however, has made a marked impact on the governors' reactions to
the program. The question has progressed from *whether* local
governments will lend financial support to *how much* they can
contribute. Presently, local government contributions range
from nearly 100 percent of local costs to near zero, with an
average of well over 30 percent of recurrent costs being
carried by local government structures.

The administrative capacity necessary for implementing a
vigorous fertility control effort is essentially in place.
On top of this, the Philippines have achieved modernization
beyond what such key indicators as the 1981 per capita GNP
($600), educational status, and access to services would sug-
gest. Universal elementary education and high-school literacy
are two of the positive legacies of the U.S. colonial period
leading to a remarkable uniformity of economic aspirations for
modernization throughout most of the otherwise regionally
diverse nation.

The adult Philippines literacy rate improved from 72 percent in 1960 to 83 percent in 1970 and 89 percent in 1980.
Literacy is split almost evenly between the sexes: 87 percent
for men and 86 percent for women in 1975. The rural rate (79
percent), however, was significantly lower in 1975 than that
for cities (93 percent). Although the percentage of females
enrolled in elementary school is slightly higher than that for
males (100 to 95), it is lower in secondary school (47 to 65).
At the secondary level, there are considerable differences
among rural and urban, regional, and income groups.

Increasing urbanization and educational opportunities
promoted the emergence of a middle class during the 1960s and
1970s. The country's professional ranks began to increase,
as did the managerial cadre filling governmental and industrial
posts. Economic expectations rose, too: Filipinos were becoming accustomed to a better life style.

A national program of rural electrification, begun in 1970,
facilitated cottage industries. Rural women, like their city
counterparts, entered the marketplace. They liked the feeling
of relative independence and the income that economic diversity
brought; they began to yearn for upward mobility for their
children and to consider more carefully the difficulty of
individual nurturing in large families. In a 1980 survey by
Outreach workers, 69.4 percent of rural women had decided they
did not want more children. If the problems of financial trans-

fers and decreasing acceptance of more effective contraceptive methods can be overcome in the near future, the program's outlook is very good.

In a 1981 statement regarding population stabilization in the Philippines, Sylvia P. Montes, deputy minister of social services and development and currently in charge of the National Family Planning Project, had the following to say about the relationship between long-term plans and population incentives:

> . . . a simple exercise wherein alternative population levels are matched with projected resource availability; assuming that self-sufficiency in basic needs is a major objective, it appears that the country could support a maximum population level of 94 to 120 million. The long-term Philippine Development Plan envisions that in the year 2000 the country shall have achieved higher economic growth, more employment opportunities, greater incomes with a more equitable income distribution, and greater access to education and other basic human services.

> The attainment of a stationary population size is implicit in the population targets of the current Five-Year Philippine Development Plan and the Long-Term Plan for 2000. These plans target the attainment of a net reproduction rate of 1 in the year 2000, so that by that year, the population level would be about 70 million, growing at a rate of 1.6 percent per annum. Carried further, these figures imply a population level of about 120 million in 2070, the year in which a stationary population level is projected to be attained.

> Considering the results of this simple exercise, it would seem that the population growth targets and the implied population levels in the current Five-Year, Ten-Year and Long-Term Development Plans may be considered realistic and acceptable.

> Various policies have been adopted to enable the Philippines to achieve population stabilization:

> 1. The goal of the National Population Policy is to achieve that quality of life which will enable every Filipino to enjoy the fruits of economic and social progress. This would mean population control education efforts from primary school to adult education would be intensified. Strong motivation and acceptable incentives to smaller families should be developed. Improved techniques alone cannot be expected to produce the desired results. It has become increasingly

*clear that incentive and motivation are as
essential as contraceptive technology in achieving fertility reduction.*

2. *Provision of employment opportunities, special
incentives such as priorities in housing, tax
exemption and the like, to defer marriage.*

3. *Promote and develop greater opportunities and
the higher awareness or knowledge of the people
on the improvement of economic and social
condition of potential growth areas, and develop
effective communication models crucial to a program of regional dispersion.*

A toughened posture by the Catholic church could, however,
cause difficulties.

The Church Steps In

From the national program's inception, the clergy's attitude regarding family planning has been far from unified.
Since the mid-1970s, premarital counseling by family planning
advisers appointed at the local government level has been
required by law, and many village priests also actively engage
in counseling individual church members to use their own conscience about contraception and the methods they select. Many
clergymen are outspoken advocates of the national fertility
control program.

The government's determination to maintain a firm separa-
tion between church and state, and the Catholic church's
recognition of its tenuous hold over its unorthodox membership
has, in fact, given rise to a tradition of compromise between
the two factions. The result is that a certain degree of
political activism by the country's Catholic clergy—particularly by its own and foreign Jesuits—is tolerated by the
government, which does not wish to tangle with popular clerics,
and by the Church, which enjoys its prominence and does not
want to risk internal divisions. Since the early days of
martial law, however, foreign priests who have been particularly
vocal in their opposition to the Marcos regime's human rights
violations have been threatened with deportation. In at least
one case, the threat was carried out.

The relative independence of Filipino Catholics was drama-
tized by their response to the Pope's encyclical of 1968. Faced
by the specter of starvation that continuing high birth rates
could bring, the Filipino clergy found the Pope's *Humane Vitae*,
in which the Church's traditional ban on artificial contraception was reiterated, to be "an unrealistic approach to a terrible problem."

In August 1973, bishops, priests, and laypersons from 18
Asian nations met in Manila to protest the infallibility of the

Pope's encyclical. The overwhelming concensus of those meeting was that developing nations could not possibly achieve
higher standards of living unless they curbed their runaway
birth rates. While rejecting forced (but not necessarily
voluntary) sterilization and abortion as contraceptive methods,
the Asian Catholics strongly advocated the freedom to practice
birth control and urged all Catholic Asians to "wholeheartedly
support all efforts toward the solution for the population
problem." In conclusion, they agreed that the Church "must
involve herself with the real problems of the time and commit
herself to a search for their solution."

A few years later, Bishop Francisco F. Claver, S.J., prel-
ate ordinary of Malaybalay, Bukidnon in Mindanao, echoed the
sentiments expressed in 1973 when he defended his work on
behalf of the nation's poor by remarking, "If we as preachers
of the Word are to be credible to the people we are preaching
to, if we are to serve them as we in truth must serve them, I
do not see how we can as a group continue to work almost
exclusively and for the most part with the rich, the powerful,
the better circumstanced."

Bishop Claver, who is the first bishop from the Igorot
tribe of Luzon's mountain province, serves as the outspoken
and controversial conscience of both the Church and the state.
A champion of human rights and fiercely opposed to martial law,
he is above all proudly Filipino. The missionary's task, he
believes, is "to Christianize but not to Westernize."

The bishop's work in behalf of political and economic
justice has caused some to think of him as a possible successor
to President Marcos. But for now, at least, his political
energies are spent much more on the grass-roots level. During
martial law, he opened church doors in the South to town-hall
meetings--in defiance of laws negating the right of assembly--
to foster a sense of political and economic self-determination
among the poor. That many of the communities under his juris-
diction are predominantly communist is seen as a threat by
many in government. To Bishop Claver, however, communism is
seen as coping behavior, as an outgrowth of political and economic necessity for people separated from the stream of
economic and political decision making.

The Philippines' leading Catholic clergyman, however, is
of quite another ilk. Jaime L. Cardinal Sin, Archbishop of
Manila, has begun to emerge as a national figure. One of 16
children, Cardinal Sin is a political craftsman whose survival
instincts have served him well. During the early days of the
national family planning program, he remained quiet, not wish-
ing to risk his personal relations with the President and Mme.
Marcos. But during the National Population Welfare Congress
which met in Manila on November 12, 1980, Cardinal Sin left no
room for doubt about his doctrinaire stand on the issue of
fertility control:

*. . . The Church believes--and I concur whole-
heartedly--that if a man and his wife decide to
limit the number of their children, they have
every right to do so. The Church believes, however
--and I agree with all my heart--that the means
used in limiting the number of children should not
do violence to nature. In short, we encourage
couples to plan the size of their families by using
natural means, not by chemical or mechanical or
surgical means.*

*In his speech before this Congress yesterday, the
President made a statement which, in my considered
opinion, renders juridical pressure on Filipino
couples superfluous and irrelevant. The President
said that the fertility level of the Filipino
people has gone down substantially. If this be so,
then our population control managers can write a
strong petition to remove these onerous juridical
and social service restrictions. Because these
restrictions, whether we admit it or not, are coercive.*

*. . . President Marcos also stated that, in the
light of the success of the program, we can now
turn our energies towards socio-economic development. There is, of course, no quarrel with socio-
economic development. Anyone in his right mind
will agree that this is highly essential to national
progress. What I find discordant is the idea that
socio-economic development is impossible unless
there is family planning.*

*Perhaps it is possible to achieve socio-economic
growth even with our present level of population
increase, if we were to take a second look at our
national priorities.*

*. . . Do we really give priority to labor over
capital? How labor-intensive, for example, are the
industries in the export-processing zones? Do they
really benefit our country or do they benefit the
multinationals more?*

*I believe that it is most unjust to instill fear
and panic in the minds of people by prophesying
imminent doom unless the population explosion is
stemmed. I believe that the poverty of the masses
is due, not to excessive population growth, but to
the obsessive avarice structured in an onerous
socio-economic and political system.*

While the Catholic church remains divided on the issue of
fertility control, the indigenous Protestant church, Iglesia
ni Cristo (Church of Christ), has long assumed a leadership
role in programs embracing both conventional contraceptive
methods and sterilization. Since its inception in 1914 as a
militantly anti-Catholic, anti-Western body, Iglesia ni Cristo
has become the largest single denomination among the Protes-
tants who make up about five percent of the country's population. The strict obedience required of its membership ranges
from church-dictated block voting in both national and local
elections to tithing. Having taken an early stand against the
large-family norm, it has become a powerful force in grass-
roots development and the establishment of public health programs.

THE MATTER OF PUBLIC HEALTH

Compared to the Philippine 1981 birth rate of 34 per 1,000,
its official death rate of 10 per thousand for the same year is
quite low--nearly as low, in fact, as that of typical industrialized countries and wealthier developing nations. The low
mortality rate, however, masks the fact that most deaths occur
among the young, whereas in industrialized countries most deaths
occur among the elderly. For this reason, life expectancy is
considerably lower in the Philippines than, say, in France.
The figures are also complicated by the relative lack of
accurate statistics on infant mortality in developing countries.
Many demographers view the Philippines' official estimated
annual infant mortality rate of 65 per 1,000--intolerably high
as it is--as being unrealistically low. Reported infant mortality rates of 90 per 1,000 in the Eastern Visayas, northern
Mindanao and the Cagayan Valley and 50 per 1,000 in central
Luzon seem excessively low in light of a 1975-77 survey of
hospital deliveries in Manila that showed an infant mortality
rate of 126 per 1,000. In any case, the nation's mortality
rate points to continuing problems of malnutrition among
infants, preschool children, and pregnant and lactating women;
low resistance to disease; and a consequent high prevalence of
life-threatening respiratory and diarrheal disease among children below the age of five.
As these mortality rates are reduced by ongoing efforts to
control disease and raise nutrition levels, the nation's population growth rate could actually increase, even in the face of
continuing fertility control efforts. To counter this, the
nation's family planning program will require at least as vigorous support as that given to the nation's health and nutrition
programs. Whether it will receive that support remains to be
seen.
During the mid-1970s, 69 percent of the nation's children
suffered from malnutrition--as much a reflection of family

feeding customs and nutritional ignorance as the unavailability
of food. Although progress has been made in training families
to grow and feed such high-protein foods as mung beans, which
do not require extensive funding or a food distribution program,
and PL 480 food is distributed to preschool children and pregnant and lactating women through the Catholic Relief Services
and CARE, the problem remains unabated.

Malaria also still plagues large sections of the Philippines. Schistosomiasis (snail fever) is a problem for the farm
and fishing populations of southern Luzon, the Visayas and
Mindanao, where it takes an economic as well as a human toll
by reducing the farmer's ability to work the hours necessary
for successful rice production.

A proliferation of rural health centers has succeeded in
extending health care to many of the nation's poor. In the
cities, low-cost health care is available in hospital clinics.
And an important portion of the nation's health care is provided by folk healers who appeal to the traditional Filipino's
mystical sense. *Mananambals* (psychic healers and birth attendants) perform healing and surgery by the concentration of
psychic energy while *mananbangs* concentrate on births only,
much as the traditional *hilots* (midwives) do. *Orasyonans*
(faith healers), meanwhile, count on prayers and incantations
to heal, and *herbolarios* (herbalists) are experts in the use
of curative herbs and plants. Mananambals, who are known as
tambalans when they practice in towns, are especially important
in such remote areas as Bohol, where there is only one doctor
for every 10,000 people. These generally uneducated healers
refuse to put a price tag on their services--which are often
highly successful--for fear of losing their healing powers.
Compensation is made in cash or kind, according to the patient's
ability to pay.

A growing number of acupuncturists are offering their
services, as are hypnotherapists, who specialize in emotional
problems as well as mind-induced anesthesia during childbirth
and surgical procedures.

Because of extremely low resistance to disease among the
country's malnourished and intensely crowded living conditions,
pneumonia and tuberculosis remain the Philippines' top killers.
But the ultimate killer is overpopulation. With a 1981 population of 49 million and an annual growth rate of 2.4 percent
which, unless it is reduced, promises a doubling of the population in just 29 years, the consequences of overpopulation are
obvious. A strong program of agricultural development has
made the country self-sufficient in rice at its current population level. But the country still depends heavily on U.S.
food surpluses for survival.

The country is dependent on food aid, but unlike many other
developing nations, it is not blindly dependent. The Philippine leadership understands the tenuous nature of the U.S. PL
480 program, and is energetically trying to step up its own

food production. Without parallel and equally vigorous efforts to reduce its population growth rate to a point of stabilization in line with its resources, however, the energy-poor country is destined to experience more and more severe food deficits and, ultimately, a declining standard of living for all its citizens.

THE MULTINATIONALS RUSH IN

Postwar (1950-73) economic development in the Philippines represented both a continuation of and a break with the colonial economic heritage of 1900-45. The economy was marked by an open dualistic structure pitting a rural sector against an urban industrial sector and linking the two to each other and to the outside world only through trade. Trade resources—land, water, and minerals—were used to produce export commodities that made possible the purchase of raw materials and machinery required by the growing urban industrial sector.

The import control policies signed jointly by the Philippines and the United States in 1956 created a sudden shift in profitability away from commercial and primary export activities to manufacturing for the domestic market. Openings for both domestic and foreign investments suddenly appeared. U.S. manufacturers, faced with the abrupt closing of their Philippine markets, rushed in to invest in production within the Philippines to serve the same markets.

An emphasis on capital-intensive large-scale manufacturing from domestic and multinational interests was enhanced during the 1950s and 1960s by incentive policies and adopted by the government of the Philippines. Small and medium-sized firms found it increasingly difficult to penetrate the bureaucratic procedures required either to qualify as a new and necessary industry in the earlier days, or to secure Board of Investments certification later. Import controls also acted as a barrier to small- and middle-sized manufacturing.

Between 1972 and 1978, the nation's total real Gross Domestic Product (GDP) grew at an average rate of 6.7 percent. While it subsequently declined to 6.0 percent in 1979 and 4.7 percent in 1980, the GDP has averaged well above the 5.1 percent level of the preceding 12 years (1960-72). Little of this, however, has found its way to the lower classes.

With its heavy concentration of industrial production, Manila, which holds only 12.6 percent of the country's population, accounted for 35.5 percent of the GDP in 1979. That year, Manila's per capita GDP was 2.8 times the national average. By contrast, the two regions with the lowest per capita GDP in 1979, the Eastern Visayas and Bicol, tallied only 48.9 and 54.2 percent of the national average, respectively—less than 20 percent of the Manila total. Overall consumption expenditures, meanwhile, were reduced from 85 percent of GNP in 1960 and 81 percent in 1972 to 75 percent in 1979. The rich were getting

richer and the poor in the rural areas weren't getting much
at all.

In 1974, the multinational presence in the country's mining
sector was diluted considerably by a decree which forced foreign firms engaged in the exploitation of the Philippines'
natural resources to sell 60 percent of their stock to Filipinos. Under a system reminiscent of the U.S. Affirmative
Action Program, foreign firms were also required to install
Filipino managers. Among those companies that were most
affected was the gigantic Benguet Consolidated, a U.S.-owned
gold and silver mining company. Under this new management,
Benguet continued its operation and, by 1977, some 70,000
ounces of gold and 90,000 ounces of silver were being mined
each year. The country's rich copper, nickel, and chromium
deposits also were being exploited profitably. By 1986, the
government's program of export expansion calls for the export
of 600,000 ounces of gold and 700 million tons of copper per
year.

The nation's oil reserves, however, have proved to be
commercially disappointing. Rather than producing the goal
of 40,000 barrels of oil a day, the huge Nido oil project off
Palawan put out only some 20,000 barrels a day in 1980. Consequently, the country remains energy poor, and the rising
costs of oil imports have shown up in inflationary costs in
every sector of the economy.

In 1979 about 36 percent of the nation's GDP was contributed by industry, with manufacturing accounting for 25.3 percent
and construction for another 7.2 percent. Agriculture contributed about 24 percent of the GDP, and the service sector produced another 39.7 percent. Due to the rapid growth of so-
called nontraditional (primarily manufactured goods) exports,
export production comprised 19.8 percent of GDP in 1980—up
from 17.6 percent in 1972 and 10.6 percent in 1960. Nontraditional exports grew from a meager 6.0 percent of total exports
in 1960 and 14 percent in 1972 to an impressive 47.5 percent
in 1980.

Traditional agricultural and mineral exports (coconut,
sugar, forestry, abaca, pineapple, tobacco, copper, gold,
silver, iron, chromite ores, and a few petroleum products),
on the other hand, dropped from 94 percent to 52.5 percent of
GDP during the same period. The nominal U.S. dollar value of
total exports increased, however, at an impressive average
annual rate of 23.4 percent between 1972 and 1980, compared
with only 5.8 percent during the previous 12 years.

The Inflationary Cycle

Despite a strong 73 percent growth in export earnings
between 1978 and 1980, the Philippines' reliance on imported
oil has resulted in a rising balance-of-payments deficit that

increased from $1.17 billion in 1978 to an estimated $2.17
billion in 1980. The dollar value of imported goods increased
by 66 percent, or $3.13 billion, during this period. Nearly
half of this increase was due to high prices paid for petroleum products, which rose by $1.37 billion, even though the
volume of oil imported declined slightly to 30.6 percent of
all commodity imports in 1980. While the costs of petroleum
imports soared, the earning from exported coconut products, a
key traditional export, declined dramatically due to a drop
in the international market for coconut oil. Sugar exports,
on the other hand, practically recovered in 1980 after a four-
year market slump.

Thus, by trying to sustain high-level activity via the
encouragement of capital-intensive and import-dependent development of industry and agriculture, the Philippine economy has
become riddled by unemployment and inflation. From an average
of 7.4 percent during the 1975-79 period, the annual rate of
inflation leaped to 21.5 percent in 1979 before leveling off
to an annual rate of 15.2 percent at the end of 1980. The
rise in oil prices was passed on to consumers as a means of
energy conservation. By August 1980, the retail price of a
liter of regular gasoline had jumped 186 percent over its cost
of P 1.66 in 1978 to a new high of P 4.75 (U.S. $2.40 per
gallon), and the price of diesel fuel had doubled.

When government retail price controls on food staples were
allowed to expire in 1979 to prevent serious production disincentives, upward price adjustments contributed heavily to
inflation. To calm this response, price controls were reim-
posed in February 1980 on rice, corn, eggs, poultry, pork,
cooking oil, sugar, canned milk, and canned fish.

Inflation cannot be attributed entirely to rising energy
costs, however. The government's policies since the late
1970s of minimum wage rates, including cost-of-living allowances to keep pace with inflation, has had a significant influence on inflation while increasing the wage gap between people
employed in such controlled sectors as organized manufacturing
(firms employing five or more people) and those working, for
example, in family-run *sari-sari* variety stores or in the
service sector. More important, however, is the high level
of deficit financing required to fund the growing capital
outlays of the government's economic development program and
the continuing lack of efficiency in terms of manufacturing
productivity relative to input.

The Two Faces of Unemployment

Marching hand in hand with overpopulation and inflation
is unemployment. Growing population pressures on scarce arable
land have burdened the economy by forcing many rural migrants
onto a relatively small capital-intensive industrial sector

unprepared and unable to absorb them. The bulk of these migrants have been left in underproductive, often part-time jobs in commerce and services not directly related to the modern sector. The result has been a perpetuation of surplus labor, the stagnation of real wages, and the persistence of open as well as disguised unemployment.

The official rate of open unemployment declined from 7.0-8.0 percent of the labor force in the late 1960s to 4.0-5.0 percent in the middle and late 1970s. Hidden unemployment in the form of underemployment, however, is rampant--particularly in seasonal agriculture and the commercial and service sectors.

Ironically, a significant contributor to unemployment is overeducation. Status in the Philippines is not as solidly fixed as it is in most traditional societies. Individuals can rise or fall, reflecting on their family's status in the process. Status depends primarily on wealth, which before land reform policies were instigated following martial law, was equated almost exclusively with land ownership. Now it is education which has become virtually an end in itself and which indeed provides just about the only avenue (other than fortuitous marriage) toward upward mobility. As a result, there is an extraordinary scramble for higher education among the nation's youth.

Since there is a far greater supply of educated and technically trained people than the Philippines can absorb, doctors and lawyers can be found driving taxis or working in construction, Ph.D.s often languish in low-paid research projects, and thousands of nurses join other Filipinos in the yearly crush at Middle Eastern, Canadian, and U.S. visa stations. Since 1969 Filipinos have accounted for the largest number of legal annual immigrants entering the U.S., and countless numbers also enter illegally each year. In 1975 alone, 32,000 Filipinos entered the U.S. legally. Many of them joined relatives already established in the United States.

The urban employment picture is predominantly one of commerce (23.8 percent) and manufacturing (12.2 percent). About 80-90 percent of all urban commercial employment, however, is composed of retail trade, which is primarily made up of small units such as the ubiquitous sari-sari stores, which employ about 65 percent of all retail-trade workers. Most sari-sari store owners are self-employed, and family members are unpaid. Manufacturing, meanwhile, claims about 16.5 percent of the urban work force, with domestic services accounting for about 12.7 percent. Most of the country's male workers are employed in agriculture, forestry, fishing, or hunting. Only about 35.9 percent of all women in the work force are employed in these areas.

By 1975, 45.3 percent of the nation's families lived below the poverty line. Increasing importation costs, inflation, industrial inefficiency, rural underdevelopment, and economic dualism have all contributed to severely unequal income dis-

tribution throughout the country. The prime contributor to
the country's economic and developmental woes, however, is
rapid population growth.

As the World Bank's 1980 report on poverty in the Philippines noted, there is a strong

> *positive relationship between family size and*
> *poverty incidence. Families with 6 members and*
> *more contained about 52 percent of the total*
> *families and accounted for 68 percent of the poor*
> *families and about 80 percent of the poor popula-*
> *tion. By far the largest number of poor families*
> *were dependent on rice and corn farming, and half*
> *of these were located in the Cagayan Valley, Bicol,*
> *and the Visayas.*

Whether or not employment figures are compiled with a conscious bias toward ignoring unpleasantries, the fact is they
omit the serious and disturbing trends of underemployment. As
a result, they present a grossly misleading picture of the
economy's ability to provide enough productive employment in
the face of a rural sector of the economy.

AGRICULTURE: AN EMPHASIS ON EXPORTS

Marcos' New Society was initiated by a decree on land
reform and the instigation of a comprehensive Agrarian Reform
Program. A tradition of oligarchal land holdings, low-produc-
tion tenant farming, and an antiquated rural credit system was
replaced by the new look of "Masagana 99." Launched on May
21, 1973, the Masagana 99 program embraced a modern mix of
"Green Revolution" technologies, easy credit, and farmer education. Its goal was to provide rice self-sufficiency and thus
ease the nation's balance of payments.

With Secretary of Agriculture Arturo R. Tanco, Jr., in
charge, the program flourished. Funding was boosted by financial and technical assistance from USAID, the United Nations,
and the World Bank. Irrigation projects sprouted on Luzon's
central plain, the nation's prime farmland, a 40-mile wide
valley extending 100 miles from the Lingayen Gulf to Manila
Bay. Modern petrochemical fertilizers and pesticides were
introduced. New high-yield rice varieties developed by the
International Rice Research Institute (IRRI) and the University
of the Philippines at Los Banos began to work their own magic:
yields were increased by more than 50 percent.

In 1976, a project jointly funded by the Philippine government and USAID began to tame the flood waters that periodically
inundated more than 42,000 hectares of the best agricultural
land in the 312,000 hectare Bicol River Basin on the southern
tip of Luzon. An irrigation and drainage system was carved in

the basin's northeastern corner. Rice and corn sharecroppers
in the densely populated region began to become amortizing
owners of the land they tilled. The farmers were collectivized
into farming cooperatives modeled on the *Samahagn Nayon* (barrio
association) system being introduced throughout the country.

Masagana 99 surpassed its goal of rice self-sufficiency:
the Philippines exported about 300,000 tons of rice in 1980, a
50 percent increase over the 1979 rice export level. But when
Green Revolution technologies were extended to other agricultural areas, it was discovered that they simply could not work
elsewhere. The nation's Agrarian Reform Program bogged down
for the very reason that visitors and social anthropologists
alike find the islands so fascinating: the only constant in
the Philippines is diversity.

To begin with, there is the uneven topography, the great
variation between regional climates and farming patterns, and
the concentration of agricultural development on export crops.
Productivity in many areas is limited by poor land quality and
the remoteness or lack of public administration assets such as
roads, water control facilities, communications networks,
markets, and slaughterhouse and cold-storage facilities. Then
there are the farmers themselves, fearful of offending an ever-
present host of mythological spirits and believing that luck
(which cannot be earned) may have a lot more to do with a good
crop than does fertilizer.

All of this, plus the lack of farm extension services,
farmgate prices, and income alternatives in the islands' most
remote areas, have perpetuated rural poverty. And rural overpopulation continues to exacerbate the problem. In its 1980
report on poverty, the World Bank concluded:

> *The most important determinants of poverty in the
> [dominant] food crop sector appear to be the small
> farm size, limited access to land [tenancy or land-
> lessness], low physical productivity, low value
> crop mix, lack of infrastructure. [The effects of
> natural disasters are also important.] . . . Poverty
> outside the food crop sector though similarly related
> to limited productive assets, is affected by special
> conditions. In coconut farming, there are large
> numbers of small holdings, a complex tenure system
> controlled by absentee landlords, a high proportion
> of overaged trees, low physical productivity, and
> lack of intercropping. . . . Sugarcane workers
> have suffered from over-supply of workers. . . .
> In the fishing sector . . . competition from com-
> mercial fishermen and motorized boats, lack of
> equipment, and overfishing of several fishing fields
> have combined to limit [the] catch and incomes . . .
> [of the poorest group, the municipal fishermen], who
> typically fish with unmotorized boats close to the
> coastal areas.*

And now the bottom has dropped out of the Philippine coconut market on the heels of an economic scandal that rocked the Marcos administration in September 1981. Coconut products are the Philippines' leading export and coconut oil its biggest seller; 80 to 85 percent of all coconut oil traded in world markets is produced in the Philippines. Between 1979 and 1981, however, coconut oil prices fell by more than 50 percent. The problem was exacerbated by a slump in sugar, copper, and timber, compounded by rising oil bills and interest payments that ate up 88 percent of the country's export earnings during the first nine months of 1981.

To counteract these influences, the United Coconut Oil Mills (known as Unicom), the dominant Philippine coconut company, tried to corner the U.S. coconut oil market with an OPEC-type maneuver dubbed "Cocopec" by some critical wags. In 1979 Unicom--whose chairman is Secretary of Defense Juan Ponce Enrile, a friend of Marcos--ordered its U.S. subsidiaries to stockpile more than 43,000 tons of Philippine coconut oil to drive up its price. The plan failed, and several U.S. firms filed a $100 million civil antitrust suit against the U.S. companies and their Philippine principals, including Unicom. Of much greater concern to the third of the population that depends on coconuts for at least part of their income, however, is a levy that essentially taxes farmers' coconut product sales. Although the levy has helped to build up the coconut industry, it has also succeeded in creating Unicom's virtual monopoly by funding its acquisition of financially troubled coconut mills. The levy also funds the replanting of hybrid coconut seedlings under an exclusive government contract held by a company owned by Eduardo M. Cojuangco, Jr., another close friend of Marcos who is also the president of Unicom.

The poor Filipino farmer, meanwhile, has exploited every available acre. Like Korea, but unlike Thailand and Malaysia, the Philippines have an extremely high ratio of population to arable land. In 1975, about 4.61 million of an estimated 4.66 million hectares of potentially arable land were under cultivation. There is simply no more room for expansion. Population pressures on Luzon and the Visayas have pushed land-hungry farmers onto Mindanao.

For years, the Muslim Moros of Mindanao have been deeply disturbed by this population spillage onto their lands. And the fact of encroachment isn't the only problem. The Moros, who consider all land to be communally owned, are not about to honor the concept of private, individual ownership. In any case, the frontiers of that relatively undeveloped island are quickly disappearing under a crush of increasingly desperate humanity.

On Mindanao and elsewhere, traditional *kaingin* (slash-and-burn agriculturists who farm in patterns) try to eke out livelihoods as their ancestors did. In the process, these shifting kaingin destroy an estimated 200,000 hectares of forest each year.

Now, because cultivation in many areas has already exceeded the limits of suitable land, homesteading farmers have taken to the steeper slopes as well, and the entire ecological balance is being upset. The rampant deforestation of these marginal farmlands has caused serious erosion and the permanent loss of soil fertility in many areas. Further down the watershed, lowland farms suffer from reduced water supplies and coastal fisheries are affected by sedimentation and threatened by the destruction of productive coral reefs. The extremely poor upland farmers, meanwhile, depend on the lowland farmers and fishermen for off-season employment as well as for goods and services.

Rain-dependent farmers, particularly those in the water-scarce Visayas, are among the poorest of the country's poor. Although export-quality rice surpluses produced in this region over the past three years (1978-81) has depressed farmgate prices somewhat, productivity is marginal. For these regions, USAID is working on a strategy to introduce diversity by alter-nately planting rice and corn.

The World Bank, meanwhile, is supporting the Kabsaka Pro-gram directed at the double-cropping of rainfed rice in Iloilo Province on Panay. And USAID has long been active in swampland aquaculture on Panay. Since fish provides Filipinos with their chief protein source, the nation's 6,000 water-girt villages play a vital nutritional role. Here, fish are harvested twice a year from ponds dug below river level and stocked with finger-lings and algae culture. The Ford Foundation and USAID are also aiding the government and landless tenant farmers to provide them with another source of protein and other nutrients from red meat and dairy products.

The Philippines have been pressing the limits of its more productive farmland for several years. Unless export crops are deemphasized, not even the most dynamic and modern program of agrarian reform can hope to catch up to and keep pace with the country's population growth. Land under perennial cropping --the coconut, fruit, coffee, abaca, rubber, and banana plan-tations--have room for expansion. But skewed as they are to the export market, cropping patterns and employment on the nation's plantations are highly responsive to foreign market prices.

Intensive land use and higher annual yields from land already under cultivation are, in fact, the only roads open to increased agricultural production. But the nation's burgeon-ing population is placing an increasingly intolerable burden on its natural resources. With water already scarce in many areas, the Philippine Inter-Agency Committee on Environmental Protection has reported the discharge of about 100,000 tons of mine tailings per year into eight major river systems. This contaminated water affects an estimated 130,000 hectares of agricultural land. (The total amount of all toxic waste gener-ated each day is about 140,000 tons.)

The country depends heavily on Mindanao's mineral and timber riches for foreign exchange. Yet the need for immediate income is often met at the expense of long-term benefits from conservation. Although the government voices strict conservation policies, thousands of square miles of commercial quality forest—particularly stands of highly-valued hardwood known as *narra*—have been cut down with no concern for the future. What remains is disappearing at a distressingly rapid rate to choruses of "Arydong kahoy," the bull bucker's cry to warn both men and forest spirits of falling trees. These spirits are thought to have the power to seriously injure or even kill a man; if they have been properly warned and still don't get out of the way, the bull bucker cannot be held responsible. Similarly, if timberland owners issue proper conservation orders that go unheeded, they cannot be held responsible, either.

The government's conservation efforts in the Cagayan Valley date from 1974, when the five largest Japanese corporations were invited to invest in agricultural and wood industries in the valley. The result was a $31 million joint Japanese-Philippine project that removed enormous sections of timberland from the private sector. The Filipinos have become entrenched capitalists; controls do not go down easily.

All sectors of the economy are becoming increasingly disillusioned and restive. Wealthy landowners complain that they receive too little for the land they are forced to sell in plots ranging from less than one hectare to about seven hectares to former tenant farmers who pay for the land over a period of 15 or so years. Peasants, on the other hand, complain that the land reform program is moving too slowly: by 1980, 61.1 percent of the country's poor depended on agriculture as their main source of income. Of these, only 20.4 percent were farmer-owners while 23.8 percent were tenant farmers, 3.9 percent were part owners, and 6.1 percent were landless farm laborers.

The hoards of poor people flocking to Manila each year from the provinces see Marcos' urban industrial blitz in terms of a rural agricultural blight. And they are not the only ones leery of the Philippines' grossly unbalanced echo economy. As Lorenz (1980) asked:

With numerous industrial projects on the drawing boards for the 1980s, how will the Philippines' government survive the adverse credit rating which has been building up in recent years amid accusations of cronyism, fiscal irresponsibility, and 'misguided' spending?

An easy scapegoat for the declining confidence in the Philippines' economy from the point of view of foreign banking institutions would be the increased oil prices which have affected every stratum of

> *Philippine society, curbing spending and drawing*
> *attention to the fragility of the energy-short*
> *economy . . .*

Where can the Philippines obtain more capital for its
ambitious industrialization program for the 1980s? Unexpectedly the International Monetary Fund and the World Bank late
last year approved an increase in the Philippines' foreign
borrowings in 1980 in spite of the past dubious record. At
the same time, as a sort of justification, the IMF and World
Bank recommended more diversified industrial production, now
concentrated heavily on electronics and garments, and an
increased scope of traditional exports.

Since then, President Marcos has encouraged the private
business sector to carry on with major industrial projects as
soon as possible, lest inflation make them even more exorbitant. Foreign borrowings were thus expected to increase further
in spite of the already over-extended position.

Meanwhile, Marcos' relations with foreign investors has
hit a new low on the all-important energy side. Rising environmental concerns have led him to take up the cause of geothermal
energy and to dump—or at least sidetrack—a planned foray into
nuclear power.

Following the Three Mile Island incident in Pennsylvania,
Marcos began to demand extra safety factors for the nation's
first nuclear power plant being designed by Westinghouse
Electric on the Bataan Peninsula, some 35 miles west of Manila.

A Shaky Future for the New Society

The Marcoses' power base is not stable. The New Society
has produced neither peace and stability for the country nor
a general state of well-being for its citizens. The nation's
persistently high population growth rate has already far outstripped the government's ability to feed, service, and appease
its society. Filipino intellectuals, university students, and
freedom-loving journalists are deeply resentful of what they
feel is a climate of oppression.

In a great show of bravado, Marcos followed the 1977 lift-
ing of the nation's 1:00-4:00 a.m. curfew with a declaration
that ended martial law on January 18, 1981. At the same time,
he won a presidential election, assuring himself another six
years of power. Former Secretary of Finance Cesar Virata was
installed as prime minister and the "new New Society" opened
its doors. But as Henry Kamm remarked in the *New York Times*
on January 25, 1981:

> *Even allowing for partisanship—and many politicians*
> *and private citizens are unprepared to believe any-*
> *thing but the worst of Mr. Marcos and his wife, Imelda*

> . . . it is difficult to reject the contention that
> the President [has insured his hold on the Philip-
> pines]. He dominates all cogs in the state machin-
> ery and the patronage that flows from it: adminis-
> tration, military and police. His control over the
> communications industry is so complete and the cult
> of his personality so assiduously developed that he
> and his candidates are assured of maximum [and
> favorable] coverage. . . . Opposition politicians
> thus foresee no more than a slim possibility of dis-
> lodging Mr. Marcos [before 1987].

The seemingly eternal warfare between the Philippine government and the Islamic-based and Libyan-backed Moro National
Liberation Front in the nation's South has also been gradually
losing its sting. Moro soldiers and leaders have extended the
olive branch in return for political appointments. They have
not, however, relinquished their guns—most of which are made
in Russia and smuggled in with alleged Libyan financing—through
the Philippine's back door, Borneo. Like the government's
concession on the matter of divorce in the Muslim-dominated
area, the decision to allow the Moros to keep their guns was a
peace-making compromise made on the basis of the fiercely-proud
Moro's equation of guns (and the traditional kris) with manli-
ness.

Whereas 85 percent of the Philippines' armed forces were
engaged in a "peace-keeping" mission in the South during the
spring of 1980, a much-reduced force comprising 60 percent of
the military was deployed against the separatists at the end
of 1981. The remaining 40 percent of the military, however,
has had its hands and weaponry busy fighting the newly resurgent
NPA. Having divested itself of its Maoist image to appease non-
communist Marcos opponents and keep pace with Mao's fall from
grace in China, the NPA has nevertheless retained both its communist character and anti-Marcos fervor.

Threats to both Marcos and the Philippine nation are mount-
ing from both within and without the country. By the end of
1981, world-market prices for coconut products, sugar, copper,
and timber had severely affected the nation's balance-of-
payments. A decline in coconut-oil exports to the U.S. has
sent the Philippines scampering off to markets in China and the
Soviet Union. Meanwhile, long-simmering sentiment against
Marcos-serving multinationalism in general and "Americanism"
in particular is causing waves of distrust to build between the
Philippines and the United States.

Meanwhile, development in the energy-, water-, and land-
short Philippines is racing against the clock. Today 3,222
Filipinos will be born. Each year, the country's growth rate
of 2.4 percent adds 1.2 million people to its poverty-burdened
population.

There may still be time to turn the tide against the
problems of overpopulation and imbalanced development that are

sweeping the country toward economic, social, and political upheaval. Unless steps are taken soon, however, and taken toward the benefit of the nation as a whole, the Philippines--and the United States--could find themselves together in the western Pacific in an untenable situation.

REFERENCES

Baradas, David B. 1975. "Non-Muslim Mindanao." Lecture presented during the Association of American College Women/ Cultural Center of the Philippines Lecture Series, Manila, January.

Beech, Keyes. 1981. "Rebels in Philippines Explode Into Action." *International Herald Tribune* (Paris), October 21.

Branigin, William. 1981. "Coconut Crash." *Washington Post*, November 14.

Casiño, Eric. 1973. "Ethnographic Art of the Philippines, An Anthropological Approach." Seminar paper. Manila: University of the Philippines.

Chaffee, Frederic H., et al. 1969. *Area Handbook for the Philippines*. Washington, D.C.: The American University.

Day, Beth. 1974. *The Philippines: Shattered Showcase of Democracy in Asia*. New York: M. Evans and Company.

Engel, Francis H. 1974. *Philippine History: A Brief Digest*. U.S. Embassy Women's Club Guide Series, March. Manila: U.S. Embassy.

Esmundo, Rafael A. "The Total Integrated Development Approach: A Human Response." Unpublished speech. Mimeographed.

Gallen, Moira. 1979. "Abortion Choices in the Philippines." *Journal of Biosocial Sciences*, no. 11.

Gleeck, Lewis E., Jr. 1974. *Americans on the Philippine Frontiers*. Manila: Carmelo & Bauermann.

Guthrie, George M. 1968. *Six Perspectives on the Philippines*. Manila: The Bookmark.

Herrin, Alejandro. 1979. "Rural Electrification and Fertility Change in the Southern Philippines." *Population and Development Review* (New York: The Population Council) 5, no. 1.

Herrin, Alejandro N. and Thomas W. Pullum. 1981. *An Impact Assessment: Population Planning II*. Report prepared for the Commission on Population, Republic of the Philippines and USAID/Philippines, Manila, April 6, 1981.

Institute of Philippine Culture. 1980. Draft of an unpublished study of the Total Integrated Development Approach. Manila.

International Labour Organization. 1974. *Sharing in Development--A Programme of Employment, Equity and Growth for the Philippines*. Geneva: International Labour Office.

Jocano, F. Landa. 1971. *Myths and Legends of the Early Filipinos*. Quezon City, Philippines: Alemar-Phoenix.

---. 1975. *Slum as a Way of Life*. Quezon City: University of the Philippines Press.

Kamm, Henry. 1981. "Marcos Lets Martial Law Go Without a Whimper." *New York Times*, January 25.

Kangas, Georgia Lee. 1977. "Makati: From Swampland to Boomtown." *Sa Atin Lamang.* Manila: Association of American College Women.

Lorenz, Keith. 1980. "Philippines Foreign Debt Seen Troubling Bankers." *Journal of Commerce*, August 27.

Molina, Antonio M. 1960. *The Philippines Through the Centuries*. Manila: University of Santo Tomas Press.

Moser, Don. 1977. "The Philippines—Better Days Still Elude an Old Friend." *National Geographic* 151, no. 3.

Nance, John. 1975. *The Gentle Tasaday*. New York: Harcourt Brace Jovanovich.

Tinsler, Douglas. 1975. *The Bicol River Basin Today*. Manila: National Media Production Center.

Chapter 3

Egypt: Solutions to the Human Paradox

Egypt is a land of extraordinary paradoxes, not the least
of which is its unique oasis-like geographic position. Existing as it does in a long, narrow strip watered by the Nile,
the country has been protected from the historic cultural
forces of migration that have shaped the rest of Africa by the
very desert that limits its development. Persians, Greeks,
Romans, Turks, Arabs, Albanians, French, and the British invaded
by sea, each laying down a distinct layer to the country's
cultural complexity. Each succeeding wave brought an elite
of its own; from 525 *B.C.* until King Farouk I was forced to
abdicate in 1952, native Egyptians were regarded as third-class
citizens in their own land.

In the person of Gamal Abdel Nasser, however, the poor
Egyptian found a heady source of hope and dignity; he was a
big man who radiated confidence.

As much of the postwar world settled down to the fact of
cold war between the United States and the Soviet Union, Egypt
gained prominence in the political designs of both superpowers.
Weak and corrupt as it was, Egypt's monarchy, with its desert
buffer, had insulated the country from both Islamic and Arabic
radicalism: there were people among the country's intellectual
and military elite who could be talked to. And both the United
States and the Soviet Union rushed in to talk about the Suez
Canal, about the oil fields being discovered by British and
U.S. oil companies in the Sinai Desert, about Egypt's position
vis-à-vis the emergence of Israel, about the need for Egypt's
rational leadership of the fractious Arab world.

King Farouk was no match for the diplomats from Washington
or for the Free Officers, a group of young Army officers led
by Col. Gamal Abdel Nasser, who were determined to free the
country from foreign domination by playing East against West.
The U.S. sanction of the bloodless revolution of 1952 (which

was carried out with a diplomatic push from the CIA) and U.S.
financial support of Nasser's subsequent presidency, under-
standably, was never publicized. In the long run, it did not
matter: Nasser eventually proved to be his own man. He was
intensely nationalistic; above all, he was a military man with
a genius for strategic manipulation. Nasser accepted economic
aid from the United States, and military aid from Russia and
Czechoslovakia, and proceeded to reduce foreign control and
ignore cold-war alignment by nationalizing just about everything in the country including the Suez Canal Company.

Nasser adopted the cause of Arab brotherhood as a rallying
point for a nation in need of focus. Similarly, the nation's
humiliation at the hands of the Israelis in 1948 was turned to
Egypt's benefit: under Nasser, the Israeli scapegoat for
Egyptian frustrations was a diversionary tactic for unpopular
reforms at home. The state broke up the nation's large landholdings and confiscated the royal family's holdings outright.
What was mistakingly judged "Arab socialism" or "Islamic
socialism" by the rest of the world swept the country toward
a course of economic development as cunningly crafted as a
military campaign. But ideology, ethnic ties, and religious
fervor had little to do with it. Nasser *was* the revolution.

Having engineered the overthrow of Mossadegh and restoration of the Shah in Iran and the overthrow of Farouk in favor
of Nasser in Egypt, the United States believed it had saved
the Middle East from communism.

The United States underestimated Nasser's zeal for national
self-determination. He had come to believe that his country's
economic future depended on the construction of the Aswan High
Dam. Piqued by Nasser's conclusion of an arms deal with the
Soviet bloc, however, Eisenhower's Secretary of State John
Foster Dulles denounced Nasser and announced the withdrawal of
American aid to the dam project in July of 1956. As a consequence, Nasser turned to the Soviet Union for capital, and for
a time the U.S. lost a major client state in the Middle East.

Buoyed by foreign financing and increasing prestige in
Africa and the Middle East, Nasser's military mind swerved from
the West to the hegemony of pan-Arabism, with himself at its
head. England's negotiation of the Baghdad Pact with Pakistan,
Iran, Turkey, and Iraq was viewed by Nasser as an attempt to
isolate Egypt. He reacted by joining the Afro-Asian states
bound in the Bandung Conference of April 1955 and providing aid
to rebels in Algeria who were seeking to oust the French. The
next year, having been denied U.S. financial backing for the
Aswan High Dam, he nationalized the Suez Canal Company, thus
alienating both the British who had controlled it and the
Israelis who were dependent on it.

A military coup in Yemen in September of 1962 opened up
the possibility of the extension of Nasser-led pan-Arabism to
the area. The five-year war seriously strained both the
Egyptian economy and Nasser's credibility: while victories

were touted over Radio Egypt by day, trains loaded with bodies
of Egyptian soldiers killed in Yemen rumbled into Cairo under
cover of darkness at night. Meanwhile, Nasser's anger mounted
over an Israeli military buildup on the Syrian border and
reports from U.N. peace-keeping troops, who had been placed on
the Egyptian-Israeli border in 1957, that Israel was slowing
moving onto Egyptian territory.

Angered and humiliated, Nasser demanded the removal of
U.N. troops from Egyptian territory. They were removed and,
fearful of an Egyptian attack, Israel quickly launched a
preemptive attack on Egypt and Jordan on June 5, 1967.

The Six-Day War was a disaster for Egypt. At its end,
Israel occupied the entire Sinai Peninsula and, as Nasser's
power diminished, Egypt became increasingly dependent on the
Soviet Union for protection against Israeli air attacks, which
lasted for three more years. Pressures from the United States
and the Soviet Union finally brought about U.N. intervention
which ended the fighting in September 1970. But a few hours
later, Gamal Abdel Nasser died, taking his dream of Egyptian-
led pan-Arabism with him. He was replaced as president by his
friend and fellow Free Officer, Anwar Sadat, and a new era of
internationalism dawned for Egypt.

OVERPOPULATION AND THE MATTER OF PRIORITIES

What President Sadat inherited in 1970 was overpopulation,
land shortages, food shortages, and an undereducated and underemployed society marked by hostility toward Israel.

First on Sadat's agenda was the settlement of the continuing conflict with Israel, which again erupted into warfare in
October 1973 and which Sadat still firmly believed could not
be put to rest until an autonomous homeland for the Palestini-
ans that had been displaced by Israel was established. Second
was strengthening the country's economy by opening the door to
foreign investment, a direct reversal of Nasser's strategy.

A pragmatic and astute leader, Sadat failed, however, to
assign any priority to the country's most serious and obvious
problem, that of Egypt's runaway birth rate. Some say that
Sadat's failure to face the country's calamitous population
problem was due to his belief that economic development would
take care of it. Others say his blindness in this vital area
was a reflection of his fatalistic belief in the Islamic tenet,
"Mashallah" (All is of God).

Most likely, the omission of fertility control from Sadat's
national priorities was due to a combination of all of the
above. The fact is that while Egypt has been making enormous
economic gains over the past decade, it must claim the dubious
distinction of being the only developing country in the world
whose growth rate has increased by 40 percent over the past ten
years. And it has increased at a time when the world outside

of Africa and the rest of the Middle East is beginning to bring its birth rate down, and despite sixteen years of nationally sponsored family planning programs.

As of mid-1981, Egypt's population stood at 43.5 million. It is now adding 100,000 people a month--1.2 million a year--to a land unable to sustain them. At its present growth rate of 3.0 percent a year, Egypt's population will double in just 23 years to more than 87 million by the year 2004. The social, economic, and political implications of such unchecked growth are also horrendous for the United States, whose interests in the volatile region depend on a strong, friendly Middle Eastern ally to balance U.S. support of Israel.

Between 1917 and 1937, when Egypt's population grew from 12.8 million to 15.9 million, members of the country's intellectual elite became increasingly aware of the potential for population problems from a growth rate that went from 1.16 percent per year in 1917 to 1.77 percent by 1937. Concern eventually spread to the Egyptian Medical Society, which obtained a *Fatwa* (religious decision) from the Grand Mufti of Egypt which sanctioned the use of *al-Azl* or other methods of fertility control.

Al-Azl is the Arabic term for isolation, or preventing the sperm from reaching the ovum. In 1945 the first birth control clinic was established and was soon abandoned by the Child Society of al Maadi near Cairo.

In 1953, in the midst of an explosion that pushed the growth rate to 2.85 percent a year between 1947 and 1960, the newly established Ministry of Social Affairs set up a National Population Commission which, in 1955, set out to establish a number of family planning clinics. In 1957 the commission became a quasi-voluntary organization, the Egyptian Association for Population Studies.

In a *Christian Science Monitor* interview on October 8, 1959, however, President Nasser declared:

> I am not a believer in calling on people to exercise
> birth control by decree or persuasion. Instead of
> teaching people how to exercise birth control, we
> would do better to teach them how to increase their
> land production and raise their standard [of living].
> In my opinion, instead of concentrating on birth
> control, we would do better to concentrate on how
> to make use of our own resources. We live in and
> make use of only 4 percent of the area of our coun-
> try. The rest is neglected and desert. If we direct
> our efforts to expanding the area in which we live
> instead of concentrating on how to reduce the popula-
> tion, we will soon find the solution.

Nasser the military man was determined to conquer the desert. The Aswan High Dam would be his primary weapon.

In 1962, however, with the miracles to be wrought by the
High Dam still six years away and food shortages becoming
apparent, Nasser's National Charter announced a new and vigorous commitment to family planning:

> *Population increase constitutes the most dangerous*
> *obstacle that faces the Egyptian people in their*
> *drive towards raising the standard of production*
> *in their country in an effective and efficient way.*
> *Attempts at family planning deserve the most sin-*
> *cere efforts by modern scientific methods.*

Government-backed fertility control had been sanctioned,
and as a result, the Supreme Council of Family Planning was
established by presidential decree in 1965. The council was
given high visibility by the presence of the prime minister,
other ministers, and the head of the Central Agency for Public
Mobilization and Statistics. The next year, an Executive
Board of Family Planning was established by order of the prime
minister and was entrusted with the instigation of a national
family planning program based on the existing health infrastructure.

A total of 2,301 health units was immediately made available for the provision of family planning services throughout
the country. During the next 12 years the number of units
grew to an impressive 3,636. To augment the new board's work,
the Egyptian Family Planning Association was charged with the
coordination of such voluntary organizations as the Cairo
Women's Club, which had for years been active in family planning in the Nile Delta. The association was to work in collaboration with the International Planned Parenthood Federation
(IPPF).

Between 1966 and 1974, the country's birth rate slowed
substantially from 41.2 per thousand to 35.7. As the following table shows, however, the birth rate began to pick up
again in 1975, while the death rate continued to decline, and
the drop in birth rate contributed to a government complacency
about the population problem typical of the earlier wartime
perspective.

The ordinarily forward-looking Sadat appeared to have slid
backward to adopt Nasser's 1959 view against fertility control.
In any case, the population problem continues to this day to
be denied its proper place in the national perspective. Why?

It is not for lack of organization or discussion. It is
certainly not for lack of outside technical, financial, and
supply assistance, or studies and reviews of the problem. The
problem continues to grow because overpopulation is not perceived by Egypt's leadership to be a problem.

Unlike many nations that lack either a public or private
organization to deliver services, Egypt enjoys the advantages
of a basically homogeneous population (90 percent Moslem, 10

percent Coptic), a common language (Arabic), and a compact
living area: one-third of the population lives in the narrow
Nile Valley between Cairo and Aswan and two-thirds live
between Cairo and the Mediterranean shore in the fertile triangle known as the Nile Delta. Furthermore, the country's
topography is not complicated by the kind of mountains that
make communications impossible in such countries as Nepal. The
nation also has a relatively well-developed system of roads and
is fully covered by radio and increasingly by television.

TABLE 3.1 *Egypt's Population Size and Growth, 1800-1981*

Year	Population (in 1,000)	Birth rate per 1,000	Death rate per 1,000	Growth rate per year (%)
1800	2,400	NA	NA	NA
1907	11,287	NA	NA	1.23
1947	17,907	NA	NA	1.14
1966	30,076	41.2	15.9	2.54
1976	38,228	36.4	11.7	2.31
1984	47,400	41.0	11.0	3.00

NA, not available.

Source: Omran 1980.

Since 1978, family planning services have obstensibly been
available at nominal cost in 291 health offices, 214 mother-
child health centers, 585 rural health centers, 1,633 rural
health units, 273 hospitals, and 640 voluntary clinics. In
fact, it is often said that there is a health unit within four
or five kilometers of every Egyptian. In addition to these
units, some 2,000 pharmacies also sell contraceptives at state-
subsidized prices. A recent survey indicates that 38 percent
of the nation's rural women obtain their contraceptive supplies
from these private pharmacies, probably because of the convenience involved and the somewhat wider selection of contraceptive brands available. Many international donors have
swept in with family planning assistance.
   This seemingly ideal family planning supply network
continues to fail because of the following factors: (a) Family planning workers are poorly trained, inadequately paid and
unaware of the microbial cause of disease. An informed understanding would remove most of the blame for infection from the
contraceptives themselves and place it where it belongs--on
the lack of sanitary conditions in clinics and hospitals. (b)
Having been promoted primarily by Westerners, family planning

measures are often viewed by traditional rural Moslem populations as intrusions and by the bureaucracy as a means of attain-
ing government sinecures. (c) Family planning programs are
split up among so many agencies that redundancy occurs. (d)
Most importantly, the leadership is either disinterested in the
need for fertility control or unaware of the problem. As the
distinguished epidemiologist Abdel R. Omran remarked in a 1980
report on Egyptian fertility, "The best description that I can
give for the Egyptian family planning program in the 1970s is
that it has become much like a wealthy yet demanding orphan
whose money everyone desires, but whose demands everyone shuns."

The level of awareness and understanding among top political leaders is critical to an assessment of influences shaping
a country's population policy and program. But while it is
safe enough to point out that no Middle Eastern country regards
rapid population growth as a primary obstacle to economic and
social development, few developmentalists are willing to point
out the underlying cause of the Middle Eastern population
problem. A fear of disturbing sensibilities prevents non-
Moslems from pointing out that, whereas it may not be a case
of leaders wearing blinders, they certainly perceive the
population problem as a Western invention unrelated to individual Moslem nations. It is this deflection of reality—as
well as foreign experts' own cultural biases—that makes so many
Western observers throw up their hands and pronounce the Middle
East inscrutable and its problems unsolvable.

There can be little mystery, however, about Egypt's high
fertility rate, given the traditional Islamic submission of the
will to Allah, the economic benefit of children sent by Allah
to tend livestock and work in cotton fields and on truck farms
at the age of six or seven and to provide for their parents in
their old age, and the low status of women outside the family.
As the Koran asserts, "men are in charge of women because Allah
has made one of them to excel the other." In rural areas
particularly, "the other" is kept in her place via a lack of
education and such cultural practices as female circumcision,
particularly in Upper Egypt. Clitoral excision serves a dual
purpose: by eliminating a prime source of sexual pleasure for
the female, it removes one basis for marital infidelity and, at
the same time, it reinforces the woman's function as a child-
bearer.

It is as natural for a poor Egyptian to want to have a
large family as it was for President Sadat to expect that a
firm commitment to expanded land reclamation and the construction of new towns would solve his country's problems. From
Sadat's viewpoint it was perfectly understandable: make the
desert bloom and the population problem would fade away.

Whether current Egyptian President Hosni Mubarak becomes
mired in the same developmental mirage remains to be seen.
The fact is, however, that land reclamation can never hope to
catch up with the food and living demands of a rapidly increas-

ing population that has already outstripped its natural resources.

AN AGRICULTURAL SOCIETY PLAGUED BY
FOOD SHORTAGES

The saying that "The Nile is Egypt and Egypt Is the Nile"
is as true today as it was before 1968, when the Aswan High
Dam harnassed the Nile's hydroelectric potential and increased
the viability of irrigation projects designed to reclaim desert
lands. The eternal struggle against the desert continues with
increased urgency as burgeoning numbers of people crowd into a
habitable area of 55,039 square kilometers--only 5.5 percent of
the total area of almost one million square kilometers. In a
traditionally agricultural society where economic pressures
have caused urban migration to the point where 48 percent of
the country's population is now crowded into urban areas (in
1907, only 19 percent of the population was urban), population
density and food shortages have given rise to increased social
unrest.

The population crunch has resulted in an escalating competition for land to meet urban and agricultural demands.
Cairo, for example, which can comfortably accommodate a maximum
of 2 million people, now has a population of 6.5 million. With
only 0.6 percent of the country's habitable area, the city holds
15 percent of its population; Greater Cairo now has 10 million
people. Nationwide, 97 percent of the population is squeezed
into 3.5 percent of the total land area. In Bulaq, an industrial slum of Cairo, the population density is the highest in
the world--more than 40,000 people per square kilometer. Such
public services as transportation and telecommunications suffer
frequent breakdowns. The housing shortage is critical. Sanitary systems are overloaded to the point of bursting. Broken
sewage lines are an increasing threat to public health.

The most serious effect of such land scarcity, however, is
the country's accelerating food deficit. Historically, Egypt
has experienced extraordinarily high agricultural yields: from
1890 to 1940, total agricultural production grew faster than
the population. From 1940 to 1968, however, the country's
population growth exceeded its production growth in all but
two years. To raise the level of food consumption, the government stepped in with heavy subsidies of the production and
retailing of a number of food staples. The result: an increasing dependence on food imports.

In 1978 alone, the nation's bill for imported food amounted
to $2 billion, up from $1.8 billion in 1977 and $1.4 billion in
1976. More than 50 percent of all food is now imported, and
livestock feed, wheat flour used for *aish baladi* (literally
"peasant bread," the round, flat pita-like bread that is the
Egyptian staple), and three-quarters of all wheat used for
direct consumption, are imported.

In 1976 Prime Minister Salem reported:

During the preceding 10 years, public expenditures
increased from about ₤E 900 million [one Egyptian
pound, or ₤ 1, is equal to $1.43 in 1976 dollars]
in 1965/66 to more than ₤E 2 billion in 1975. During
the same period, government revenues increased from
₤E 500 million to only ₤E 1 billion, resulting in a
deficit of ₤E 400 million in 1965 and a colossal ₤E
1 billion in 1975. . . . The rates of consumption
increased from 67% of the national income in 1965
to 80% in 1975. . . . Local production cannot meet
consumption except in the range of 43% in relation
to corn, 80% in relation to maize, 70% in relation
to beans and lentils, and 80% in relation to sugar.
The rate of increase in consumption of industrial
products was much higher.

An immediate consequence of government food subsidies and
imports is an increasing balance-of-payments deficit and
dependence on foreign economic aid. A long-range consequence
is a perpetual cycle of overpopulation and hunger: studies
show that increased caloric intake in the country has succeeded in lowering mortality while raising natural fertility
and, of course, the more people there are the greater the
demand on food supplies.

Although President Sadat based much of his country's
development on a policy of land reclamation, expectations
inflated by the hope of the Aswan High Dam have been deflated
by the dam's contribution of a mere 15 percent to the country's arable land. And today this 15 percent adds but three
percent to the agricultural product on which 50 percent of
the labor force depends for its livelihood. Furthermore,
while the cost of energy-intensive land reclamation is enormous (it costs about ₤E 1,000 to reclaim one feddan of land
from the desert) some 40,000 feddans of potentially arable
land a year are converted to construction sites.

At best, the land contributed by the High Dam can accommodate four to five million people, a number replaced at Egypt's
current rate of population growth in just four to five years.
Every ten years the country adds the equivalent of Australia's
entire population, without the resources of that continent.

From 1960 to 1980, while the country's population was
growing by 16 million people, the amount of cropped land was
increasing by only 1.1 million feddans, and even that farmland
increase is shown to be misleading when overall productivity
is examined. Deprived of the Nile's nutrient-rich flood
waters, which existed prior to construction of the dam, farmlands are subject to decreasing soil quality. Farmers complain
that state-provided fertilizers often arrive too late and in
quantities too small to be effective. Intense irrigation,

TABLE 3.2 *Population Growth Versus Cultivated and Cropped Land, 1821–1980*

Year	Population	Cultivated area (x 1,000 feddans)[a]	Per capita cultivated area	Cropped area (x 1,000 feddans)[a]	Per capita cropped area
1821	4,230,000	3,053	0.78	3,053	0.73
1907	11,190,000	5,374	0.48	7,595	0.67
1947	17,907,000	5,761	0.32	9,133	0.51
1960	26,085,000	5,900	0.23	10,200	0.39
1976	37,866,000	6,300	0.17	11,211[b]	0.30
1980	17,400,000	6,300	0.15	11,250[b]	0.27

[a]One feddan is equal to 1.03 acres.

[b]Estimate from Omran 1980.

Source: Egyptian Central Agency for Public Mobilization and Statistics, with corrections from Mohammed A. El-Badry in *Demography*, 1965.

based on energy- and water-wasteful systems designed 50 years
ago, raises the soil's salinity. Yield potentials are further
reduced by the government's policy of selective output control:
farmers are unwilling to alternate subsidized crops with non-
subsidized crops.

Subsidies of petroleum products and fuels plus land reform
and a general increase in workers' wages have also had the
unplanned consequence of strengthening the traditional economic
value of large families. The number of farms under five feddans increased from 38 percent of the total cultivated area in
1961 to 66 percent in 1975. While these farms typically employ
far more labor than larger farms, comparatively little labor is
hired from outside the family. When farm family size outstrips
small-farm per capita income, excess family members typically
head for the city.

AN ECONOMIC BOOM, A DEVELOPMENTAL BUST

The aspect of Middle Eastern development that Westerners
and westward-looking national leaders find most baffling is
the fact that, unlike other areas of the world, economic
development bears little relation to fertility rates in the
Middle East. When there is a relation, it is apt to be an
adverse one in which fertility--particularly in rural areas--
actually increases rather than decreases. Egypt is a strong
case in point.

To get the country's war-drained economy moving at the end
of 1973, President Sadat reversed the nation's economic course
from Nasser's stand against foreign investment. Foreign
exchange controls were suddenly relaxed, and an open door
policy, Al-Infitah, invited foreign investors in. Although
state ownership in the petroleum, mining, transport, and power
sectors was not affected, and allocative controls were continued in such areas as agriculture and construction materials,
foreign as well as domestic concerns were vigorously encouraged
to invest in the country. The turnabout achieved dramatic
results.

The Saudis and Kuwaitis leaped in with investments enabling
Egypt to import greater quantities of capital goods and raw
materials to boost the country's productive capacity. With the
signing of the Camp David accords, the United States replaced
Saudi Arabia and Kuwait as the nation's largest creditor; about
$3.6 billion in bilateral loans were outstanding by mid-1980.
Between 1974 and 1980, the real gross national product (GNP)
grew by 8.0 percent per year and industrial production (including petroleum) rose by about 20 percent per year while exports,
paced by increases in oil sales, grew by more than 30 percent
per year. Meanwhile, as productivity picked up at home, more
and more Egyptians left the country in search of higher-paying
jobs in such oil-boom nations as Libya, Saudi Arabia, Kuwait,

and Algeria. By 1979, some 1 million Egyptians of all skill
levels--about 10 percent of the nation's labor force--were
working outside of the country. Migrant worker remittances to
their families at home have become the second largest source
of foreign exchange. This, plus the fact that 41 percent of
the population is under the age of 15 and the military continues to divert large portions of the work force, has depleted
the job market and increased wages.

Egypt's continuing encouragement of exploration and
development activities by foreign oil companies brought in a
record 36 new contracts in 1980 with planned expenditures
valued at $875 million. Additional agreements also are being
made for the exploration of expected large natural gas reserves.
Domestic price increases on domestic petroleum prices, however,
have done little to close the gap between subsidized domestic
and world energy prices. This difference, of course, affects
the real cost of food and industrial production.

The country's economic boom has resulted in markedly
increased demands for domestic and imported foods and other
consumer goods. (Until Al-Infitah provided sources of foreign
exchange, commodities such as cosmetics, for example, were
virtually unobtainable except on the thriving black market.)
The nation's elite who, until Al-Infitah hid their wealth for
fear of financial empoundment and other government reprisals,
have come out of the economic closet with blatant consumerism.

The buyer's market now thriving in Cairo and Alexandria
has created a pinch of its own: inflation is on the rise. The
first effect of Al-Infitah in the 1974-77 period was an increase
in wages of 62.3 percent in construction, 50 percent in agriculture, 15.3 percent in services, and 12.7 percent in mining
and industry. During the same period, however, consumer prices
increased by 32.7 percent. By mid-1980, the official estimation of the rate of inflation was 30 percent; some observers
believe that a 50 percent inflation rate was closer to the
truth.

The economic forecast for the immediate future is good.
During 1982 oil export revenues expanded by about 20 percent.
Suez Canal earnings are projected to grow at 10 percent per
year and tourism receipts to increase by 13 percent a year,
unless growing social unrest and a trend toward militant Islamic
fundamentalism scare tourists away. Migrant worker remittances
are expected to increase by $1 billion annually. Import prices
are expected to rise 9.0 to 10 percent each year.

Steady improvements have been made in the country's balance
of payments. During 1980, major foreign exchange earnings
increased by almost 40 percent and the balance-of-payments
deficit dropped below 8.0 percent of the gross domestic product
(GDP). By the end of 1980, foreign exchange reserves were
estimated at over $1 billion--equivalent to slightly less than
two months' import requirements.

Like the majority of leaders of both developed and developing nations, however, Sadat counted on a socioeconomic boom

brought on by the development of Egyptian oil. The country is heavily oil dependent, and relies on low state-subsidized prices. Export earnings are linked to oil, as are migrant worker remittances. But oil is a finite resource: the vigorous exploration and development of Egyptian oil fields being undertaken now will boost Egyptian (and U.S. and British) coffers now, but will ultimately hasten their depletion.

As for the migrant workers on whom the government counts for foreign exchange and population pressure release: as oil reserves near depletion in the labor-importing countries over the next fifteen years or so, the need for migrant workers will dwindle with oil revenues. Meanwhile, Middle Eastern countries are already beginning to depend more and more on unskilled labor from East Asia. Unless Egypt's economy is turned to the development of labor- rather than energy-intensive industrial and agricultural systems, and based squarely on a national policy of population stabilization, the country's burgeoning population will soon undercut the country's economic plans.

Employment is down, but underemployment is up. While the growth of manufactured goods declined in real terms from 1976 to 1980, agricultural production remained sluggish: during the 1970s, real agricultural output grew at the rate of 1.3 percent per year, less than one-half the rate of population growth.

At the bottom of the scale, educational levels, particularly among women, remain severely low; at the top of the scale, a surplus of college-educated people has maintained pressure on the government to hire all Egyptians with college degrees. Wages, however, cannot keep pace with such inflated employment demands, members of the country's bureaucracy must take on two or three jobs to make ends meet.

Meanwhile, the economic boom has obscured the nation's population issue. Emigration by workers continues to be viewed as a constant factor in population reduction despite the fact that workers' absences are only temporary and have the effect of merely postponing rather than actually reducing their wives' fertility. And Egypt remains a poor developing country where even an overall per capita income of only $370 a year blurs the picture of an increasing gap between the financially squeezed lower classes and upper class consumers.

Unless Egypt takes immediate steps to effectively reduce its population growth rate, it will never ba able to feed and service its people. Nasser's plan for self-determination was based on the promise of the Aswan High Dam and military might. Sadat's plan for self-sufficiency was based on the expectation of continuing foreign aid and the benefits of finite oil resources. Unlike Nasser, however, Sadat was either unable or unwilling to face the fact that the country's economic and social problems are rooted in the overpopulation of a limited land area. Whether the country's new leadership will be able or willing to set a more realistic developmental course remains to be seen.

PUBLIC HEALTH AND THE SOCIAL SETTING

In 1973 the Supreme Council for Population and Family Planning and the Population and Family Planning Board (PFPB) produced a policy embracing a nine-point approach to fertility
reduction: raising the standard of living of the family,
education, employment of women, mechanizing agriculture, industrializing the countryside, reducing infant mortality, social
security, information and publicity, and specific services,
including family planning. Unfortunately, these remedies were
based on Western prescriptions. Much of what is good for most
of the rest of the world turns out to be incompatible with
Islamic realities in the Middle East in general and Egypt in
particular.

Egypt's insupportable fertility rate is a product of apathy,
fatalism, and misinformation. As we have noted previously, the
immediate result of increased food consumption and effective
public health measures has been *increased* fertility, particularly in the rural areas, where it is highest to begin with.
Egyptian as well as foreign population experts tend to be
mystified by this phenomenon which is an extraordinary departure
from family planning experiences throughout most of the rest of
the world. It is not surprising, however, when placed in its
proper cultural context.

Generally speaking, the healthier a woman is, the more
children she is able to have. And the fact is, the Egyptian
woman and her husband want to have what Westerners (but not
Egyptians) consider to be a large family of five or six children. Voluntary family planning programs can work only in so
far as they respond to the desires of the targeted population.
Large families are a voluntary response to conditions under
which parents must rely on their children for sustenance and
security as well as for joy and companionship in life at the
bleak marginal survival level. Even when these conditions are
alleviated, the *perception* of them and of the consequent need
for large families is apt to linger. In Egypt as in the rest
of the Middle East, large families, a product of ingrained
Islamic fatalism, are validated by historical economic requirements and perpetuated by current socioeconomic and public health
conditions.

Although great strides have been made in the public health
sector with smallpox having been eradicated and cholera brought
under control, a number of endemic, life-threatening diseases
still plague the country. A national program of polio and
measles immunization has failed to control those diseases;
tuberculosis, hepatitis, rabies, and trachoma and other eye
diseases run rampant. About 61 percent of farmers and farm
laborers and 23 percent of people in other occupations are
infected with schistosomiasis, or "snail fever," which has persisted since the pharaonic era and has increased since the
country's conversion to perennial agriculture.

With cereal grains making up 80 percent of the calories
and 50 percent of the protein consumed by the average Egyptian,
malnourishment is a continuing problem. About 32 percent of
all rural children and 14 percent of urban children are seriously anemic. Most diets are severely lacking in vitamins C,
A, and B complex. Add to this a general lack of rural sanitation and overall hygienic awareness, with an infant mortality
rate that still hovers about 90 per thousand births.

Despite the continuing prevalence of life-threatening
disease and malnutrition, however, public health conditions
have improved significantly since the revolution. Their
improvement, in fact, is a major factor in the country's
population growth upswing over the past ten years.

From the beginning of the twentieth century until 1947,
the country's crude death rate was around 25 per thousand a
year. After World War II, however, international attention
focused on the issue of worldwide disease control. Eventually,
teams of World Health Organization (WHO) physicians and technicians came into Egypt with schemes for controlling epidemics
(overpopulation, however, was not and is not viewed by WHO as
a communicable disease of epidemic proportions). The introduction of antibiotics, chemotherapy, disease-reducing insecti-
cides and environmental control, immunization programs, and
the extension of rural health service delivery systems have
lowered the crude death rate to 11 per thousand per year, compared to the U.S. death rate of 9.0 per thousand.

Health conditions have not improved dramatically enough
for the poor Egyptian to perceive them as having changed. A
1980 study of 1,010 rural Egyptian women, for example, indicates that declines in child mortality are not likely to produce
substantial declines in fertility habits in the near future.
Women who had lost one or more children wanted an average of
about 1.4 additional children; those who had lost no children
preferred, on the average, slightly less than one additional
child. Infant deaths are in fact considered to be so much a
part of the birth-death cycle that few of the women studied
could remember exactly how many children she had lost, and
almost none of them knew the dates of their children's births
and deaths.

The study also found, however, that women living in villages with low infant mortality rates were more likely to use
contraceptives in planning their families than were women
living in villages with high mortality rates. Furthermore,
the increased knowledge of family planning and greater educational opportunities for women are likely to have an impact
on reducing excess fertility. Thus, by lowering the infant
mortality rate substantially below the current rate, fertility
rates may also be lowered in the future.

The Egyptian man, who looks on children as gifts from God
and believes that Allah provides all, and the Egyptian woman,
whose place in society is relative to her position as a mother,

will continue to have large families until they are convinced
otherwise. Even a strictly and immediately enforced program
of national incentives and disincentives for fertility control
will take time, something that Egypt does not have.

The immediate result of agricultural mechanization is
worker displacement and migration to cities, not fertility
reduction. The immediate result of pushing industry onto agricultural lands is increased displacement of critical cropland,
not fertility reduction. A study shows that employment opportunities for women in rural areas do not result in reduced
fertility either. The study concluded that, although women's
employment in urban areas acts to reduce fertility, women's
employment in rural areas has the opposite effect.

Since the 1952 revolution, the government of Egypt has
made a strong commitment to educational development. The
problem with this is that the educational developments which
currently claim about five percent of the nation's GDP have
been undertaken as the result of political pressure rather
than careful, overall planning.

Pressures to provide the urban middle class with secondary
and higher education plus policies to support technical education have not been echoed by pressures to expand primary education in rural areas. While the opportunities for secondary,
college, and technical training have expanded far beyond the
country's ability to absorb such numbers of highly educated
people with rising expectations, the growth of primary schools
has fallen behind the growth in numbers of children of primary
school age.

As would be expected in a society where the status of women
enrolled in school, while over 85 percent of males of equivalent
age are in school. This is considerably lower than the average
female primary enrollment rate of 68 percent for girls in other
Middle Eastern and North African countries and of the 81 percent rate of female enrollments in the middle-income countries
of the world.

Susan H. Cochrane of the World Bank has come up with an
interesting hypothesis. Since a woman's desired family size
decreases as she becomes more highly educated, Cochrane suggests
that

> . . . *expenditures to reduce the country's food
> deficit may be more productive when they are spent
> towards educating a girl through preparatory school
> and thus reducing fertility than when they are
> spent on reclaiming a feddan of land.*

By the year 2000, each feddan of land reclaimed at the cost of
ʰE 1,000 in 1976 prices can feed between 2.5 and 5.0 people.
However, if that money were used to educate 3.3 girls through
preparatory school, they would each have at least one less
child on the average than if they remained uneducated.

Similarly, the age of female marriage impacts on the country's fertility rate; women who marry relatively late are likely to be educated and to be contraceptive users. The legal age of marriage in Egypt, however, is 16 for females and 18 for males, and the encouraged early marriage of females in many rural areas is still prevalent. The reason is twofold: while a female child is of relatively low economic value to a rural family, her virginity is a marital requirement.

In such poor regions as Faiyum, where land reclamation has failed to produce expected results, children have become an economic liability. Because the land no longer supports the crush of available child labor, young boys are sent to cities to work and girls are married off as soon as possible. To circumvent the legal marriage age of 16, families often neglect to record the births of females. Then, when a girl reaches the age of 14 or so, she can be presented to the mullah as being 16 and therefore of marriageable age. This practice not only sends young brides off to a lifetime of maternal bondage, but isolates them from educational opportunities; the absence of a birth certificate means a female is ineligible for school enrollment.

Child marriages and hence childbearing by children is encouraged throughout the Islamic world and obviously contributes in a major way to high fertility rates in all Islamic societies since the women's reproductive years often cover the age span of 15 to 45. During this time, the woman can be expected to have 10 to 12 pregnancies at a minimum. This spectrum of reproductive behavior over a 30-year period typically unfolds as follows: 12 pregnancies produce nine or ten live births, of whom seven or eight survive beyond the age of one. Of these, about five or six children will survive beyond the age of five.

A WEALTH OF PROGRAMS, A PAUCITY OF COMMITMENT

Egypt's strategic position and puzzling population problem hold an almost mystical allure for international population-oriented agencies. Their programs have become problems in themselves. As Sheikh Muhammed Abduh, an Egyptian in London protested in 1884: "Do not attempt to do us any more good. Your good has done us too much harm already."

Since 1977, USAID has pledged $45 million for family planning programs in Egypt. By the end of 1981, $17 million of this had been spent and an additional $100 million was earmarked for allocation over the next four to five years. USAID's projects include: an integrated social service and family planning project in one of the country's 25 states, a rural health project including a family planning component in four states, an urban health project including a family planning component in Cairo, support for the Ministry of Health's Department of

Family Planning, support to the State Information Service for
Information, Education and Communication, a myriad of other
projects in population education and social work, etc.

Between 1976 and 1981, UNFPA spent $10 million to support
a major population and development project in 12 states. An
additional allocation of $13 million to $16 million over the
next five years will extend the project to 12 more states.
World Bank loans in the mid-1970s for $5 million and in Novem-
ber 1978 for $25 million, plus $8 million from the British
Overseas Development Ministry, have supported the construction
of health centers with a small component on experimental home
visiting (1973-77) and a community-based integrated family
planning and health project in seven states. This $33 million
loan and grant was made on the basis of expected matching funds
of $33 million from the Egyptian government. In reality, how-
ever, such matching—mostly in kind in staff and facilities—
falls short of its obligations.

Other agencies—CARE, UNICEF, and German and Swedish
agencies among them—have made their input. Without all this
help, Egypt undoubtedly would have done nothing at all about
its population problem. Ironically, however, the abundance of
input may have a great deal to do with the programs' relative
lack of results: Egypt's family planning programs have become
a means for an overblown bureaucracy to ensure its own surviv-
ability.

Meanwhile, with the population growth rate having increased
from 2.3 percent a year in 1972 to 3.0 percent per year in 1981,
survey data indicate that only 20 percent of reproductive-age
couples in the Nile Delta use contraceptives today; in less
developed Upper Egypt, a mere 6.0 percent of such couples use
contraceptives. The rate in the main urban areas such as Cairo
and Alexandria is estimated to be above 30 percent, although
data are not always reliable. In interpreting these figures,
one should remember that most national family planning programs,
such as those in India, the Philippines, Korea, and Indonesia,
have achieved 12-15 percent prevalence of contraceptive use
within three or four years of the program's inception.

Like most underdeveloped countries eager to acquire economic
sophistication, Egypt has many five-year plans and annual modi-
fications of those plans. From 1962 to 1979, however, no
mention was made of the need for reducing the country's high
fertility rate in any of a succession of five-year plans.
Instead, Egyptian economists simply accepted a population growth
rate of about 3.0 percent a year and came to the conclusion
that, since the population was growing at such a rapid rate,
more land needed to be reclaimed and cultivated, additional
jobs had to be created, and new houses and whole new towns had
to be built. Growth became the keynote of planning that
ignored the biggest growth industry of all, the country's
population.

In December 1979, having been pressed by the community of
donor nations for a statement on the need for fertility control,

the Egyptian government prepared a modification to its rolling five-year plan to place population concerns front and center. The issue of the country's high growth rate would be addressed and with a vigorous, multifaceted attack. The donor community heralded Egypt's new posture at a meeting convened by the World Bank in Paris. A year and a half later, however, it was discovered by a USAID population officer that the new statement had not been acted upon, that few knew of its existence, and that, in fact, it had never even been translated into Arabic.

In addition to perceptions at the top, the level of awareness at the technocratic level of government is a vital consideration in the potential success of any national program. In Egypt, such awareness is present, although it is difficult to estimate how widespread and deeply felt it may be. Egypt is known for its wealth of human resources and trained manpower; obviously, within its vast governmental system, public and private sectors, and multitude of universities, there are those who have an accurate understanding of the population dilemma and the impact of rapid growth rates on Egypt's prospects for development, security, and economic survival. At best, however, this perception is not universally shared, and one can frequently encounter an economist, statistician, or other technically trained person making the claim that Egypt has no population problem, that it is only short of land.

Obviously, a major contributor to the lack of understanding has been the absence of a clear call to action on the population problem from the top. A common problem in one-party states, dictatorships, or near dictatorships is that no one is inclined to risk his job by giving the boss the bad news. Similarly, foreign technical specialists and assistance agencies, particularly such agencies as the World Bank and those operating under the aegis of the United Nations, are loathe to make waves for the fear of ruffling international sensibilities. The result is that when the issue is raised by donor agencies or foreign emissaries, such insulated leaders tend to dismiss it as some kind of Western alarmist thinking not genuinely related to the real issues of internal development.

Problems in program implementation begin in the headquarters of the Ministry of Health in Cairo, where responsibility for managing family planning activities is given low priority. For example, no central staff unit exists to implement services, commodity procurement, distribution, training, and all the other elements of a full-blown service effort within the ministry itself. Instead, one physician and an assistant have been endowed with nominal responsibility for the entire nationwide service delivery.

The $45 million USAID-assisted program is supported on the Egyptian side by only two professionals, hardly enough to manage the paper work associated with the receipt of U.S. foreign assistance, let alone move resources of that magnitude with any speed and effectiveness. Worse still is the project assisted by the World Bank (a $25 million soft loan plus $8 million grant), to be matched by an equivalent amount of Egyptian pounds. In this instance, the principal government officer responsible for implementing the Ministry of Health's World Bank loan is himself opposed to fertility control. Although this fact is well known within both the donor community and the government of Egypt, no corrective action has been taken to date. In the words of one U.S. foreign aid official, "It is analagous to having a $66 million water sanitation project in which the chief engineer is opposed to clean water."

Furthermore, despite the fact that the 3,636 units obstensibly providing contraceptive services throughout the country are adequately staffed and reasonably equipped, their staffs have not been trained in specific fertility control methods. Most physicians are unable to do IUD insertions, nurses are not instructed on how to distribute oral contraceptives, and most of the country's supply of condoms has yet to be moved from warehouses to clinics.

The Supreme Council for Population and Family Planning, which was designed to give prestige and visibility to the program, seldom meets. Support from both local and international donors suffers from a lack of coordination. Condom shipments are stalled in warehouses, the flow of other contraceptive supplies is frequently interrupted, and brands are sometimes changed, confusing consumers.

Pills, which are manufactured locally with imported raw materials, are sold under the foreign licensors' international commercial labels. Their manufacture, however, depends on the availability of foreign exchange, another variable. Interruptions in pill distribution are particularly serious since the pill is used by more than 70 percent of the nation's contraceptive users.

The IUD is not adequately supported by the program, and surgical methods are not promoted at all. Sterilization, in fact, has officially been ruled out of the program in response to a newspaper article voicing unexpectedly negative views on the subject by leaders of the PFPB, the director of family planning in the Ministry of Health, and the minister of religious affairs.

A particularly sad commentary on the state of awareness at the top level of the Egyptian government is made by the extraordinary appointment of a man who is totally ambiguous about the country's population problem to head the nation's information service. A major thrust of the family planning efforts outlined by the PFPB in 1973, one which has received heavy USAID funding and technical assistance, was to be carried by the nation's radio and television stations. Yet the new director of information services, who is fresh from a stint as Egypt's representative to the Vatican and carries

the title of ambassador, believes that family planning information is "too delicate a subject" to be aired to the public.

THE PROGNOSIS

Given such a poor performance record, the prognosis for
Egypt's family planning future is guarded at best. Nevertheless, there still exist the advantages of a homogeneous
population, a good communications system, and an extensive
and adequately staffed health organization. Moreover, recent
attempts at energizing village councils in the population
project managed by the PFPB have begun to demonstrate that
prevalence levels can increase if community action becomes
associated with the delivery of family planning services.
This program, until recently a pilot effort supported by the
UNFPA in 12 rural governorates, will soon receive additional
assistance from USAID for its extension to all rural states
over the next two years.

On the commercial side, a nonprofit organization established to market contraceptives has already pioneered the
commercial marketing of IUDs for a fixed price via a referral
system to local physicians agreeing to perform IUD insertions
at moderate cost. This program, managed by an affiliate of
the Egyptian Family Planning Association called The Family of
the Future, is now marketing condoms. Soon, low-dose oral
contraceptives will be marketed in major urban areas throughout the country.

A nationwide education campaign initiated in 1980 has
reached corners of the country previously untouched by family
planning information. The program, which has been well
institutionalized and has been producing a steady stream of
information, literature, and radio and T.V. appeals, will
undoubtedly suffer from the insensitivity (or oversensitivity)
of the new director of information services.

Were the family planning effort to be pursued with just
moderate vigor, it would be reasonable to expect that 30-35
percent of reproductive couples in Egypt would be using contraceptives effectively within ten years. This would have the
effect of reducing Egypt's crude birth rate from today's 41
per thousand to roughly 30 per thousand and reducing its growth
rate from 3.0 to 2.0 percent for a doubling time of 35 rather
than 23 years. The immediate goal is to improve the delivery
of family planning services to people who already want them.

Even if the Ministry of Health managed to pull itself
together and acquire a staff large and strong enough to implement an effective contraceptive program, and if all the training and logistics and informational obstacles were overcome,
what would the prognosis be then? It is reasonable to assume
that in Egypt, as in many other traditional developing countries, the majority of unwanted fertility can be eliminated.

In Egypt this would mean reducing the completed family size from about six to something just under an average of four. However, to move from four to three and from three to two, as the society must if it is to achieve population stabilization, would require a new set of measures and a new kind of political organization. Fundamentally, it would require a social contract in which individual families recognize they would have to control their fertility for their own and society's greater good. Couples should be given the incentive and disincentive to fulfill this contract. This would be much like the imposition of speed limits on crowded city streets that are necessary for public safety and survival. Since very few in Egypt are willing to discuss these kinds of measures today, it would be pointless to speculate about the willingness or ability of the nation to implement such measures in the next five or ten years.

It is equally difficult to speculate about what can be expected from the international donor community. One could project, however, that countries with severe food deficits such as Egypt will not forever be able to count on food subsidies from the affluent West, whether these subsidies are in the form of low-interest loans or outright grants as is the case today. Ultimately, too, the U.S. public may very well demand greater performance from countries and bureaucracies that do not choose to place priorities on reducing their high fertility rates while increasing their demands for assistance from the industrialized West.

Debate over U.S. foreign aid to Egypt has already begun, as was reported by Harley (1981) in the *Christian Science Monitor*:

> *Egypt has been receiving a whopping 44 percent of the food that the U.S. sells on easy terms under Title I of the Food for Peace Program.*
>
> *But lawmakers are no longer convinced that it's such a good idea.*
>
> *The House Foreign Affairs Committee is expected to debate legislation . . . that would put a ceiling of 30 percent on aid to any one nation.*
>
> *At stake are delicate trade-offs between the goal of helping to feed a strategically vital country, like Egypt, and the desire to have a more evenhanded aid program that would encourage long-term food sufficiency in poor countries themselves.*
>
> *Until now, support for Egypt has been treated like something of a sacred cow. Egypt's strategic importance has discouraged U.S. lawmakers from tampering with the steadily rising aid programs for fear of negative effects on Egyptian President Anwar Sadat's delicate domestic economy.*
>
> *The Egyptians have used Title I aid—worth $312 million this year—to help bring down food prices*

*and ease consumer burdens. . . . Some congressmen
and agricultural economists also are convinced that
the large influx of U.S. food is discouraging
Egyptian farmers from producing. With its present
approach to Egypt, argues University of Chicago
Prof. Theodore Schultz, the United States has been
'underwriting a bad Egyptian policy' that pays
farmers far less than the world standard for their
crops.*

Food and technical assistance to Egypt is based on skewed
perceptions of need by both the Egyptian leadership and the
donor community. All of the assistance and developmental
programs both sides can come up with won't amount to much
unless Egypt's population growth rate is reduced significantly
and immediately. And this will not happen unless the Egyptian
leadership makes a sincere commitment toward the reduction of
the country's fertility rate and assigns prime priority to it.
Unless food and technical assistance to Egypt is tied to a
firm national population policy, it becomes increasingly
counterproductive by raising economic expectations and solidi-
fying dependence on foreign aid while obscuring the underlying
causes of economic and developmental stagnation.

Egypt's land reclamation program has been defeated by its
population growth rate. The country simple does not have
enough arable land to feed even its current population. To
nourish its population by the year 2000 with the amounts of
animal protein now available to Latin Americans, for example,
would require 40 percent more agricultural land than is needed
at present consumption levels. Food self-sufficiency by the
year 2000 could be achieved only by a maximum increase of crop
yields, a minimum increase in population, constant food consumption per capita, and a 30 percent increase--an additional
3.27 million feddans--of cropped land.

In an atmosphere of decreasing inclination and ability on
the part of affluent nations to subsidize the rapidly increasing food requirements of unchecked populations, the political
ramifications of an increasingly hungry population are potentially explosive. As Omran (1980) pointed out

*. . . the increasing pressures on resources are
finding political repercussions in the form of
resentment, distrust of the government, and--at
least once--open protest. The government is being
blamed for food shortages, disappearances of commodities from the market, and unavailability of
certain needs. The government has been spending
huge amounts of money in subsidies of food and other
commodities in order to keep certain consumer items
available to the masses. When in January 1976, the
government announced a reduction of the subsidy for*

*bread, open protest in the street erupted and the
government had to withdraw its plan. The relative
unavailability of certain items--especially for the
poor--increases the awareness of maldistribution of
wealth and the friction between classes. The new
policy of opening the country to foreign investment,
sound as it may be, has put the Egyptians in the
unenviable position of competing for land, housing
and business in their own country with means that
are much less than those of foreigners, be they Arabs
or others. Such competition has sent land and housing prices skyrocketing, and apartments that used to
be available at reasonable prices are now beyond the
reach of the poor; even those who have money resent
spending a fortune to have a place to live.*

By mid-1981, Egypt had become a powder keg. In the face
of social and economic disillusionment, anti-Western, anti-U.S.,
anti-Israel, anti-Christian, and anti-Sadat sentiments were
finding increasingly volatile expression. The radical Moslem
Brotherhood and other extremist Moslem groups such as *Al-Takfir
wal-Higra* had penetrated deep into the Military. Many Egyptians
looked on Sadat as a U.S. puppet and felt betrayed by the Camp
David peace accords between Sadat and Begin.

In response to Sadat's secular and pro-Western policies,
a wave of militant Islamic fundamentalism swept across the
country. Purdah blanketed even the U.S. University of Cairo,
where growing numbers of female students took to shrouding
themselves from head to toe in the name of Islamic nationalism.
The long nightshirt-style *gallabiya* commonly worn by village
males and urban traditionalists made a comeback in middle-class
activist circles.

The Marxist National Progressive Unionist Party was stepping
up its demands for a return to Nasser's socialism to save the
nation's economy. University student dissidents organized into
a network of Islamic societies known as *El Gamaa El Islamia*
protested against Sadat's opening of the country to Western
investment, products, and personnel and the underemployment of
Egyptian college graduates.

The threat of a religious revolt pushed Sadat's dream of
a democracy for Egypt ever further from his grasp. The Soviet
Union and President Muammar Qaddafi of Libya, meanwhile, were
beginning to inch forward from the wings where they awaited
Egypt's liberation from U.S. influence.

In mid-September 1981, the political situation took a
dramatic turn. On Sadat's orders, more than 1,600 oppositionists were rounded up and jailed. Among them were Islamic and
Coptic militants, political activists, lawyers, journalists,
and professors charged with fomenting sectarian sedition, under-
mining national stability, or simply violating the Law of Shame,
which makes a crime of the propagation of rumors damaging to the
state. For one brief month, the climate seemed to have cooled.

But then, on October 6, 1981, while viewing a military parade near Cairo, President Sadat was assassinated. The Egyptian people lost a strong, courageous leader whose zeal on behalf of the development of his people eventually turned many of those people against him.

It is certain that Egypt needs U.S. aid; the Soviets are unable to provide assistance to the extent of that now being provided by the United States, and neither Saudi Arabia, Kuwait, nor Libya are development-minded. On the other hand, the United States needs Egypt as a base for its interests in the generally hostile region, to counteract Russian designs in the area, and to act as a brake on destabilizing Israeli expansionism.

Land and reclamation cannot fill Egypt's grain silos; oil revenues cannot forever be counted on to stock Egyptian stores with the necessities and luxuries Egyptians have come to expect. Meanwhile, Egypt's population of 47.4 million is sure to double and continue to increase beyond that. Whether it doubles in just 23 years at the current 3.0 percent growth rate or in 70 years at 1.0 percent is an issue that is critical to the country's strength, development, and autonomy.

The day is approaching when this type of massive donor assistance will end, and this could very well be hastened by a new Western perception of Egypt as an unstable country. Egypt has far more people than it can feed, service, or contain. Unless fertility control is made a firm national priority, Egypt might very well become another Iran.

In January 1981, U.S. Ambassador to Egypt Alfred L. Atherton, Jr., and Ambassador (retired) Marshall Green made a presentation to President and Mrs. Sadat at their home on the consequences of Egypt's rapid population growth. Sadat, who listened carefully but said little, finally remarked, "It's a nightmare."

Under the present regime, Mubarak has attempted to support the family planning program and strengthen population policy. During a ministerial presentation on the relationship between population growth and development planning, he urged his ministers to support and cooperate with the family planning program.

Recently he has instructed the plan organization to hold a conference focusing on the population problem. He has suggested various policy options aimed at lowering fertility, including raising the legal age for marriage. Mubarak has done this in spite of expressed opposition by Moslem fundamentalists and the Ministry of Religious Affairs.

Mubarak has instructed the Ministry of Information and Communications to develop an active program of promoting an awareness of the population problem and to provide information to the public on the availability of contraceptives. A program integrating population information into the school curriculum is also under way.

How successful Mubarak will be in overcoming the religious opposition and the stifling bureaucracy of the existing program has yet to be determined.

REFERENCES

Copeland, Miles. 1969. *The Game of Nations*. New York:
    Simon and Schuster.

"Democracy with a Bite." 1981. *Time*, September 21.

El-Khorazaty, M. Nabil. 1980. "Factors Affecting Family
    Planning Use and Attitudes in Rural Egypt." Paper pre-
    sented at a seminar, "The Demographic Situation in Egypt,"
    Cairo University, December 15-18.

Futures Group. 1980. *Egypt--The Effects of Population
    Factors on Social and Economic Development* (RAPID, Resour-
    ces for the Awareness of Population Impacts on Development,
    USAID).

Jansen, Godfrey. 1981. "Moslems and the Modern World." *The
    Economist*, January 3.

Kelley, Allen C., Atef Khalifa, and M. Nabil El-Khorazaty. 1979.
    Demographic Change and Development in Rural Egypt. Draft.

Marx, Robert E. 1980. "Egypt: Current Food Situation."
    Report prepared for the U.S. Department of State, Inter-
    national Economics Division, January 8.

Omran, Abdel R. 1980. *Reassessment of the Prospects for
    Fertility Decline in Egypt: Is Development a Prerequi-
    site?* University of North Carolina, Chapel Hill, June.

Rizk, I.A., C.S. Stokes, and M.R. Nelson. 1980. "The Influ-
    ence of Individual and Community-Level Child Mortality on
    Fertility in Egypt." Paper presented at the annual meet-
    ing of the Population Association of America, Denver,
    April 10-12.

U.S. Agency for International Development (USAID). 1980.
    Mission to Arab Republic of Egypt. Agricultural Sector
    Strategy Update, January.

---. 1980. Mission to Arab Republic of Egypt. Population
    Strategy Update, January.

---. 1981. Report on the Egyptian Economy and Debt Repayment
    Prospects. January.

Vicker, Ray. 1980. "Fate of Sadat's Regime May Hinge on Its
    Success In Improving the Ordinary Egyptian's Hard Life."
    Wall Street Journal, August 22.

Zachariah, K.C., et al. 1981. *Some Issues in Population and Human Resource Development in Egypt*. Study prepared for the World Bank, report no. 3175-EGT, May 12.

Chapter 4

Bangladesh: On the Thin Edge

THE PHYSICAL SETTING

Bangladesh is essentially a flat, swampy, alluvial plain
built up by centuries of sedimentation from three great river
systems converging near the Bay of Bengal. These rivers--
the Ganges, the Brahmaputra, the Meghna--and the lesser rivers
feeding into them give up their separate identities in a
mingled maze of swamplands and waterways along the southern
coast. Much of the country is less than 30 feet above sea
level; the abundant presence of water makes it look from the
air like jigsaw puzzle pieces floating on a vast, flat lake.
Between monsoons, however, the land masses are withered by
drought.

The land is fertile but inhospitable. Population density
in the country's 55,126 square miles--an area slightly smaller
than the state of Wisconsin--is the highest in the world
except for such small city-states as Hong Kong and Singapore.
Whereas Wisconsin's density is about 8.7 people per square
mile, Bangladesh is burdened by a density of nearly 1,700
people per square mile. No place in the country is free from
the crush of humanity and human settlements. One of the reasons that recurrent hurricanes take enormous human tolls is
that people are pushed onto land geographically unsuited for
habitation.

The country is practically without natural resources.
There are sizable but underdeveloped natural gas reserves,
some low-quality coal, and soil so rich that Bengalis have
been given to boasting that "you have only to stick a twig
in the ground and it will grow."

The forest blanketing 15 percent of the country is gradually
disappearing, and the flat, riverine beauty of the land makes it
extraordinarily vulnerable to vicious natural disasters.

Human life is constantly threatened by the scourges of river flooding, cyclones, disease, and famine. Overpopulation has set the stage for periodic starvation; rice, Bangladesh's primary food crop, is consistently insufficient to meet the country's own needs. The tropical climate and lack of adequate sanitation encourage disease, especially after storms and floods.

About 90 percent of all Bangladeshis live in rural areas where they are dependent on agricultural production for survival. But nature and overpopulation have made survival marginal at best. Most transportation in the rural areas is by foot or boat and barge. There are 3,000 miles of navigable rivers, but less than 700 miles of surfaced roads. The predominance of river water and marshy ground makes road building difficult and costly, and rebuilding at the end of each year's monsoon season is essential. For this reason, development projects are seriously constrained; journeys of only a few miles quickly become exhausting, all-day undertakings.

The nation is plagued by malnourishment, an 80 percent illiteracy rate and an average per capita GNP of only $100 a year. With a population the size of that of all the countries of Central America from the United States to Columbia combined, Bangladesh is ranked by the World Bank as being second only to Kampuchea in terms of poverty.

With a growth rate of 2.7 percent per year, Bangladesh's population will double in just 25.6 years.

THE EVOLUTION OF A NATION

In its earliest incarnation, when it was fused with the current Indian state of West Bengal in the subcontinental Hindu region known as Bengal, the area now making up Muslim Bangladesh was neither poor nor Muslim. Until the European maritime revolution brought colonial entrepreneurs to Asia in the early sixteenth century, Bengal was a rich country famous for its fine silks and muslins. As the centers of trade shifted to far away metropolises, however, the Bengalis were left with an economy based on high-quality jute and rice.

The area around the Bengali capital of Dacca began its inexorable decline; for several centuries, Bengalis in the Dacca region found themselves tucked away at the end of someone else's empire.

Ethnically, Bengal was a racial melting pot of ancient proto-Australoids (Veddas), Indo-European Armenoids, Mongoloids, and Mediterranean Aryans. With the advent of Islam in the eighth century A.D., Arabs, Persians, and Turks migrated in large numbers, gradually sifting into the relatively remote area now known as Bangladesh. Although a number of small tribal groups have retained their native ethnic purity, the vast majority of Bangladeshis—about 98 percent of them—are now Bengali, an admixture that is at once a linguistic and an ethnic grouping.

From the eighth to the twelfth centuries *A.D.*, Bengal was ruled by the Buddhist Pāla dynasty based in neighboring Bihar (India). An influx of semi-independent Muslims from Turkey and Afghanistan controlled various parts of Bengal from the twelfth century, but it was the Mughal Empire that eventually changed both the character and the culture of the area.

The first Mughal, Bābur—a descendant of the Turkish conqueror Timur and of Chagatai, the second son of the Mongol ruler Genghis Khan—swept onto the subcontinent in 1526. A two-century period of violence, pomp, and glory unequaled in the region's history had begun. The Mughals, who were known as much for their administrative excellence as for their artistic splendor, gradually integrated Hindus and Muslims into a united Indian state. By the end of the sixteenth century, Bābur's grandson Akbar had pushed the empire's boundaries northward from Delhi to encompass the entire subcontinental stretch from Afghanistan to the Bay of Bengal. And Islam had begun to take root in what is now Bangladesh.

The Mughal Empire's decline during the eighteenth century gave rise to a new dynasty in Bengal, Bihar, and Orissa. Its rulers, known as the Nawabs of Bengal, soon found themselves faced by the powerful force of British colonization. From 1757 to 1764, the British, who in 1690 had established themselves in Calcutta in western Bengal, took over the Nawabs' realm, and Bengal became the base for British expansion in India.

Although Islam was the religion of the powerful during both the Turko-Afghan and Mughal periods, Hinduism in the Bangladesh region was tenacious. As late as 1872 there were more than 18 million Hindus in Bengal, compared to about 16 million Muslims. Beginning in the 1890s, however, migration and attrition gradually tilted the religious balance in favor of the Muslims. Ascetic divines and Sufi (mystics) won converts among lower-caste Hindus. Meanwhile, waves of Muslims from northern India and other countries began to arrive. Aided by the Hindu ban on widows' remarriage, the Muslims' high fertility patterns soon left the Hindus far behind in terms of both population size and politico-economic power.

Assam was joined to Bengal from 1838 to 1874, but in 1954 the government of India was separated from that of Bengal. With the bloody revolt that ended British rule over India in 1947 and the even bloodier aftermath of partition among Hindus, Muslims, and Sikhs that ensued, 7 to 8 million Muslims fled India for the north, and about the same number of Hindus made the nightmare journey in the opposite direction. Some 200,000 people traveling in both directions were slain.

At the end of the terrible civil war that tore families as well as a mighty nation apart, Pakistan was born and Bengal was split in two. West Bengal, along with Bihar and Orissa,

became part of the Republic of India. East Bengal went to the
predominantly Muslim state of Pakistan, and became known as
East Pakistan. More than a thousand miles of Indian territory
separated East Pakistan from Pakistan's other four provinces
and its capital, which eventually moved from Karachi to Rawal-
pindi/Islamabad. Culturally and psychologically, East Pakistan
was a whole world away.

Punjabis--Muslims who had fled Sikh control of the Indian
Punjab--took charge of Pakistan while the Bengalis, though an
overall numerical majority in the new country, were generally
left to chafe at their position as political outsiders. East
Pakistan was also left out of the nation's economic drive. The
industrial structure built by Pakistan in its eastern province
consisted primarily of jute mills to replace those built under
British rule which were now located across the Indian border
in Calcutta. East Pakistan's relentless population increase
was matched by its economic decline. It had become an impoverished and isolated feudal state.

Independent At Last

East and West Pakistan had three things in common: Muslim
majorities, fear of India, and a mutual interest in East Pakistan's thriving jute and tea export industries. But for 24
years, development in East Pakistan was primarily a one-way
street leading to West Pakistan. The large foreign exchange
earnings generated by the East's jute and tea industries were
consumed by the expansion of the West's more broadly based
industry. During the years 1960-65, the annual rate of economic growth per capita in the West was 4.4 percent; in the
East, it was only 2.6 percent. West Pakistan also cornered
the market on the preponderance of foreign aid to Pakistan.

An example of favored treatment for the West was the great
Indus Basin scheme for hydroelectric development. At the
initiative of the World Bank, Pakistan signed an agreement
with India in September 1960 that conceded the right of India
to draw off water from the eastern Punjab rivers. In return,
Pakistan received massive assistance in exploiting the resources
of the upper Indus. Having organized the country's expertise
in technology and management, Pakistan skillfully negotiated for
billion-dollar assistance from such friends as the United States
and the World Bank for the construction of the Mangla Dam, the
world's largest irrigation project, which opened in 1967, and
the Tarbelea Dam, which was completed in the mid-1970s.

Pakistan also received immense military assistance from
the United States, partially in exchange for surveillance posts
along its borders with the Soviet Union and China and for
assistance with the Nixon administration's rapprochement with
Pakistan's friend, China. The Pakistani air force was equipped
with subsonic planes and modern missiles, while an armored

division was outfitted with Patton tanks. East Pakistan, meanwhile, was making friends of its own.

On August 9, 1971, East Pakistan signed a treaty of peace, friendship, and cooperation with the Soviet Union, calling for mutual consultation in the event of attack or threat of attack on either. East Pakistan was not only losing its fear of India, but of West Pakistan as well.

In November 1970, a catastrophic cyclone and tidal wave slammed into East Pakistan, ravaging a 3,000-square-mile area of the Ganges River delta. A half-million people were swept from the face of the earth in a matter of only a few hours. East Pakistan's exorbitant population growth rate meant that these people were replaced in less than three months. But the apparent indifference of Pakistan's leadership to the human suffering and resource destruction left in the cyclone's wake loosed a flood of Bengali nationalism. Autonomy came to be viewed as the only road to survival.

East Pakistan's poor socioeconomic structure had been shattered, but the Bengali spirit had gained new strength and determination. An unresolved war with India over Kashmir in 1965 and internal strife in Pakistan had weakened the presidency of Ayub Khan, who finally retreated behind a curtain of dictatorship.

Ayub's jailing of the popular Sheikh Mujibur Rahman (Mujib) who, as head of the powerful party known as the Awami League, was an avowed supporter of independence for East Pakistan, had proved politically disastrous. Ayub resigned on March 24, 1969, and General Yahya Khan assumed the title of president. The nation was placed under martial law.

The national election of December 1970 sent shock waves through Pakistan. Mujib's Awami League achieved a national majority that surprised even his supporters. When the new assembly rejected Mujib's demands for East Pakistani independence and Yahya Khan suspended the East's Constituent Assembly on March 1, 1971, Mujib ordered a boycott and general strike throughout East Pakistan. He received total support from the Bengalis; even the judges refused to acknowledge the authority of the president.

Full-scale warfare between government troops and Awami League supporters soon broke out in the East. Mujib and many of his colleagues were thrown into prison, and others escaped to India, proclaiming East Pakistan an autonomous state. As the fighting raged, the East's intelligentsia and leadership were systematically decimated; an astounding 10 million Bengalis fled across the border into India. The country, which was still reeling from the effects of the cyclone of November 1970, was plunged into chaos.

On December 3, 1971, war broke out between India and Pakistan. Although the Pakistani military was at least the equal of India's Russian-outfitted forces, it was no match for India's determined numbers. India--which favored East

Pakistani independence primarily for the economic disruption it would cause West Pakistan--carried out a successful invasion of East Pakistan. On December 16, the Pakistani army was forced to surrender at Dacca. The independent People's Republic of Bangladesh (Bengali Homeland) had been established with Sheikh Mujib at its head.

Postwar Problems

The Bangladeshis had little time to celebrate. The new nation was faced with a formidable combination of social, economic, and sometimes political problems arising out of the ten-month civil war. The new nation was divided into four regions: Dacca, Chittagong, Rajshahi, and Khulna. These divisions were in turn subdivided into about 422 *thanas* (literally "circles," each having a population of between 100,000 and 200,000 people), and the thanas were subdivided into 4,350 unions, consisting of groups of villages. In 1974 the census reported the existence of a total of 68,385 villages.

The restoration of law and order posed a major obstacle to reconstruction and rehabilitation efforts. Weapons had to be recalled from youths who had joined the liberation forces; citizens accused of war crimes had to be arrested and detained in an orderly fashion; members of non-Bengali communities-- primarily Biharis who had entered East Pakistan following partition in 1947--were frequently open to charges of collaboration; the army and police were in disarray. Administrative tasks were further complicated by the state of emotional shock in which the people had emerged from a civil war that had produced enormous acts of inhumanity, including the systematic terrorization and massacres of civilians.

Then the effects of monsoon flooding in 1972, the gradual return of Muslim refugees from India, and the 10-20 million displaced persons already in Bangladesh began to be felt. The country was faced with mass starvation and epidemics of smallpox and cholera brought from India by the refugees. Widespread famine was averted and disease eventually brought under control by massive foreign assistance programs led by the United States.

The administration of adequate supplies of relief and rehabilitation materials was hampered, however, by the destruction of road and rail communications (particularly bridges), the obstruction of major ports and channels by sunken vessels, and by increases in the price of essential items on the open market at a time when employment opportunities were scarce and when smuggling and hoarding were financially profitable. A fixed-price ration shop distribution system was unable to meet the acute demand for some time, although the United Nations Relief Operation in Dacca gave technical assistance to transport facilities. Stores of perishable food and medicines sat in dockside warehouses.

During 1972 a total of 50 agencies rushed to Bangladesh's aid. Between two and three million tons of foodstuffs were imported as part of millions of dollars of aid accompanied by hundreds of international experts sent by the United States, the United Nations, India, and other countries willing to help Bangladesh get on its feet. The United Nations Children's Fund (UNICEF) sponsored a nationwide child-feeding program to combat malnutrition. Wherever possible, the Bangladesh government pursued a policy of test relief, using imported, donated, or locally acquired food as payment in kind for manual work on public projects. The incidence of malnutrition inevitably skyrocketed in the worst affected areas, but the prospect of widespread starvation was defused.

Amidst this turmoil, Mujib managed to form a government. On December 16, 1972, Bangladesh's constitution was approved and a parliamentary form of government established. With Mujib as prime minister, the presidency was relegated to a ceremonial post on the model of India's system.

Mujib, however, had had no previous governing experience. Despite his immense popularity, he proved unequal to the task of dealing with the difficulties of constant politicking throughout government and industry, corruption at senior ministerial levels, and the depleted layer of bureaucratic expertise remaining from the slaughter of civil servants by the Pakistan army. In 1974 and 1975, the lack of administrative experience began to take its toll.

Under Pakistan's rule, all but a handful of Bengali civil servants had been confined to lowly positions; those who were left were as unprepared for their new responsibilities as Mujib was for his. Mujib was practically on his own. Although he was a skilled politician and adept even at handling the long lines of people who flocked to him with grievances, he was at a loss when it came to trying to run an economy, let alone trying to build up such a poor country as Bangladesh.

In August 1975 Sheikh Mujib, the "father of independence," was murdered along with his entire family by a group of dissident army majors. For three months, the country floundered on the brink of anarchy while various army factions jostled for power and finally persuaded the original group of dissident officers to leave the country. Then in November 1975, Major General Zia ur-Rahman--or Zia, as he became known affectionately to his people--emerged as the strong man (not to be confused with General Zia-ul-Haq of Pakistan).

Pushing for Progress

Zia quickly established order under the aegis of martial law. Then in June 1978, he established his own grass-roots credentials with an overwhelming 4-to-1 presidential election

victory. And his support was solidified in early 1979 when
his Bangladesh Nationalist Party won 203 of the 300 seats in
a parliamentary election. Although 36 of the country's 50 or
so political parties contended that the election had been
rigged, the victory left no doubt about the new president's
popularity.

Zia was a nationalistic dynamo who brought a sense of
order and discipline to a chaotic Bangladesh; he worked with
seemingly superhuman vigor to get his country moving. Under
his leadership, the government worked diligently to push
forward on all fronts; Zia attempted developmental approaches
that previous regimes lacked either the imagination or the
political will to promote.

"We must work hard to pull this country up by its boot-
straps," Zia is quoted in a Bangladesh review as having said.
"There is no substitute for hard work. I on my own cannot do
it, nor can ten individuals. But everyone pulling together
can do everything."

Zia led by example, by tirelessly touring each of the
districts of Bangladesh by foot and country boat to reach and
throw his weight behind development projects in even the most
inaccessible parts of the country. He had his critics, but
few of them came from the country's masses, and during the
five and a half years of his leadership, not one case of
personal corruption was levied against him.

His vigor and incorruptibility paid off in unprecedented
support for equally unprecedented programs of fertility control and economic development. His programs, however, were
constrained by the country's lack of nearly all resources
except the one that troubled him most: people. Zia viewed
overpopulation as the most serious and far-reaching peril
facing the Bangladeshi people. Unlike most Third World
leaders and unlike almost all other Muslim leaders, Zia had
a full and realistic understanding of the dire consequences
of his country's high population growth rate.

On May 30, 1981, however, President Zia was gunned down
much as Mujib had been, by a mutinous army officer. But Zia's
legacy survived his assassination. The reins of government
were passed on to 76-year-old Abdus Sattar, who was himself
elevated to the presidency by a landslide victory in November
1981 on a platform echoing Zia's dedication to the developmental priorities of population control, increased food production, and the promise of literacy.

President Sattar, a former supreme court justice, was not
able to unite the country behind him the way that Zia did.
Political stability is a prime requisite for economic development in Bangladesh, and economic development, planned around
the culturally unpopular notion of fertility control, is
necessary for political stability. On March 25, 1982, Army
Chief of Staff Lt. Gen. Ershad declared martial law and took
over the government. He declared four goals for the new

government: streamlining government machinery and weeding out corruption, gearing up the economy, ensuring people's participation in governmental activities and establishing a viable democratic system, and general elections on the basis of adult franchise.

General Ershad is a strong supporter of family planning. The new emphasis in the program is on decentralization and promotion of sterilization services. Individual and community benefits are also anticipated.

BANGLADESHI SOCIETY

Bangladesh is, after Indonesia, the largest Muslim country in the world. Eighty-five percent of its people profess a faith in Islam, while about 14 percent are Hindu. The remaining one percent are divided among Buddhism, Christianity, and animism. Since 98 percent of the people are Bengalis who speak a common language, the population is basically homogeneous.

Economically, however, the population is sharply divided between wealthy landowners and impoverished farm laborers. And hopes for democracy are limited by cultural realities. What democratic sense that is not erased by the Islamic denigration of females is wiped out by the fact of too many people in too small a place.

The lifetime prospects for a child born in Bangladesh today are indeed grim. The country's rural 90 percent are crowded into 68,385 villages. Home is typically a one-room mud-and-dung hut devoid of electricity and sanitation. Potable water is scarce. Increasing demands for the cow dung and crop leavings traditionally used for cooking and heating fires have drastically reduced their availability, too. The scavenging for crop residues for use as domestic fuel is also contributing to a decrease in soil quality, since the leavings when plowed under form a natural fertilizer for vital croplands. Although about 15 percent of the country is covered by forest, the commercial wood industry is vastly underdeveloped and no effort at all has been made so far to turn the nation's forest potential toward a domestic fuel industry.

Public Health

The life-death cycle in Bangladesh is a short and painful one. While the annual death rate is between 16 and 20 per thousand, the infant mortality rate is between 136 and 150 per thousand births. One-fifth of all children born today will die before the age of five. For those who survive childhood, life expectancy is a mere 47-51 years.

One-third of all pregnant and lactating women suffer from severe caloric deficiency, a fact that translates into extreme

vulnerability to disease for both mothers and their children.
Pneumonia and diarrheal diseases are the major causes of
infant deaths, and tetanus is a major cause of neonatal mortality. Overcrowding under unsanitary conditions perpetuates
the prevalence of scabies, respiratory infections, and worm
infestations.

About 15 percent of children below the age of five are
victims of acute and chronic malnutrition. The growth of an
additional 60 percent of the nation's children is stunted by
chronic undernutrition. Communicable diseases such as malaria,
tuberculosis, and leprosy also account for a high proportion
of illness and death. As Rafferty (1980) noted:

> *Health services available to most villagers
> consist generally of the traditional village midwife
> (dai), local indigenous health practitioners, and
> occasional visits by field-based health and family
> planning workers. Doctors and hospitals are so
> remote in terms of travel time as to be considered
> only at times of serious need and even then are
> likely to be beyond reach. Bangladesh now [1979]
> has an estimated 7,000 physicians, only some 1,750
> of whom are located in the rural areas--a ratio of
> about one doctor per 46,200 rural people.*
>
> *Medical education is hospital oriented with
> little emphasis on public health. Government health
> clinics are not a highly respected source of health
> care and are characteristically underutilized. The
> cadre of rural health workers that has been built up
> in recent years suffers from lack of motivation and
> supervision and, with the exception of the earlier
> smallpox and malaria campaigns, there is little
> indication that they are delivering any effective
> health services to the rural poor.*

Education

Although former President Zia gave education top priority
in Bangladeshi development, the educational picture remains
as depressing as the public health situation. From 1973 to
1980 the number of schools and colleges was increased by 33
percent; the primary-school enrollment of females rose by 50
percent while the enrollment for males increased by 30-35 percent; overall secondary-school enrollment increased by 35
percent; there were substantial enrollment increases in the
engineering colleges and in polytechnic, commercial, and
vocational training institutions; and universities were generally upgraded and their enrollments boosted by 33 percent.
All of which makes the country sound as though it is in the
midst of an educational boom until it is pointed out that

improvements took off from an almost negligible base, particularly in the case of female education.

In any case, most of the recent improvements in the country's fledgling educational system have been quantitative rather than qualitative. In many respects, past educational policies and programs have served to perpetuate or even compound imbalances, inequities, and distortions in the country's school system. An excessively male-oriented, urban-focused, elitist structure of education has remained virtually unchanged over the past decade. The result: while the illiteracy rate has stuck at about 80 percent, the urban-rural and male-female educational gaps have widened considerably. Thirty percent of all males over the age of ten are literate to some degree, while only 12 percent of the nation's females are literate.

Education in Bangladesh suffers as much from poor management and an inadequate system of teacher training as from the traditional lack of a coherent national educational policy tailored to the needs of the nation as a whole. More than half of the students entering grade one leave school before grade five, and the costs of predominantly private (and sexually segregated) secondary schools are far beyond the reach of the average Bangladeshi. Furthermore, an overwhelming emphasis on liberal arts in higher education is reflected by acute unemployment--as high as 25 percent--among university graduates.

As in most developing countries, Bangladesh's educational system is geared to the expectations of the elite and subject to pressures from urban middle- and upper-class interest groups. Between 1973 and 1980, only 57 percent of the education budget was actually spent; despite the priority supposedly given to primary and nonformal education, the amount spent on primary education was only half of that spent on university education, and there was no real progress at all in the area of nonformal training.

Between 1973 and 1978, a target of a six-fold increase in female teachers to attract female students and serve as role models for them was met by a mere doubling. And only half of the new primary schools planned for 1979-80 were actually constructed. Meanwhile, the high primary dropout rate continued unabated due to a lack of improvement in the quality of facilities, materials, curricula, teaching, and supervision.

Educational strategies have not only failed to be implemented, but the shares of both the development and revenue budgets earmarked for education declined during the 1970s. As of 1976, the percentage of gross domestic product (GDP) designated for education was little more than one-third of the average for all developing countries and less than half that for Asian countries.

The educational thrust lacked both staff and management capable of translating plans and policies into action, and supervising and evaluating ongoing programs. The Public Works

Department delayed primary-school construction; the Textbook Board failed to procure necessary materials; the release of funds allocated under a succession of annual development programs ran into tangles of red tape.

In 1980 a new five-year development plan again put education in the spotlight. The new plan calls for even greater--and one would hope, genuine--emphasis on primary education and mass literacy programs.

The focus is to be on functional education linked with employment in rural areas and urban slums. The development of community schools is aimed at providing vocational training of out-of-school children and adults--40 million of them in the 11-45 age group--in just five years. Science and technology are to become basic components of the educational system, and the rural-urban disparity in educational services is to be reduced. The budgetary goal is for outlays for primary mass education, which averaged about 13 percent of total development financing for education during 1973-80, to reach 50 percent (41 percent for primary and 9.0 percent for mass literacy) by 1985. Most importantly, the development of women's education is to be accelerated. Secondary schools for girls are almost nonexistent in rural Bangladesh today.

The program has far-reaching potential. But at Bangladesh's current population growth rate of 2.7 percent per year and the high dependency burden placed by 43 percent of the population being under 15 years of age, there can be little room for long-range optimism. According to studies on the relationship between education levels and contraceptive use done by demographers Rafiqul H. Chaudhury (1978) and Mohammed Alauddin (1979), women's education is the major key to fertility reduction. That key, however, is hidden deep within the folds of Bengali and Islamic traditionalism.

THE STATUS OF WOMEN--A GLIMPSE BEHIND THE CULTURAL CURTAIN

Deprived of education and confined to a domestic role, the Bangladeshi woman spends her life under the protection and, therefore, under the control of an adult male--first her father, then her husband, and later her son. She lacks both economic and social status, is subject to overwork and undernutrition, and is totally without authority. Her status in Bengali culture is secured only through childbearing. And even in this area she lacks authority: since wives are typically about ten years younger than their husbands, they are subordinate to their husbands in all matters, including such critical child-bearing decisions as an offspring's education, future employment, and marriage partner.

Rural Bangladeshi women are, in fact, the most disadvantaged of all Bangladeshis. These women, who can be divided into three

sociological groups, may have significantly different life
styles, but their ultimate status is the same: inferior and
isolated. According to a study undertaken by Louisa B. Gomes
(1980) for the U.S. Agency for International Development
(USAID) in Dacca, the poorest of the three groups are desti-
tute women—widows, divorcees, and abandoned women—who must
beg or hire themselves out as laborers or servants to survive.
About 15 percent of all rural women fall into this category.

About 70 percent of all rural women fit into the second
group, which consists of wives of landless farm laborers or
daily wage earners, sharecroppers, or small farmers with
landholdings of less than 1-1/2 acres. These women are
employed solely within their own households, without the
benefits of either pay or outside help.

The third group of women, who make up about 15 percent of
the total of rural women, is somewhat better off. These are
the wives of merchants, professionals, and relatively large
landowners (with holdings of more than 1-1/2 acres) who can
afford to hire domestic servants and thus are allowed a little
more freedom. This group includes most of the educated rural
women who have reached the equivalent of grade eight to ten
and who are usually the first to take advantage of opportunities for training and employment. Employment outside the
home, however, is always in addition to, rather than a substitute for, household duties.

The Ideal of Purdah

Women's behavior clearly reflects on a rural Bangladeshi
family's status. The cultural ideal of womanhood encompasses
strict *purdah* and a complete sexual division of labor that
empowers men with all work and decision making that might be
construed as even vaguely intellectual. An extended family
structure usually permits a smooth transition for a woman
through the stages of her life and continued security after
her husband's death. But it drastically restricts her freedom
and leaves almost no opportunity at all for self-development.

Although only relatively wealthy families can afford to
adhere to the ideal of strict purdah, the influence and power
it symbolizes for the male prompts nearly all families to
enforce it as completely as possible. And although the purdah
system that reduces a woman to a shadowy object is dying out
in much of the Middle East and most of South Asia, it is still
rigidly adhered to in Bangladesh.

Purdah (literally, "the curtain") involves more than the
seclusion of women. It regulates nearly every aspect of a
woman's life, and especially her physical mobility. Strict
purdah means that a woman stays within the family compound,
which is usually surrounded by a wall of vegetation and sometimes has screens of woven rushes to hide the inner courtyard.

She is never seen by males other than those in the immediate
family.

The maintenance of such strict purdah is possible for only
a few households in a village, and the strictness varies somewhat according to region. But all villagers look to the
households practicing strict purdah as the most prestigious
and respected, as bringing honor to the entire village, and to
purdah as the most desirable life style for women. Conversely,
a lapse in purdah brings an immediate loss of prestige to a
family.

Although there is evidence that attitudes toward purdah
are slowly changing and that the rigidity of purdah is decreasing due to economic stress, women still remain generally
confined to their homesteads. Some women may leave the compound to fetch water from a community handpump or well, to
wash clothes in a pond, pick vegetables from a garden plot or
gather firewood, but women rarely if ever venture to the market. Indeed, it is entirely possible to travel overland for
days through rural villages and not once encounter or even
glimpse a woman in the market buying, selling, or mixing with
others.

While a typical rural Bangladeshi man works from an average
of 10 to 12 hours each day, a woman works from 10 to 14 hours.
Women's duties include seed preparation, grain storage, vegetable and fruit growing, poultry raising, livestock care, food
processing and preservation, household maintenance and repair,
fuel gathering, and post-harvest rice procuring—all activities
critical to the rural and household economy.

Women also play a dominant role in such cottage crafts as
the production of fish nets, baskets, mats, jute products,
quilts, rope, fabrics, and some food products for both local
and foreign markets. In spite of the fact that handicraft
production may be a full-time occupation for some women, they
are nevertheless dependent on men to supply the necessary raw
materials and to market their products.

Bangladeshi women not only work longer hours than their
male counterparts but, due primarily to overwork, undernourish-
ment, vulnerability to disease, and the physical strain of
frequent pregnancy and childbearing, they live shorter lives.

In many villages, a feudal relationship between rich and
poor women serves to benefit both. Women from poor households,
for example, may be expected to perform such services as helping with rice husking and milling, fetching water, cooking for
holiday feasts, and clearing the courtyard of drying rice when
rain threatens. Sometimes payment is made in the form of a
portion of the food being processed or prepared; often, no
immediate compensation is either made or expected for services
rendered.

Throughout the year, however, village elites give sustenance
and support to the poor in the form of food on religious occasions or saris and relief goods after such natural calamities as

floods and hurricanes. Goods are also distributed to the poor
to insure loyalty at election time, as a form of gratitude to
Allah for prayers granted, to mark baby-naming and circumcision
ceremonies, and on death anniversaries. Rich families also
often provide small loans without the burden of interest or
stigma of publicity.

The Norm of Early Marriage

Whether rich or poor, the rural Bangladeshi female approaches womanhood as a child bride, a child wife, and a child mother.
Although the practice of marrying off females at the age of 11
or 12 (or even younger) is becoming increasingly rare and
females are not legally eligible for marriage until the age of
16, early marriage is still the norm. Some village girls today
do pass the onset of puberty without marrying, a situation most
villagers consider to be a social problem tied to disruptive
modernization. But even though an unmarried girl is obviously
as old as 16 or 17, her relatives will try to conceal the fact
by claiming that she is only 12 or 13.
Nine of ten Bangladeshi females are married in their teens,
however, and a high proportion of these young brides enter
marriage before or immediately following the onset of menstruation. The proportion of 15- to 19-year-old Bangladeshi females
who are married is, in fact, the highest on the entire subcontinent.
The tradition of early marriage is valued as conducive to
smooth postmarital adjustment since the new daughter-in-law has
not yet developed an independent personality and is therefore
still malleable. Furthermore, since premarital virginity is
highly prized by Bengalis, early marriage assures the groom of
a virginal bride and assures her parents of a marriageable
daughter. Females who lose their virginity before marriage
become social liabilities and potential economic burdens to
their parents.
The decision to have children is almost never left up to
the woman. Instead, her childbearing is prescribed by her
social status, which in turn is often dictated by important
family members, by her overall status in terms of the number
and sex of children previously born, and by her family's
economic situation. The young bride begins bearing children
soon, if not immediately after marriage. She is typically
totally unaware of the concept let alone the merits of spacing
births, and continues to produce an average of around seven
live children after about 12 pregnancies. Spacing that does
occur is usually due to the two to three years of lactation
amenorrhea (infertility during breast-feeding) which is common
among Bangladesh's malnourished women.
It is not uncommon for Bangladeshi women to become pregnant
as many as 16 or 17 times during their childbearing years. And

it is not surprising that the great majority of adult female deaths in the 12 to 50 year age range are maternity related. Approximately 27,000 women die each year in childbirth, while about 8,000 more die from abortions induced by a variety of unsanitary folk methods.

As the following table shows, in 1975 nearly half of all 15-year-old Bangladeshi females were married, and this proportion rose to 90 percent for 19-year-olds. Meanwhile, only about 7.0 percent of women aged 20-24 were unmarried compared, for example, to 54 percent in Sri Lanka.

TABLE 4.1 *Percentage of Females Married, According to Age, 1975*

Current age	12	13	14	15	16	17	18	19	20
Percent married	7	14	25	47	60	76	85	90	93

Source: International Statistical Institute, 1979.

Women's Development: A Male Prerogative

Since 1975, a number of steps have been taken to open the way for Bangladeshi women's participation in development programs, to insure their legal rights and to raise their status. President Zia constantly seized and created opportunities to speak out in favor of full female participation in all sectors of society and initiated programs toward this end. While this concern generally failed to be translated into action by officials beneath him, Bangladesh's constitution now states that equal opportunity is guaranteed to all citizens regardless of sex.

Campaigns against the dowry system and other social customs connected with early marriage are receiving some attention, and the government has ruled that 10 percent of all vacancies in both government and nongovernment sectors must be set aside for women. At the lower levels, at least, these vacancies are being filled as specified. Thirty appointed seats in the national assembly are also now reserved for women and, in 1978, a separate Ministry of Women's Affairs was created.

Change is in the wind, but the wind blows weakly. Toward the end of Zia's life, Bangladeshi newspapers were splashed with accounts of Zia's impassioned addresses to groups of women on the importance of their full participation in all sectors of Bangladeshi development. Two and three times a week, the newspapers hailed Zia's conviction that the nation's very future depended on its women. Significantly, however, none of these glowing front-page accounts mentioned a word about the need for men to let their women step forward.

The Value of Children

Bangladesh's traditional large-family norm is a consequence of cultural quasi-tribal security, economic necessity, and abiding faith in the Islamic tenet that Allah will provide. The value given to children, especially to sons, and the importance placed on having both sons and daughters to make a family complete have a strong bearing on Bengali fertility behavior.

As Salahuddin (cited in Javillonar et al., 1979) has observed, "Girls are made fully conscious that unlike their brothers who are assets to the family, they are only liabilities." This preference for male children is as prominent among the professional elite and urban middle class as it is for the country's rural population. Other studies of rural fertility by Mead Cain show that male children are net producers by age 12, compensate for their total consumption by age 15, and additionally compensate for a sister's total consumption by age 22. Moreover, under Sunni law, sons are the inheritors and managers of land. Large landowning families receive even more benefits from their sons than do less affluent families, since wealthier parental households control their sons' contributions for a longer period of time.

Village children begin their economically useful lives as early as age 6. By about age 8, some 29 percent of boys and 78 percent of girls are put to work in the household. These percentages, of course, increase with age: over 60 percent of boys and 93 percent of girls by age 10, and nearly all boys and girls by age 12 have entered the household labor force.

Children are also a built-in social security system for their parents. About 95 percent of all rural Bangladeshi women depend on financial assistance from their children in their old age; for about 74 percent of these women, this is their only means of support. Nearly all Bangladeshi women expect to live out their widowhood or divorced life with their sons.

As Cain (1977) reported, wealthy parents not only have, on the average, more living sons (2.8) as compared to the poor (1.8), but they also enjoy greater old age support than the poor. The sons of rich parents also tend to stay with the family longer. Among large landowners, for example, the mean age of departure from their parents' homes for more than 80 percent of these relatively privileged sons is 28.5 years. Only about 65 percent of the sons of landless families live with their parents and, when they leave, they do so at a much earlier age (22.3 years at the mean).

In addition to these economic fertility boosters, the woman's dependence on childbearing for social status cannot be overemphasized. The possibility of polygamy under Islamic law and the ease with which a husband can divorce a wife make children, especially male children, the ties that bind a husband to his wife and a wife to her home.

MANAGING PROBLEMS AND AGENDAS

Each month Bangladesh adds 200,000 people (2.4 million people a year) to its population-strangled land. For almost 30 years, concern about the natural calamity of overpopulation in the area has gained momentum. But over the same 30 years—despite other natural calamities such as population-decimating cyclones and floods and a violent civil war that shook loose a shifting refugee mass equal to the population of Hungary—the nation's population growth rate also has gained momentum.

Neither environmental, economic. and political upheavals nor endemic disease and malnutrition have slowed the course toward catastrophic population of a country with shortages of energy, food, and land. And, as Table 4.2 shows, the policies and personal exhortations of an exceptionally aware and dynamic leader had equally small impact on the cultural forces opposing what Zia realistically termed "population control."

TABLE 4.2 *Population and Growth Rate, 1931-81*

Year	Population (millions)	Intercensus average yearly growth rate
1931–1951		1.0%
1951	42.6	
		2.52%
1961	53.4	
		3.2%
1974	76.4	
		3.1%
1980	90.6	
		2.7%
1984	96.4*	

*Population Reference Bureau midyear estimate.

Source: Alauddin 1980, and Population Reference Bureau 1981.

It took Bangladesh's population 64 years to double from 28.9 million in 1901 to 57.5 million in 1965 and 38 years to double from 38.2 million in 1936 to 76.4 million in 1974. At its 1984 annual growth rate of about 2.7 percent, however, it will take a mere 25.6 years for the country's 1984 population to double to 199 million by midyear 2010. At the same time

that the population doubles, of course, the per capita availability of cropland decreases accordingly.

TABLE 4.3 *Declining Cropland per Person*

Year	Net cropped area (x 1,000 acres)	Total Population (in millions)	Land-to-person ratio (acres per person)
1961	19,138	54.5	0.35
1974	20,550	76.4	0.27
1980	21,000	90.6	0.23

Source: USAID 1981.

The Bangladesh government cannot provide for the nation's
unrestrained and unsupportable annual birth rate of 46 per
1,000. Yet the anti-birth control forces abounding in Bengali
society present formidable barriers to the necessary achievement of a small-family norm. Economic development in itself
cannot be expected to have an immediate impact on the runaway
fertility rate promoted and perpetuated by a culture that keeps
its women under wraps and allows them to experience social
status only as childbearers.
    In fact, it is generally the case that the larger a fam-
ily's landholdings, the more children that will be born to it.
The reasons for this seemingly perverse fact are the same
reasons that urban women tend to produce slightly more children
than rural women in Bangladesh: the relative absence of economic stress plus better nutrition, health care, and living
conditions and stricter adherence to purdah among the middle
and upper classes result in more children.

TABLE 4.4 *Average Number of Children Born, According to*
          Husband's Landholdings, 1978

	None	1 acre	1-1.9 acres	2-2.9 acres	3+ acres
Total Fertility Rate	6.8	7.1	7.3	7.4	7.7

Source: Stoeckel et al. 1979.

Education and Fertility

In the same way that economic status is associated with increased fertility, primary education seems to relate positively to elevated fertility levels for both men and women. Secondary and higher education for both sexes, however, relates markedly to a sharp reduction in fertility. The 1974 census reported that women with no schooling had, on the average, 3.9 live births; those with primary education, 3.4 live births; and those with secondary or higher education, 2.6 live births.

The educational level of husbands is not as significant as that of wives in lowering the average fertility, unless they are educated above the secondary level. In fact, women whose husbands have achieved primary or secondary education tend to have the highest fertility rates. The relatively low fertility rates among the nation's poorest uneducated people and affluent secondary- and college-educated people reflect both economic status and contraceptive acceptance.

The poor have fewer live births due to the women's general malnourishment and an increasing acceptance of sterilization by both males and females in response to economic stress. The highly educated affluent have fewer children due to delayed marriage for women (while they are in school), greater awareness and access to contraceptive methods and their merits, the presence of servants and thus relative freedom of women from menial labor, and higher expectations for their children's education and employment.

Religion and Fertility

Religion also plays an important role in fertility behavior. Muslim women in their twenties and thirties are a bit more fertile than Hindu women of the same age and also appear to bear more children in their later years. Much of this is due to the relaxation or nonexistence of purdah among Hindus who are more frequently educated at higher levels, marry later, and practice contraception more regularly than Muslims.

The implications of this fertility difference, combined with massive Hindu emigrations following partition in 1947 and again before and after the civil war of 1971, do not auger well for population control efforts in Bangladesh.

The Bangladesh Fertility Survey of 1978 also found that 7.5 percent of the country's Muslims and 10.3 percent of the non-Muslims were contraceptive users. Meanwhile, nearly 70 percent of Muslims as compared to about 63 percent of non-Muslims had no intention of using contraceptives.

Social Acceptability and Demand
for Family Planning

The Koran does not place any prohibition at all on any form of contraception. *Azl* (now taken to mean *coitus interruptus*, or withdrawal) was practiced by the prophet Mohammed's companions and literally translates into contraception in general. Traditional contraceptive methods—Azl, rhythm, abstinence, prolonged breast-feeding, and induced abortion—have long been used by even the most religious Bangladeshi Muslims to delay pregnancies during times of extreme economic stress or when a woman is severely ill. Today, with the exception of induced abortion, these traditional methods account for about one-fourth of all contraceptive use.

Additional children are looked on as gifts from Allah who, of course, will provide for them. The fact that too many children may plunge a family into total economic despair (and a woman into an early grave) is quite incomprehensible to the traditional Muslim whose initiative has been stifled by a centuries-old security blanket of fatalism.

Once several children have been born, however—and especially if at least two of the children are sons—the desire to limit the number of additional births increases considerably. This is evidenced by the significant number of high-parity women who seek either sterilization or abortion or a combination of abortion and immediate sterilization. Estimates of the numbers of women who want to limit births but fail to do so run as high as 25 percent of all married women between the ages of 12 and 50. The primary reason given for their hesitation is the fear of side effects from the use of modern contraceptives.

Furthermore, rural lower-middle-class Bangladeshis tend to take their fertility cues from the wealthier large landowning families for whom the strict observance of prestige-elevating purdah and large-family size go hand in hand. At the lowest end of the economic scale, however, tradition is slowly giving way to pragmatism as the basic arithmetic of numbers and lack of food availability confront those with little chance to improve their economic lot.

In more developed countries, the pattern of demographic transition from large to small families has been established as proceeding from the top downward. In those countries, the small-family movement has been led by high-income, educated couples anxious to limit the number of children under their support as a means of raising their own standard of living and increasing their children's future prospects. Not so in Bangladesh. Here, the society is beginning to experience what some refer to as the bottom-up demographic transition phenomenon.

Reports from such family planning sources as the Bangladesh Ministry of Health and Population Control and Elizabeth Marum of USAID/Dacca indicate that a transition to small-family acceptance is moving, albeit in low gear, from the bottom of Bangladeshi society upward. The transition is being led by the poorest of the poor, by people who must struggle simply to survive from one day to the next.

Marum found in 1981, for example, that the contraceptive use rate among 355 extremely poor women employed as day laborers in road building and other earth-moving projects was 26 percent, about twice the national average. Moreover, the rate of contraceptive use by these women existed in the absence of any special or intensified family planning motivational or service delivery activities.

Although the bottom-up phenomenon offers hope for population control in Bangladesh, such factors as the lack of secondary education and related early marriage for rural females contribute an increasingly unsupportable burden of both wanted and unwanted children. Other contributors to the prospect of sustained high fertility rates are the continuing pattern of early and almost universal marriage, the concentration of female marriages within a short 15- to 19-year age range, and the current age structure--43 percent of Bangladesh's population is under 15 years of age; only 3.0 percent is above the age of 64. As increasing numbers of young women enter their reproductive years, in fact, the nation's crude birth rate may actually rise. The concentrated age range of marriages also contributes to a concentration of births: two-thirds of all Bangladeshi children are born to women in their twenties. The result: an extremely short time between generations.

As previously noted, voiced intentions do not make a viable educational system. Nor does the presence of laws guarantee either their acceptance or enforcement; rural families obviously are neither impressed nor bound by the 16-year minimum age of marriage for females; many of them do not even know the law exists. For that matter, a law prohibiting abortion has been on the books since British colonial times, but it obviously is never enforced.

Similarly, the concentration of family planning information and services in urban areas does nothing either to promote or service small-family desires among the nation's rural 90 percent. Despite the Bangladesh leadership's vigorous support of the country's national population control program, only about 13 percent of all Bangladeshi married couples of reproductive age (MCRAs) are protected by contraceptive use.

So far, at least, neither a top-down nor bottom-up approach to population control has succeeded in turning the nation's population problem around.

The National Family Planning Program

As long ago as 1953, attempts were made by concerned East Pakistanis to arouse interest in the area's rapid population

growth. Volunteers established the East Pakistan Family
Planning Association which, in 1964, would become an affili-
ate of the International Planned Parenthood Federation (IPPF).
Although this organization received only nominal help from the
Pakistan government, it did manage to sponsor a number of
urban clinic-based family planning activities.

In 1955 the Pakistan government finally recognized the
nation's high fertility rate as a problem, and in its First
Five-Year Development Plan, allocated Rs. 50,000 (about $10,000
of soft-currency loans made by the United States under its
Public Law 480 [PL 480]) to the East Pakistan Family Planning
Association. It was not until 1960, however, that the government actually involved itself directly in family planning
efforts.

The Second Five-Year Plan (1960-65) set aside Rs. 30.5
million ($3.9 million) for family planning programs. Objec-
tives included: the establishment of family planning clinics
and supply distribution points in existing health centers, the
training of motivational and clinical personnel, and the promotion of research and administrative projects in the area of
family planning.

Several urban postpartum family planning clinics were
established via government initiative. Family planning training programs for doctors were set up in existing hospitals.
The establishment of research and evaluation centers made way
for an important experiment in rural-based family planning by
the Comilla Academy for Rural Development. Although the
project achieved only a modest contraceptive use rate of about
six percent of fertile couples in the area, it did prove that
family planning services could be administered as a normal
adjunct to ongoing health programs.

The Second Five-Year Plan aimed at reaching ten percent
of the nation's reproductive-age women. Due to the absence of
effective contraceptives and inadequate field staffing and
funding, however, the plan barely began to reach its goal. In
fact, less than ten percent of the eligible population even
visited the clinics, and only 9.4 million of the Rs. 30.5
million allocated were actually spent. Disrupted by war with
India in 1965 and weakened by a reliance on relatively ineffective contraceptive methods—condoms, diaphragms, and vaginal
jelly—the program's acceptance rate remained at less than two
percent of the nation's potential contraceptors.

The Third Five-Year Plan (1965-70) greatly expanded both
the family planning program itself and the funds earmarked for
it. Some Rs. 234 million were plugged into a system geared
to: making family planning services available to the entire
population by 1970, including training and research as an
integral part of the program, and reducing the crude death rate
from 20 to 15 per thousand, and thus the growth rate from 3.0+
to 2.5 percent per year.

Heightened emphasis on expansion and motivation resulted
in the Pakistani government's establishment of an autonomous

National Family Planning Board in 1966. Independent of the national health service, the board's mission was to implement the family planning program in cooperation with other relevant government units.

Family planning offices were set up in each of the nation's 400 thanas; each of these was staffed by one thana family planning officer and supporting office personnel. An eventual total of 25,000 traditional birth attendants (dais)--most of them illiterate and village-based women--were appointed to act as part-time workers. Chief male organizers were also appointed to supervise the dais' home visits. By 1968, all hospitals, dispensaries, and health centers, plus a large number of individual doctors, were involved in contraceptive service activities based primarily on the newly introduced IUD (Lippes loop) and sterilization.

Nineteen permanent district-level clinics and 345 permanent thana family planning clinics grew up throughout the country, and a female paramedic, called a "lady family planning visitor" --the forerunner of today's family welfare visitor (FWV)--was posted in each thana clinic to dispense conventional contraceptives and insert IUDs. Thanas without clinics were served by a number of mobile IUD teams. The 25,000 dais worked on a monetary incentive basis, and similar incentives were introduced for doctors as well. Government doctors, private practitioners, clients, and recruiters all received per-case cash payments for sterilizations.

During the late 1960s, however, public opposition to family planning took a violent turn. Family Planning Association offices were stormed; clinics were ravaged by fire. On top of this, the program's lack of clear policy, its administrative weaknesses, and dearth of full-time fieldworkers vastly reduced its effectiveness. The IUD, which made its debut during this period, became a scapegoat for public protest and, in fact, remains unpopular today. Reports of large numbers of vasectomies in the late 1960s were later acknowledged to be grossly inflated.

According to the National Impact Survey, by 1968 about 66 percent of the targeted couples had heard about some method of family planning. But only about 7.0 percent had ever practiced a modern method of contraception, and only 3.9-4.0 percent were currently practicing. And program operations were again disrupted by the political and military events culminating in the independence of the People's Republic of Bangladesh on December 16, 1971.

The Postindependence Program

For almost two years, from 1972 to 1974, the family planning program was stopped dead in its tracks while the new nation struggled with postwar recovery and the requirements

of establishing a sovereign government. When the subject of
fertility control was finally readdressed, it was answered by
a long and interest-centered debate within the government of
Bangladesh—first on whether there should be a family planning
program at all, and then on the form it should take.

Protagonists in the latter argument were divided into two
camps: those who fully appreciated the importance of fertility
control to the nation's total prospects for development favored
a single-purpose program, while others—with the support of WHO
and, subsequently, the World Bank and some of its associated
donors—pushed a program that would combine family planning
with malaria and smallpox eradication and other preventive
health services. Although the national family planning program
was eventually reorganized, this oscillation between "integrated" and "vertical" programs has persisted to the present
and, in fact, remains a root cause of its incoherent organization and structure.

In 1973, USAID began bilateral family planning support to
Bangladesh. At that time, USAID's principal short-term objective was to introduce the birth control pill on a broad scale
and to build up an ample in-country stock of contraceptive
commodities. For these purposes, USAID supplied over $1.5
million in grant funds for a two-year period. At the same
time, the Pathfinder Fund and the Association for Voluntary
Sterilization (both AID-funded) set up Bangladesh's first high-
quality, full-service clinics to train doctors in clinical
contraceptive techniques as well as to augment service delivery
capacity. And in 1974, the United Nations Fund for Population
Activities (UNFPA) agreed to provide $10 million of assistance
for fieldworker training and salaries, warehouse construction,
vehicles, and related support.

In late 1973, the government of Bangladesh announced that
family planning was to be integrated with health services. The
new government's First Five-Year Plan (1973-78) promised that
strong pressure would be exerted to achieve a decline in fertility that would reach replacement level by the year 2000. The
Ministry of Health was renamed the Ministry of Health and Family
Planning. And the existing secretary of health took on the
direction of the central units and field structure of the Family
Planning Board for this integration attempt.

Nearly 12,000 male workers of the vertical malaria and
smallpox program were given several weeks' training. Called
"family welfare workers" (FWWs), they began operating in
January 1974 as multipurpose workers responsible for the delivery of rudimentary preventive health and family planning information and supplies during their regular visiting rounds. At
the same time, the network of between 450 and 500 primarily
female paramedic-staffed thana and urban family planning clinics
—which had remained virtually dormant since 1971—was reactivated. Funding for both the FWW training and clinic renovations
was provided by USAID.

At the outset, "integration" was planned to occur at the fieldworker level only; over the FWWs' heads, separate chains of command and separate sources of salaries remained intact at every level. The National Family Planning Board, which had been carried over from the East Pakistan period and which had bitterly opposed integration, never became fully reconciled to it and was less than wholehearted in attempts to make it work. Equally important, the FWW training was inadequate, a serious matter since birth control pills were being introduced into the program for the first time outside of a clinical setting.

Workers were ill prepared to offer clients reliable answers to their questions, doubts, and fears. Also, they not only had an unrealistically long list of curative and preventive health duties to perform, but were frequently called away for special assignments such as periodic mosquito spraying for malaria control, intensive smallpox eradication campaigns, disaster relief, election duty, and rice procurement drives. It is not surprising that an evaluation team's study of the program's first year of operation concluded that family planning was not receiving attention commensurate with the urgency of the population problem.

"Verticality" Revisited

In January 1975, the government decided to revert to a "vertical" family planning program. The Health Division of the Ministry of Health and Family Planning was split into a Health Division and a Population and Family Planning Division, and the parental body became known as the Ministry of Health, Population and Family Planning. Three months later, responsibility for maternal and child health (MCH) services was transferred from the Health Division to the Population and Family Planning Division, and a National Population Council was formed.

The new fieldworker cadre consisted of three women and one man per union, recruited as home-visiting MCH/FP workers, a total of about 18,000 new full-time employees. The women were dubbed family welfare assistants (FWAs), and the men, family planning assistants (FPAs). Their principal qualifications were secondary-level education and established residence in the area of assignment.

Under this plan, the Health Division's 12,000 or so family welfare workers were to continue to distribute contraceptives during their home visits, concentrating on males as potential acceptors and thus, theoretically, complementing the PCFPD's fieldworkers. Although the FWWs continued to distribute birth control pills and condoms from their remaining stocks, this was on an ever decreasing scale and to the disregard of the PCFPD.

Meanwhile, a Family Planning Social Marketing Project began operations under the aegis of the Ministry of Health, Population

Control and Family Planning. The project facilitated the highly subsidized commercial sale of pills and condoms; funding for the nationwide project came from USAID through its intermediary contractor, Population Services International (PSI).

In January 1975, vestiges of the Pakistani National Family Planning Board (which had managed the vertical program of the Pakistan period and opposed the integration attempt of 1974) were assimilated on paper into a new PCFP Directorate meant to be the implementing arm of the PCFP Division. By the time September rolled around and the new Directorate's organizational structure and staffing pattern were approved, however, two important program changes had been made.

First, some 8,000 part-time dais and 4,000 chief male organizers--holdovers from the Pakistani program who had not been used in the postindependence period--had been reactivated and permitted to distribute contraceptives to homes. But they had not been given any special training on birth control pills, with which they had had no previous experience.

Second, it had been decided to distribute pills and condoms free instead of continuing to sell them at the nominal prices of three U.S. cents per monthly cycle of pills and five U.S. cents per dozen condoms, as had been the case since the integrated program's inception. The question of whether or not to charge for contraceptives had long been an issue within the government; the decision to provide them free appears to have been an arbitrary one, unsupported by field study.

Considering that the family planning program had lain dormant from March 1971 through 1973, the integrated program begun in January 1974 had in effect been a nonstarter. Since the majority of new field staff were not recruited and trained until late 1976, it is not surprising that the Bangladesh Fertility Survey of 1975-76 showed little change in fertility since 1966-68.

The 1975-76 estimated total fertility rate (in effect, completed family size) was about 6.3 compared to about 6.0 during the 1966-68 period. About 82 percent of those interviewed knew about family planning, compared with only 66 percent in 1966-68. However, only 8.0 percent of the reproductive-age couples were practicing contraception at the time of the 1975-76 survey, of whom less than 5.0 percent were using modern and a little more than 3.0 percent were using traditional methods. (Modern methods included pills, IUDs, condoms, injections, and sterilization; traditional methods included azl [withdrawal], abstinence, rhythm, foam, and diaphragms.)

In 1976, with the nationwide, highly subsidized commercial sale of pills and condoms having gotten underway the previous year, USAID funded a second phase of its earlier bilateral project to the tune of $15.3 million for three years. Meanwhile, in 1976, the World Bank initiated its first major project in Bangladesh, a five-year $45 million grant-loan provided primarily for construction and salaries.

In 1976, the Bangladeshi government declared that overpopulation was the country's number one problem. The demographic target was revised to achieve a Net Reproduction Rate
(NRR), or replacement level of fertility, of one by 1985,
which would stabilize the population at 120 million by the
year 2000. (This goal was patently unrealistic, however;
there was no conceivable way that reproductive behavior would
change from a six-child family to a two-child family size in
just ten years.) Abortion ("menstrual regulation") was given
government sanction as an official program method. The PCFP
Division was put through yet another major organizational
reshuffling and was eventually reunited in the renamed Ministry of Health and Population Control.

In 1977, a nine-week voluntary sterilization campaign
launched in 150 sites throughout the country resulted in a
total of 65,000 sterilizations and the adoption of sterilization as an official program method. Ninety percent of the
program's fieldworkers--12,227 FWAs and 4,392 FPAs--had by
this time been recruited, trained, and in some fashion, posted.

In mid-1979, the program structure was further modified by
the merger of the program's implementing arm, the Directorate,
with its policy arm, the Division. This constituted the final
absorption, organizationally and on paper at least, of the old
extra-ministerial vertical program and its personnel into the
ministerial program. Deputy secretary positions for implementation were established for each of Bangladesh's four geographical divisions, and greater authority was delegated to the
district-level administrators by upgrading their title to that
of deputy director.

Between 1975 and 1979, the national program established
operational linkages among all governmental and private agencies and laid out a division of labor. Work in the urban areas
was assigned to the existing governmental hospitals, private
clinics, commercial suppliers, and voluntary agencies. The
government program, meanwhile, concentrated on motivation and
service delivery in the rural areas. Local community leaders
and other important opinion-swayers were nominally involved in
the program. The result was a contraceptive prevalence rate
that increased from an estimated 8.0 percent during 1975-76 to
close to 13 percent during 1979. Prevalence rates of even 30
percent and higher were achieved in some areas where intensified projects were operating.

In 1979, the government target was again revised, this
time downward, to the achievement of an NRR of one by 1990.
At the same time, the UNFPA made a second five-year project
commitment, this time for $50 million. Partly because of its
decision to become involved in family planning in China and
partly due to its inability to recruit bilateral donors to help
meet the promised project funding, however, the UNFPA commitment may have to be cut considerably from the ambitious $50
million level.

With the program again at a virtual standstill, the government announced in early 1980 that family planning would again be integrated with health services. This was to be accomplished by brief retraining of fieldworkers and by administrative reorganization. Clinical and nonclinical (or "motivational") activities were to be managed through separate vertical chains of supervision.

At the thana level and below, the thana health administrator (typically a young physician) was placed over the thana family planning officer as a direct supervisor. Health fieldworkers--the village welfare workers from the malaria-smallpox cadre who were given family planning responsibilities in 1974 but subsequently were ignored--were now to be retrained and again required to provide contraceptive services along with health care. At the district level, fieldworkers and supervisors continued to report to the civil surgeon on matters related to health and to the deputy director on population affairs. In Dacca, however, there are two divisions for formal administrative purposes, but only one secretary responsible for both health and population matters.

Integration was no sooner announced than, in May-June 1980, family planning fieldworkers staged a two-month protest strike.

Some field staffers still complained that they had not "integrated" and were unable to do so until they received more explicit and satisfactory details from Dacca as to how such technical problems as supervisory and salary relations were to be resolved.

As a result of strike negotiations and other bureaucratic necessities, costs for 1981 have been estimated at about $30 per continuous user for modern temporary methods; sterilization is estimated at $5 per client. By comparison, annual user costs for nongovernmental organizations are about $10 per user per year and for those buying supplies from the social marketing project about $7 per user.

When it comes to financing for the program, USAID's 1980 evaluation of Bangladesh's national program concludes:

Traditionally the Bangladesh government has not contributed significantly to family planning program costs because of the willingness of foreign donors to support this sector. In the national budgeting process, items that are of little or no interest to international funding agencies have the first call on the government's own resources. Population is an area in which external funds have been abundantly available.

The government has been committed to the program financially, however, even though it has not had to expend large amounts of its own resources and even though it is difficult to isolate precisely the portion that it has financed. . . . In June 1980,

> *the government began to assume financial responsibility for the salaries of 8,000 family welfare assistants (initially funded by the World Bank), which can be taken as a concrete illustration of its commitment to assume costs of parts of the program originally financed by donors.*

Problems and Prognoses

A successful population program, of course, is one that produces a great enough reduction in the population growth rate to clear the way for a better standard of living for the majority of the nation's people through a viable, self-sustaining economy. In Bangladesh, the population and family planning program has not yet had this ultimate impact.

The numbers are not impressive; a contraceptive use prevalence rate of 13 percent in 1981 would indicate failure in almost any other setting. Yet against a backdrop of severe cultural constraints, political upheavals, and organizational vacillations, the program has achieved an increase in contraceptive prevalence from about 8.3 percent of all reproductive-age couples in 1975-76 to about 12.7 percent by mid-1979. And a slight decrease in the crude birth rate from about 47 to 46 per thousand means that an estimated 2.4 million births, an entire year's population increase, were averted during 1976-80.

A strong point in the country's developmental favor is an aware leadership dedicated to the principle of fertility control. Furthermore, contraceptive use levels of more than 30 percent that have been reached by intensive community-based distribution projects demonstrate that much more can be accomplished with the right mix of inputs--supervision, training, community participation, and commodity support. Were a strong system of integrated incentives included in the program, results might be achieved even faster. Such incentives might include, for example, government-subsidized tube-wells for communities achieving a specified overall growth rate, free secondary education for the first two children born to a family, and income-generating projects for women.

The government program's limited effectiveness in promoting and delivering family planning services is due in large measure to the general handicaps under which all Bangladeshi national programs suffer: the grappling for a "right" path in the highly politicized environment of this young nation with its bureaucracies, a weak physical infrastructure, traditional political patronage relationships, and a widespread fatalism among the peasantry expressed in the belief that Allah will provide. The well articulated policy of the top leadership not only suffers from ineffectiveness on the part of bureaucrats charged with implementation, but from disruptions and staff disenchantment caused by repeated reorganizations.

Despite these serious problems, however, the national population control program is generally regarded as one of the most effective of all the Bangladeshi government's programs. A functioning national structure providing family planning services and information is now in place.

President Zia's commitment to population control was both unequivocal and energetic and, among Third World leaders, matched only by the commitment of Indonesia's President Suharto. Zia's zeal also was contagious; nearly equal enthusiasm is evident within the senior ranks of the Planning Commission and the Ministry of Health and Population Control, where the long-term prospects and problems of economic and social development loom in sharp focus. Bangladesh, in fact, is the only country in the world that actually includes the term *population control* in the name of a ministry charged with implementing population programs. And so far at least, General Ershad has promised that his administration will follow Zia's example.

Bangladesh's top-level concern over the nation's population policy is reflected in the following excerpt from the Second Five-Year Plan, 1980-85:

Any meaningful population strategy must involve the notion that fertility will decline drastically and that decline cannot be delayed. Thus, the only recourse open to us is to vigorously pursue the policy of achieving NRR=1 by 1990. Experiences of other countries faced with similar circumstances show that such drastic reduction of fertility has not been achieved. But only by tracing a path that might appear today unachievable, can we hope to provide a future that has some sense at all. Certain unique factors present possibilities for a vigorous and successful population programme. These are:

(a) Population problem has been recognized as the number one problem of the nation and family planning programme has gained highest political support;

(b) The government has committed itself to allocate required resources for population control activities along with agriculture and energy sectors;

(c) The land-to-man ratio has led to such a critical condition of extreme poverty that majority of people become compelled to control fertility for sheer survival;

(d) People seem to be ready for rapid change, social mobilization, economic development, and fertility control; and

(e) Studies show that there is an unmet demand for family planning to the extent of 30-40 percent of the fertile couples.

*The nation is faced with the challenge of meeting
these unique opportunities with a vigorous, pragmatic
and unconventional population policy with a view to
achieving this optimistic population target.*

The above policy ranks, with that of the People's Republic
of China, as the most forthright, vigorous, and ambitious of
any nation in the world. But to assume that Bangladesh is
indeed ready for rapid change is presumptuous at this stage.
The program may not even be feasible without restructuring
social and economic policies. Although traditional opposition
to family planning and fertility control is still strong in
the countryside at a local community level, it no longer
appears to be an inhibiting factor to the formulation of
national population policy. Furthermore, opposition parties
have not made an issue of the necessity for fertility control.
A comparable commitment, however, is yet to be widely
internalized throughout the other parts of the government,
including even the Ministry of Health and Population Control.
Efforts are under way to gain the support of such critical
bodies as the Ministries of Agriculture, Education, Information,
and Broadcasting and Home Affairs. But the service structure
of the Ministry of Health and Population Control, although
increasingly strong and better staffed, is not yet fully
energized to carry out the ambitious task set for it by the
central government.
The task, in fact, may indeed be too ambitious, or at
least may appear to be so. Virtually all development goals
adopted by the government of Bangladesh under President Zia
were intentionally set high--in many cases, unrealistically
high--in the belief that this would act to prod people toward
more realistic goals. The government's ambitious population
growth reduction goals are certainly a case in point: they
are almost certainly unachievable in the time frame given.
Because these goals are perceived to be unrealistic, service
delivery staff tend to ignore them. Fieldworkers do not take
the targets assigned to them very seriously. In fact, not one
of the fieldworkers has been fired for not achieving his/her
target. And, as the 1980 USAID evaluation report points out,

*to the extent that actual economic planning and
investment decisions are based on these unrealistic
assumptions and projections of population change,
serious misallocations of resources would result, and
the entire development planning mechanism could become distorted, proven faulty, and, over time, lose
credibility.*

Field personnel are not only demoralized by seemingly
unreachable goals and a history of organizational instability,
they tend to be confused when it comes to distinguishing

between "cumulative new acceptors" and "current users" (or prevalence). This contributes to a major shortcoming of the national program, the lack of adequate attention to increasing the numbers of actual contraceptive users.

Too often the recruitment of new acceptors is given nearly exclusive priority, while follow-up activities are neglected. Related to this is the serious and almost universal underestimation at all field levels of current population size and, hence, of the number of reproductive-age couples to be targeted by the program.

One must rely on what service delivery records are kept and on the personal observations of both internal and foreign assessment personnel--a particular problem for the program's major donors, USAID, UNFPA, and the World Bank, who must back up their support with statistics.

The three major outside donors, however, generally receive extremely high marks from both high-level Bangladeshis and foreign observers for their innovative support and effort coordination. In fact, without financial and technical assistance from USAID, which remains the program's principal donor with a support budget of about $65 million for 1981-83, the nationwide delivery of family planning services and the introduction of pills and sterilization undoubtedly would never have gotten off the ground. USAID and its Dacca population staff have been criticized only for their failure to provide a choice of oral contraceptives and for impeding Bangladesh's attempts to meet the active demand for abortion, a service that often serves as a means of introducing more practical, but equally effective, contraception.

USAID is now seeking to introduce a variety of oral contraceptive brands into the program. As for abortion, however, current and strictly enforced laws and regulations prevent any U.S. government agency from providing any assistance whatsoever in the area of abortion.

Commodity Management and Training Weaknesses

On the Bangladeshi side, commodity management suffers from inadequate attention at all levels. As of November 1980, the position of the deputy director for materials procurement in the Ministry of Health and Population Control had been vacant for more than 12 months. Moreover, there was a severe lack of experienced central staff. District and thana supply levels were less than adequate and remain so; less than one month's supply is often available, and funds are frequently unavailable for transport of stocks from district warehouses to thana storerooms. The result is that the three central warehouses are periodically filled beyond capacity, and it is often impossible to remove older stocks because they are literally buried beneath more recently received shipments.

The inadequate training of field personnel further hampers program effectiveness. Some 1,500 family welfare visitors (FWVs), clinic-based female MCH paramedics, serve as the major clinical support group in the sterilization program and are also responsible for IUD insertions. While these FWVs, who have completed an 18-month course beyond the equivalent of a tenth-grade education, have a considerable factual knowledge, they receive so little actual clinical experience during their training that they are unable to do the tasks required of them.

The delivery system's major weakness, however, is in the training and performance of its vital fieldworkers. The training of these FWAs, FPAs, and FWWs has been seriously lacking in both practical and motivational aspects. Moreover, their supervision is so halfhearted that they have virtually lost their effectiveness as family planning promoters and pill and condom distributors.

Private Population Programs

Over 100 private and voluntary organizations lend their administrative talents and enthusiasm to Bangladesh's population effort. Some of these organizations, as described below, are notable for their enhancement of community participation in family planning and equal services.

The Bangladesh Association for Voluntary Sterilization (BAVS), which is supported by the International Project of the Association for Voluntary Sterilization, is currently expanding its operations from 22 to 24 clinics. With more than 200,000 sterilizations to its credit by the end of 1983, the BAVS has clearly demonstrated the acceptability of this contraceptive method, and the high quality of its clinical service has set a standard for expanded governmental voluntary sterilization services throughout the country. As a result, the Bangladeshi government counts heavily on BAVS for sterilization training of government physicians and as a model of patient screening, evaluation of preoperative sedative regimens and postoperative care.

The previously mentioned Family Planning Social Marketing Project opened its doors in 1976 for the commercial sale of pills and condoms at highly subsidized and therefore highly affordable prices. Supported by Population Services International, the project operates through a network of 26 wholesalers who stock over 60,000 retail outlets throughout the country. From a 1976 sales level of approximately 9.7 million condoms and 480,000 cycles of pills, annual sales increased to a November 1979–October 1980 total of more than 35 million condoms, 585,000 cycles of pills, 4 million foam tablets, and 43,000 cycles of Ovacon^R low-dose pills introduced in June 1980. As of October 1980, the project had provided 438,000 couple-years of protection—a growth of 314 percent. And the project's

future plans include branching out into the sale of such MCH
products as oral rehydration salts to counteract the dehydration
caused by diarrhea, a major contributor to infant mortality.

Family Planning International Assistance (FPIA) was established in Bangladesh in 1976 as a regional office. From the
very beginning, however, much of its work has been devoted to
the support of activities within Bangladesh itself.

An example of FPIA innovation was its National Doctor
Project under which 5,000 "national doctors" (primary health-
care workers given special training in India) were to be prepared to do vasectomies. Although national doctors are a step
below physicians with MBBS degrees (the lowest degree of
specialization for practicing physicians in the British medical
system), they tend to have busy private practices at the union
level and are therefore in a good position to promote and
provide contraceptive services. However, motivational problems,
inadequate instruction, and too few cases for adequate practical
training resulted in the training of only 380 such doctors.

Concerned Women for Family Planning (CWFP) is a voluntary
organization started in Dacca by a small group of women from
the United States who, through their experience with smallpox
and cholera campaigns and a child-feeding program, were able to
pinpoint women who were eager to practice family planning,
including voluntary sterilization. CWFP was originally based
in the founders' own homes. Advice was given on available
clinic facilities, transportation was provided to clinics, and
oral contraceptives were distributed at the neighborhood level
on a one-to-one basis. As the program expanded, volunteer
residents in new neighborhoods were enlisted as family planning
agents and their homes as supply points for contraceptives.
And CWFP continues to encourage all women interested in family
planning to begin neighborhood distribution programs in their
own homes and to become actively involved in working in family
planning centers and in the frank and open discussion of family
planning methods and merits.

The Pathfinder Fund's work in Bangladesh has been particularly effective because its country director, a highly respected
Bangladeshi, knows the country well and has close and good
working relations with principal population and family planning
officials. In addition to carrying out regular family planning
activities with USAID funding, Pathfinder also uses non-AID
funds to support nine abortion service and training activities
with the tacit approval of the Bangladeshi government.

From these Pathfinder "model menstrual regulation (abortion)
clinics," clients desiring sterilization are referred to medical
college outpatient clinics, where sterilizations are performed
by physicians--many of whom are women--who are also experienced
at doing abortions. Although this system has proven acceptable,
Pathfinder's work in the abortion-sterilization area is nevertheless hampered by the problem of obtaining funding for sterilization following abortion. Because the U.S. government prohibits

the use of AID funds for abortion, Pathfinder scrupulously maintains separate accounts for the segregation of family planning and abortion-related activities.

Contraceptive Acceptance

In a vaccination program some deaths will occur. Such deaths in mass innoculation programs usually can be traced to hepatitis from dirty needles, from a breakdown in refrigeration necessary for vaccine effectiveness, or from the inability of a few recipients to tolerate the vaccine itself. The launching of such a public health campaign, therefore, is based on the formulation of relative-risk hypotheses which, in turn, are based on former programs and perfected on accumulated experience.

Similarly, the concept of relative risk has been used for more than a decade in large-scale family planning programs; the basic, incontrovertible fact is that far more women die from unwanted pregnancies than from the side effects of contraception. The following Bangladesh mortality data are illustrative of considerations of relative risk for alternative family planning methods, particularly sterilization:

Mortality Rate per 10,000 Cases (approximate)

Childbirth	70
Abortion (folk methods)	250
Sterilization (female)	2
Sterilization (male)	3

Source: USAID 1981.

In other words, childbirth in Bangladesh is at least 35 times more hazardous than female sterilization (tubal ligation). And when one considers that the average woman who accepts voluntary sterilization would have two or three more children if she remained unprotected, the relative risk in favor of widespread sterilization availability increases dramatically.

Although sterilization promises to make a significant contribution to family planning in Bangladesh, it must be pointed out that the method is typically accepted by contraceptive users who already have an average of 4+ children. Sterilization does not address the other 80 percent of women, most of whom are in the prime reproductive ages of 20 to 29.

THE ECONOMIC PICTURE

Economic development in Bangladesh is hampered by a severely limited resource base and a vastly underdeveloped physical and social structure. The major problem, however, is the nation's virtually unrestrained birth rate.

Extreme poverty, reflected in widespread malnutrition and low per capita incomes averaging $100 per year in terms of GDP, inhibits savings and capital formation. A severe dearth of skilled labor power limits the country's managerial capacity and labor-force productivity. An illiteracy rate of 80 percent constrains the dissemination of knowledge that could lead to improved technology. An increasingly intolerable burden of overpopulation underlies high rates of unemployment, under-employment, and landlessness; whatever economic growth is achieved is immediately absorbed.

Bangladesh has always been, and continues to be, an agrarian society. The relative economic importance of industry and services has risen somewhat in recent years, but agriculture still accounts for well over half of the nation's GDP, provides employment for more than three-quarters of the labor force, and directly or indirectly accounts for over 90 percent of the country's exports.

During 1980, government revenues increased considerably more than expenditures, resulting in a Tk 1.7 billion (about $106 million at the 1980 rate of 16 takas per U.S. dollar) increase in the current surplus. This, however, was accompanied by a net erosion in the financial position of public enter-prises and corporation, by a very large (Tk 2.4 billion, or $150 million) increase in the capital account of the food budget, consisting of food import costs and loan repayments, and by a substantial (Tk 1.7 billion, or $106 million) shortfall in commodity aid receipts. Consequently, the large 32 percent increase in development expenditure was sustained only due to the government's unplanned deficit financing of Tk 2.9 billion ($181 million), equivalent to 9.0 percent of total government expenditure.*

Bangladesh's 1980 budgetary problems stemmed primarily from the necessity to import large volumes of food grains to counter-act crop losses due to drought in 1979 and to feed its burgeon-ing population. In addition, the government's lag in adjusting domestic petroleum prices to the higher international prices resulted in large World Bank-financed subsidies for energy. The total level of subsidies of petroleum and food grains increased from 1.3 percent of GDP in 1979 to 3.2 percent of GDP in 1980. At the same time, World Bank financing of the overall 1980 budgetary deficit amounted to Tk 2.9 billion ($181 mil-lion), while the petroleum subsidy came to nearly Tk 1.5 billion ($93 million).

Food transactions clearly overshadowed other developments in the nation's budget, and together with increased oil prices

---

*Unless otherwise specified, all statistics in this section are from World Bank (1981).

and costs and declining jute goods prices caused further
deterioration in the nation's balance of payments. In 1980,
Bangladesh's balance-of-payments deficit rose sharply to
nearly Tk 25.6 billion ($1.6 billion or 13.5 percent of GDP)
from a deficit level of Tk 12.8 billion ($800 million or 9.0
percent of GDP) in 1979. At the end of 1980, the country had
cash reserves equivalent to only about one month's imports.
Meanwhile, export earnings were projected to grow by only 5.0
percent, whereas imports were expected to rise by about 12
percent.

THE AGRICULTURAL SECTOR

Farming throughout the world is a gamble with nature. In
Bangladesh, however, where food storage facilities are inadequate and food distribution schemes often don't deliver, the
outcome of that gamble can become a life or death matter for
millions of people. The nation's vulnerability to the vagaries
of weather was apparent during the devastating cyclone of 1970.
In 1979, the nation's croplands were again devastated, this
time by drought.

The drought of 1979 was both unusually severe and prolonged;
for successive rice crops were direly affected. *Aman* (long-
stemmed, deep-water rice) and *boro* (dry-season rice) crops fell
well below 1978 output levels, while fishery yields fell by 28
percent. The 1980 *aus* (short-stemmed rice grown during the dry
season) and aman crops also were depressed as a result of the
drought. Although inadequate diesel fuel deliveries to farmers
using tubewells and low-lift pumps were major contributors to
the poor boro harvest of 1979, the crop recovered in the winter
of 1980 and, in fact, boro and wheat both produced record yields
that year. However, the combination of drought and poor farm-
input management meant that agricultural value added rose by
barely 0.5 percent for 1980 as a whole, while the population
was growing by 2.7 percent. The hungry nation again faced
starvation.

The government of Bangladesh was forced to act quickly to
avert widespread famine. Near minimum levels of grain consumption were maintained, and severely depleted grain stocks
were rebuilt by the importation of 2.7 million tons of food
grains during 1980. The nation's grain storage capacity, which
was never great enough to hold the reserves necessary to feed
the country's burgeoning population during poor crop years, was
becoming strained. And then the rains came.

The 1980 monsoon not only came early, it was extraordinarily
heavy and long as well. Severe regional flooding caused aus
crop losses in some districts. The overall effect of the heavy
rain and flooding, however, was beneficial. With grain production for 1981 beginning to top the 1980 level by 12-13 percent,
the government found itself in the midst of a bewildering grain

glut. After two years of domestic food grain output that fell
far behind population growth, grain supplies suddenly overran
storage capacity.

Surface and groundwater supplies were again ample, and
the number of tubewells and low-lift pumps in use increased.
Fuel supplies for pumps, seeds, and fertilizers were again
available in quantities large enough to substantially increase
planted acreage. The result was that the total food grain
production for 1981 was projected to reach some 15.05 million
tons, only slightly below the 15.4 million-ton target set by
the government for that year.

There is, however, cause for concern about Bangladesh's
prospects for maintaining this growth. During 1984 the margin
between government grain purchase prices and farm production
costs appeared to be adequate to provide the incentive necessary for increased production. To keep production incentive
up, the government is forced into the position of procuring as
much food grain as is physically possible and turning increasing budgetary resources to the construction of storage facilities. In addition to capital, this takes time.

Although the World Bank made a new loan of $40 million to
Bangladesh in May of 1981 for a four-year project in agricultural development, the country's agricultural picture is
framed by factors beyond the nation's control. Weather conditions, which swing in varying degrees from monsoon flooding to
drought, are the most obvious and most unpredictable constraints
to viable agricultural planning. Deteriorating watershed
conditions, however, are now beginning to loom ominously and
indeed could, by the year 2000, be the most significant environmental problem facing the nation. Bangladesh is dependent
on water running off the Himalayan watershed. However, should
growing population pressures in Nepal and the Indian state of
Assam continue to lead to large-scale removal of trees in
those fuel-deficient areas, Bangladesh could be subject to
even more frequent and damaging floods that would threaten both
agricultural productivity and the physical safety of large
portions of its population.

A severe watershed crisis did occur, in fact, in 1976 when
India withdrew enormous amounts of watershed in the Ganges to
flush out industrial waste sludge accumulated in the port of
Calcutta. The fact that this was done during the dry season,
when the water was needed in Bangladesh for irrigation, was of
little interest to its gigantic neighbor.

The government of Bangladesh is fighting an uphill battle
with government subsidies on food grains and agricultural
inputs, particularly fertilizer. While the historical jute
subsidy was virtually eliminated in 1980 by the increase in
international jute goods prices that year, food grain and
fertilizer subsidies remain stubbornly entrenched. Although
the government has managed to reduce these subsidies through
successive upward adjustments in prices, the need for increased

food production following the 1979 drought and substantial
increases in international fertilizer prices have precluded
drastic reductions in subsidies.

While the food grain subsidy presented in the budget is
somewhat misleading since it does not include subsidization
effected by donor agency soft-currency loans for the commercial
importation of food grains or food-surplus imports from the
United States under U.S. PL 480, the economic subsidy mentioned
above takes these factors into account. Similarly, the fertilizer subsidy shown in the government's budget is understated
since the purchase price for domestically produced fertilizer
does not fully reflect the real cost of either the capital or
natural gas feed stock used in the domestic production of urea
fertilizer.

Land Ownership and Farm Employment

The poorest of the poor in Bangladesh are among the most
deprived people on earth. The Bangladesh Land Occupancy Survey
taken in 1978 showed that 54 percent of rural Bangladeshis
were attached to households that owned no arable land. Moreover, nearly half of all landholdings were of less than one
acre. Only 29 percent of Bangladesh's cultivatable land is
directly owner-cultivated and dependent primarily on family
labor; the rest is sharecropped or cultivated by hired laborers. Tenancy is, at best, unstable since tenants can be turned
off their land at the whim of their landlords. Furthermore,
tenants are usually expected to pay for all agricultural inputs
and still hand over from 50 to 66 percent of their crops to
landlords.

The implications are striking even for a poor country; the
highly skewed land ownership pattern means that a few rich
families benefit inordinately from agricultural production.
According to the Land Occupancy Survey, about 14 percent of
the households owned 85 percent of the land. This situation
is heightened by agriculture ministry studies which found that
some landowners had more than 200 acres, even though the official ceiling is 30 acres.

Local politics are based on a series of patron-client
relationships. The landless have no say in politics, and can
only hope that their patrons win and that benefits—foremost
among them is employment—will therefore trickle down to them.
As their numbers increase, democracy moves further and further
from the reach of the illiterate, landless masses. A poor
harvest plunges marginal families into the depths of despera-
tion. They fall even further into debt, and distress sales of
their land increase; parts of their meager landholdings often
must be sold just to buy the family's next meal. Over the
past few years, distress sales of land have been continuing
at a rate that increases the numbers of landless people by five
percent each year.

This situation is desperately serious since land is the only basis of livelihood for the vast majority of rural Bangladeshis. Unlike wealthier Asian countries, there is relatively little off-farm employment available. Many landless people thus either remain in the countryside, hoping to get enough day labor at harvest time and off-season odd jobs to sustain life the rest of the year, or they drift to the towns on the chance of finding work as a rickshaw-puller or knick-knack seller. Although the cities are unable to absorb this steady migratory flow, it has kept the rate of unemployment (including seasonal underemployment) at about the 30 to 35 percent of the rural work force that it was in 1971.

With the rate of rural unemployment stabilized, however, the rate of rural employment is on the rise. Given that Bangladesh's population is headed toward a total of 150 million or more by the year 2000, the numbers of desperately poor will be astronomical and disaster a certainty unless drastic, swift steps are taken. These must include an equalization of incomes and the encouragement of all Bangladeshis to feel they have a genuine stake in their country and to plan their families and futures accordingly.

The Jute Market

Energy-deficient Bangladesh's balance of payments hinges to an extraordinary degree on its one major export crop, jute. In 1979, raw jute production reached a record high of 6.7 million bales, and about the same amount was produced again in 1980. World demand for raw jute suffered, however, from the world recession. Moreover, while the prolonged drought of 1979 did not affect jute quantity, it did affect its quality: at least 55 percent of the crop was extremely poor grade.

The jute export picture was further complicated by a vast surplus of carryover stocks amounting to 2.3 million bales; depressed foreign and domestic markets were unable to absorb the additional supply. The result was that in 1980, raw jute exports were locked into the 1979 level of 1.97 million bales.

Efforts to step up the production of such jute goods as sacking, which use lower quality jute, were thwarted by power shortages and labor strikes. In the face of these difficulties, the production of goods from low-grade jute did top the 1979 level by 22,000 tons. But the world market was unable to absorb even this small production increase. And, while jute goods exports actually declined by 18,000 tons in 1980, jute goods stocks rose considerably, and raw jute stocks reached a record level of 3.6 million bales.

The depressed market caused farmgate prices on raw jute to fall to less than half of the official minimum market price in some areas. As a relief measure in the most severely affected areas, the public jute companies purchased some 0.4

million bales of low-quality jute at an official discounted
price and additional credit was extended to private jute buyers.
Although these measures helped some growers to unload their
crops and kept raw jute prices from plunging even further for
a large proportion of growers, relief was nowhere in sight.

Forced by financial and storage considerations to suspend
its price support policy in July 1980 and stuck with enormous
stocks of low-grade jute, the government faced another problem:
farmers reacted to falling jute prices by severe cutbacks in
land area planted with jute. The decrease from 1.87 million
acres sown to jute in 1980 to 1.35 million acres in 1981,
combined with late sowing and waterlogging, resulted in a 1981
jute crop that produced only 4.2 million bales. However, the
1981 crop quality was much higher than in the two previous
years, prices recovered, and the door was opened to an experiment in free enterprise.

Public jute corporations were freed to pursue a flexible
jute purchasing policy. Although they were required to give
priority to purchases from border areas (to reduce smuggling)
and from jute growers' cooperatives aimed at concentrating
cultivation under the Intensive Jute Cultivation Scheme, the
corporations were allowed for the first time to buy the
quantities and grades they needed at free market prices. Without effective market pricing support and stabilization to reduce
market uncertainties and provide production incentives, however,
the future of the 3 million small jute cultivators remains precarious.

Agricultural Inputs and Infrastructure

Agricultural growth in Bangladesh is heavily dependent
upon the development of the nearly nonexistent agricultural and
rural infrastructure and on the vastly increased availability
and utilization of modern farm inputs. The job is formidable
and costly, particularly in light of the government bureaucracy's ineptitude and lethargy. Farmers, however, are making
strong demands for modern agricultural inputs and, although
uneven, some significant progress has been made over the past
five years (1977-82).

Annual Development Program allocations for agricultural
development, including rural development and water and flood
control, increased from Tk 3.5 billion ($219 million) in 1978
to Tk 4.7 billion ($294 million) in 1979 and to Tk 6.7 billion
($419 million) in 1980. In 1980, however, a mere 27 percent of
the year's total development expenditure was actually spent on
agricultural development. This was well below the 34 percent
average for 1973-75 and even below the 28 percent average for
1978-79. For 1981, the government allocated Tk 8.4 billion
($525 million) for agriculture in an effort to reverse this
expenditure lag trend.

A significant, if uneven, increase has been achieved in the number of modern irrigation facilities made operational. The number of tubewells operated under the Bangladesh Agricultural Development Corporation (BADC) has grown considerably: deep tubewells more than doubled and shallow tubewells nearly quadrupled between 1977 and 1980. There was, however, a slow-down in the rate of tubewell installation in 1980 due partly to heavy monsoon flooding that year. The number of low-lift pumps fielded, however, increased only from 23,400 pumps in 1977 to 38,600 in 1980. And low-lift pumps are the irrigation backbone of this low-lying country.

Meanwhile, greater attention to maintenance, fuel delivery, and prime area development has paid off in an overall improve-ment in irrigation efficiency: the total acreage irrigated by BADC equipment during 1977-80 increased by nearly 70 percent. At current prices, the demand for irrigation equipment is high; if the government succeeds in providing adequate credit and reducing distribution lags, availabilities should improve markedly.

In the past, the other government organization involved in water development, the Bangladesh Water Development Board (BWDB), concentrated on large-scale flood control, drainage, and gravity irrigation schemes which are capital-intensive and require long gestation periods. With World Bank support, how-ever, the BWDB began in 1979 to stress smaller, low-cost-per-acre, short-gestation projects. Some large irrigation schemes are now also operating, and the acreage irrigated by BWDB gravity schemes increased two and a half times from 1977, to 240,000 acres in 1980.

Fertilizer consumption has grown rapidly in recent years, and more than doubled between 1978 and 1981. Despite this progress, however, many severe problems remain.

Fertilizer distribution and application rates are extremely uneven among regions, partly because of the lack of accessibil-ity to transport facilities. Even more critical are the rigidities and supply bottlenecks prevalent in the centralized marketing system operated by BADC. Because of this, the government moved in 1979 to put fertilizer distribution at the wholesale level into the private sector. As a consequence, BADC now operates in most cases from intermediate-level primary distribution points, while private traders handle retail and local wholesale distribution. So far the results from this shift have been favorable. Not so favorable, however, has been the distribution of pesticides, which has been handled entirely by the private sector.

The past failure of government delivery systems to guaran-tee the ready availability of inputs has severely hampered the dissemination of green revolution high-yield technology that could markedly increase agricultural production both by increas-ing crop outputs and allowing for crop rotation. The avail-ability of seeds, however, is no longer the problem it was in the past, due to heavy imports of wheat seed early in 1981.

Balance-of-Trade Problems

The Government of Bangladesh counts heavily on foreign
donor assistance when making up its annual budgets. But a
realistic look at future donor potential would find a need
for extreme caution. Unless Bangladesh's developmental plans
are pulled more firmly into line with the nation's own
resources and management is upgraded enormously to remove
obstacles to program implementation and greatly reduce waste,
those plans are surely doomed to failure. And unless the
nation as a whole is made to realize that its future depends
on an immediate and drastic reduction in its population
growth rate and on sweeping social reforms, the nation's very
existence cannot be viewed with anything but pessimism.

THE INDUSTRIAL SECTOR

The Bangladeshi leadership's desperate attempts to vital-
ize national development are nowhere so apparent and so
ineffective as in the country's small manufacturing sector
and miniscule mining subsector. A flurry of costly short-term
actions has resulted in industrial activity which in 1980-81
accounted for only 8.0 percent of GDP. And the industrial
forecast for the immediate future is not much brighter.

Most of the present industrial sector was built up following independence, when some 28 percent of the nation's total
investment capital was funneled into industry. From the very
beginning, however, such industrial incentives as an over-
valued exchange rate and high tariff barriers led to serious
distortions in the sector's actual development, particularly
in the late 1960s. Although the newly independent government
nationalized about 85 percent of industrial capital assets,
poor management, the loss of markets, and shortages of raw
materials during the early 1970s caused a marked deterioration
in capital utilization and labor productivity. At the same
time, the remaining private sector, hampered by an overbearing
bureaucracy, was unwilling to invest its dwindling resources
in industry.

In 1975 the government began to redefine its approach to
industrial development. A liberalization of the foreign
exchange situation has ensured that imported raw materials are
made available to the private sector. Financial limits on the
size of individual projects in the private sector have been
increased, and the scope of sectors open to private investment
has been expanded; private investment is now permitted in the
cotton textile industry, for example. The availability of
term financing to the private sector also has increased but,
although investment approval procedures have been simplified,
they are still excessively cumbersome and still tend to favor
public enterprises over the private sector, particularly in
the allocation of import licenses.

In 1980, the level of public industrial investment was roughly three times that of private investment. Public investment, however, was dominated by a small number of large-scale, long-gestation projects in the fertilizer and engineering sectors. More than 65 percent of all public industrial investment between 1976 and 1981 was concentrated in five major import substitution projects: the Ashuganj Fertilizer Factory, the Bangladesh Machine Tools Factory, the Chittagong Drydock and Heavy Steel Structure, the General Electric Manufacturing Plant, and the Insulator and Sanitary Ware Factory.

A World Bank study found that some of these investments, particularly those in the engineering sector, were poorly conceived and resulted in an enormous waste of investable resources. The concentration of resources in large-scale projects also meant that many long needed investments to improve capacity utilization and productivity within existing plants were unduly postponed.

Both public and private industrial investment is still heavily oriented toward the domestic market. And, although earnings from nontraditional exports (those other than jute and tea) have grown rapidly due to favorable prices, increases in volume have been relatively small due to inadequate incentives and insufficient investments in export-oriented sectors. On the one hand, there has been progressive improvement in governmental policies toward the private sector and efforts made to improve operational efficiency within existing public enterprises. On the other hand, the public investment program has not been geared to raising actual productivity or preparing for long-range industrial export goals.

Against this backdrop, the government of Bangladesh in 1981 committed itself to a new five-year plan aimed at: (a) expanding the domestic production of essential "basic needs" (such as cloth and bicycles) and mass consumption commodities; (b) providing for the domestic manufacture of inputs necessary to achieve major plan targets in other sectors, including self-sufficiency in food grains and the spread of rural electrification; (c) maximizing the use of local raw materials and natural resources; (d) creating wider employment opportunities and promoting balanced regional development through the promotion of small-scale, labor-intensive rural industries; and (e) improving the balance-of-payments position by accelerating the growth of export-oriented and import-substituting industries.

Laudable as these highly ambitious objectives are, the seemingly long-range goals of the new five-year plan are actually built on a short-term base. The public investment program remains oriented almost entirely toward the domestic market, and it includes some highly capital-intensive projects whose economic profitability is questionable and whose source, the foreign assistance community, is not a guaranteed constant

over the long term. The plan's overwhelming emphasis on a
domestic market is also viewed by outside economists as
inappropriate; the fact is, the domestic market in the impoverished country is extremely limited.

As it stands now, the industrial sector, despite massive
resource inputs, is not expected to become a leading sector
of the economy. In fact, the energy expended in wasteful and
apparently misguided industrial rehabilitation and expansion
is viewed by many as leading to the further postponement of
the nation's primary long-range needs, including food self-
sufficiency, that eventually must be met by the nation's own
self-generated resources.

SURVIVAL: A QUESTION MARK

The reality of Bangladesh is harsh. It is so energy
deficient that, despite abundant potential supplies of natural
gas estimated at about 7 trillion cubic feet (the equivalent
of 160 million tons of oil), it must import all of the oil
and liquid petroleum products it consumes which amounted to
about two-thirds of its 1981 export earnings. With its malnourished population growing at the enormous rate of 2.7 percent per year, it is questionable whether the foreign donor
community, lured to Bangladesh by the personal energy and
charisma of the late President Zia, will continue to supply
funding.

The young nation is groping for answers to its age-old
problems. But time is not on Bangladesh's side. In an
increasingly energy- and power-hungry world where the most
affluent nations are compassionless, Bangladesh's continuing
failure to reduce its birth rate, to feed and educate its
people, to overhaul its development-stifling social structure,
could very well spell total economic, social, and political
collapse in the not very distant future. Bangladesh's future
and the very survival of the majority of its people depend on
the will of its population to address and redress economic
and social problems.

REFERENCES

Alauddin, Mohammad. 1980. *Socio-Economic Determinants of
     Fertility in Bangladesh: A Review.* Dacca: Institute of
     Social Welfare and Research, University of Dacca.

Cain, Mead T. 1977a. *Economic Class, Economic Mobility, and
     the Developmental Cycle of Household: A Case Study in
     Rural Bangladesh.* Dacca: Bangladesh Institute of Develop-
     ment Studies.

———. 1977b. "The Economic Activities of Children in a Village in Bangladesh (Char Gopalpur)." *Population and Development Review* 3, no. 3.

Cain, Mead, A.B.M. Mozumder, and Khorshed Alam. *Labor Market Structure, Child Employment, and Reproductive Behavior in Rural South Asia*. Population Council Center for Policy Working Paper, no. 56. New York: Population Council.

Chaudhury, Rafiqul Huda. 1978. "Female Status and Fertility Behaviour in a Metropolitan Urban Area of Bangladesh." In *Population Studies*. Dacca.

Encyclopaedia Britannica. 1977. 15th Ed.

Gomes, Louisa B. 1980. "Changing Role of Women in Bangladesh." Report on works on women in Bangladesh, 1973–79, prepared for USAID/Dacca.

Hong, Sawon. 1980. *Demographic Characteristics of Bangladesh*. Dacca.

International Statistical Institute. 1979. *The Bangladesh Fertility Survey, 1975——A Summary of Findings*. World Fertility Survey. The Hague.

Jansen, William H. 1978. *Profiles of Poverty in Bangladesh: A Preliminary Report*. Dacca: USAID.

Javillonar, Gloria, Lanric Zivetz, Susan Thompson, and Janet Griffith. 1979. *Rural Development, Women's Roles in Fertility in Developing Countries; Review of the Literature*. Raleigh, North Carolina: Research Triangle Institute and South East Consortium for International Development.

Maloney, Clarence, K.M. Ashraful Aziz, and Profulla C. Sarker. 1980. *Beliefs and Fertility in Bangladesh*. Dacca: Institute of Bangladesh Studies, Rajshahi University.

Marum, Elizabeth. 1981. *Women in Food for Work in Bangladesh*. Dacca: USAID.

National Research Council, Committee on Population and Demography. 1981. *Estimation of Recent Trends in Fertility and Mortality in Bangladesh*. Washington, D.C.: National Academy Press.

Palmore, James A., and Mercedes B. Concepcion. 1981. "Desired Family Size and Contraceptive Use: An 11-Country Comparison." *International Family Planning Perspectives* (New York: The Alan Guttmacher Institute) 7, no. 1.

Population Reference Bureau. 1980. *Population Data Sheet: Family Planning & Marriage, 1970–1980*. Washington, D.C.

———. 1981. *1981 Population Data Sheet*. Washington, D.C.

Rafferty, Kevin. 1980. "Bangladesh." *1979 Asia and Pacific Annual Review*. Singapore.

Schidlovsky, John. 1981. "Victor in Bangladesh Faces Herculean Task." *The Sun* (Baltimore), November 17, 1981.

Stoeckel, J., A.K.M. Chowdhury, and M. Alauddin. 1979. *Fertility and Socio-Economic Status in Rural Bangladesh: Differentials and Linkage*. Population Council Center for Policy Working Paper, no. 8. New York: Population Council.

USAID. 1980. *U.S. Assistance to the Family Planning and Population Program in Bangladesh, 1972–1980*. Report of a program evaluation carried out by Barbara L. K. Pillsbury, Lenni W. Kangas, and Alan J. Margolis, October 27–November 22, 1980.

U.S. Council on Environmental Quality and Department of State. 1981. *The Global 2000 Report to the President*. Washington, D.C.

Westinghouse. 1980. *Bangladesh Contraceptive Prevalence Survey*. Dacca.

World Bank. 1981. *Current Economic Situation and Review of the Second Plan*. Vols. 2 and 3 of *Bangladesh*. Washington, D.C.

Chapter 5

Mexico:
The Population-Energy Symbiosis

THE POTENTIAL FOR CONFLICT

In 1980, the United States opened its doors to a total of 808,000 legal immigrants and refugees. That same year, from 800,000 to 1 million Mexican nationals entered the country clandestinely. Although it is impossible to tally numbers that do not exist, estimates on the number of illegal aliens now in the United States run from 8 to 12 million. An estimated 65 to 75 percent of these are Mexican citizens. With high inflation and unemployment, much of the current public demand for immigration reform is focused on the Mexican-American border.

For more than a century there has been a continuous flow of Mexican emigrants to the United States. As the numbers of legal and illegal immigrants have swelled over the years, so have the social, economic, and political problems that accompany massive population shifts. For 60 years, people in the United States have become increasingly concerned about their government's inability to enforce equitable immigration controls; over the past decade, public and governmental debate over effective and humane remedies for illegal immigration from Mexico has intensified. What is needed, however, is an honest appraisal of the underlying causes of the problem on both sides of the border. It is no more realistic for the United States to view illegal immigration as a problem rooted only in Mexico than it is for Mexicans to view the solutions to their problems as lying north of the border.

Embarrassment shared by these governments threatens to cripple relations between the two countries. Mexico, with its increasingly dualistic society, is burdened by a rapidly growing population. The outward migration of large numbers of its unemployed and underemployed people has become necessary for the maintenance of political stability. Furthermore, money

earned in the United States has become a life-sustaining source
of income for many families in the central plateau region in
which the vast majority of Mexican migration originates.

The United States, on the other hand, is anxious to maintain its preferred customer standing with Pemex, the Mexican
government's oil monopoly, and needs Mexico's cooperation in
policing drug and other criminal traffic. Moreover, the United
States has relied on Mexican migrant labor for harvesting its
fruit and vegetable crops. Both nations depend on American
grain surpluses--Mexico to feed its increasing population and
the United States to ease its balance-of-trade deficit with
local export dollars.

The problem of illegal immigration is at once startlingly
simple and extraordinarily complex. The Mexicans come because
they see temporary or permanent residence in the United States
as the only way out of an accelerating cycle of poverty in
their own country; they come because they see emigration as the
only way to secure a better life for themselves and their
families. They come because they have no place else to go.

The underlying causes of migration and the dangerous
dilemmas it poses for both Mexico and the United States, however, are as complex as human nature itself. Impoverished
Mexicans, imbued with the belief that large families can be
equated with economic and social security, have moved into a
deepening pit of poverty. By overpopulating their land, they
have smothered their means of sustainability. Similarly,
people in the United States, imbued with the belief that energy
equates with GNP, have industrialized themselves into a state
of increasing expectations. By building their society on the
massive consumption of no-longer cheap or plentiful fossil
fuels, they have polluted their environment and made their life
style rather precarious.

MIGRATION AS A WAY OF LIFE

In the 1880s, when the first major migrations from Mexico
to the United States began to occur, the United States was just
beginning its industrial boom. The native-born population was
small. The Thirteenth Amendment to the Constitution had abol-
ished slavery in 1865; the passage of the Chinese Exclusion Act
of 1882 had staunched the flow of Chinese coolie labor to build
the nation's railroads. The country teemed with industrial
fervor, but it lacked a cheap and readily available labor force.

Immigrants from Ireland, Scandinavia, and southern and
eastern Europe lent their skills to factories and mines in the
country's rapidly industrializing East and coal- and iron-rich
South, East, and Midwest. And Mexicans, who worked hard and
asked little, were put to work as laborers on a railroad line
that opened in 1884 with regular passenger service between
Mexico City and El Paso, Texas. Eventually, these workers left

the railroad behind them and migrated further north to seek
their fortunes in the stockyards of Chicago, Detroit, Gary, and
Kansas City. And they stayed to found the large Mexican communities now existing in those cities far north of the border.

At the dawn of the twentieth century, an agricultural
industry began to blossom in the American Southwest. Plans
for extensive irrigation projects called for a strong, unskilled
labor force. Migrant Mexicans filled the need; they became the
backbone of Southwestern agriculture for about $1.00 to $1.25
a day.

South of the border, however, things were taking an explosive turn. In 1910 the Mexican Revolution erupted. As a
result, food supplies were disrupted; inflation skyrocketed
while employment plummeted. The irony that a revolution fought
in the name of *Tierra y Libertad* ("Land and Liberty") should
end with a massive displacement of people did not escape the
Mexican peon's notice. Large numbers of rural Mexicans began
to migrate to Mexico's urban centers. Also from 1911 through
1915, tens of thousands of Mexicans were officially dubbed
"economic refugees" and welcomed to the United States.

As poor white and black laborers moved north and east in
search of higher wages in Chicago, Detroit, and New York, the
demand for farm labor became critical in the South and Southwest. The curtailment of European immigration by World War I
and a tightening of immigration laws in 1917, plus America's
own entry into the war, created drastic labor shortages in
Southwest and Northern industrial centers. Mexicans flooded in
to fill the gaps.

At the end of World War I, however, an economic recession
touched off mass repatriation campaigns against formerly welcome
Mexican aliens. Texans and Oklahomans attacked Mexicans while
they worked and destroyed their homes and property. During
1920 and 1921, nearly 100,000 Mexicans fled the country they
had looked to for salvation. But they soon discovered that
Mexico had changed, too, and that it had changed for the worse.

Land reform had begun, but a power struggle between the
government and the Catholic church was brewing. In 1926,
President Calles (1924-28) instituted vigorously anticlerical
measures; in retaliation, the church suspended all religious
ceremonies and approved (many say sponsored) a rebel group in
western Mexico known as the *Cristeros*. Since the Cristero
Rebellion took place in the central plateau region from which
most U.S.-bound migrants came, thousands of workers were again
forced northward to the United States. From 1927 to 1929,
most of them entered California and Arizona via a new railroad
line linking Guadalajara with Nogales, Arizona.

Until 1929, the United States had a virtual open-door policy
toward Mexico. But in 1924, the door closed an inch with the
establishment of the U.S. Border Patrol; restrictionist feeling
was growing again. The pro-employer Coolidge and Hoover admin-
istrations tried to cool demands for Mexican immigration quotas

by strengthening border controls and, in August of 1928, U.S. consular officers were ordered to deny visas to Mexican illiterates under a provision of the 1917 Immigration Act. Head taxes and visa fees were also imposed on Mexican immigrants for the first time. And in 1929, Congress made it a felony to enter the United States without a visa.

As the Great Depression swept across the country in 1929, another mass repatriation campaign was launched against Mexican immigrants. The results of this drive were much greater than in the early 1920s: some 415,000 Mexicans were deported between 1929 and 1935, and about 85,000 more left "voluntarily." As in 1920-21, the numbers of Mexicans who were expelled also included substantial numbers of U.S.-born Mexican-Americans. Mexican immigration was reduced to a mere trickle.

Labor shortages created by World War II mobilization, however, brought about another flow of Mexican migration, and in 1942 the *bracero* program was established under the terms of a bilateral agreement between the United States and Mexico. Over the 22 years of the program's operation, some five million braceros (strong-armed ones) were imported to work in Western and Southwestern agriculture. Huge migrant-labor camps were set up by employers.

During the first decade of the bracero program, the red tape involved in job listing and recruiting kept employment demand ahead of bracero supply. The Mexicans still managed to come, albeit illegally, and many of them eventually dropped out of the migrant labor force to apply for legal immigrant status, which was relatively easy to get during the late 1950s and early 1960s.

At the end of the Korean War, however, unemployment rose sharply in the United States. The result: another repatriation campaign. This time, more than 1 million Mexican migrants were expelled during the mass 1953-54 roundup and deportation campaign known as Operation Wetback. Expulsion was not the last word for many of those caught by Operation Wetback, however: between 1953 and 1956 the bracero contract labor program was expanded to more than twice its original size. Many Mexican deportees soon found their way back to the United States as legal braceros.

Then, in the late 1950s and early 1960s, the immigration door began to close again. Organized labor and religious groups became increasingly vocal in their opposition to the bracero program. In response, the U.S. Department of Labor instigated increasingly restrictive regulations for the hiring of contract laborers. Moreover, the rapid mechanization of cotton harvesting, the prime source of bracero employment, reduced the need for migrant labor. In 1964, the bracero program was unilaterally terminated by an act of Congress.

With the bracero program defunct, migration went underground. During the period that bracero contracts were falling off, increasing numbers of Mexican farm workers applied for

permanent resident visas. In the late 1960s, however, such
visas were hard to come by. Many former and potential braceros
continued to migrate to the United States, but as illegals.
Since rural unemployment was also on the rise in Mexico clandestine migration began to swell.

Meanwhile, a series of amendments to the Immigration and
Nationality Act, which became effective on July 1, 1968,
drastically cut the number of visas available to Mexicans.
These amendments made legal migration to the United States
extremely difficult for other than immediate relatives (spouse,
child, or parent) of U.S. citizens or legal permanent resident
aliens. "Unconnected" migrants were required to show proof of
job offers from U.S. employers who, in turn, were required to
obtain certificates from the U.S. Department of Labor stating
that no domestic workers were available to fill the jobs and
that the hiring of immigrants would not have an adverse effect
on local wages and working conditions.

The amendments also restricted the number of admittable
Mexican nationals from about 62,000 per year to 40,000, thereby
extending the waiting period for visa applicants. On the other
hand, the amendments opened up a new category of visa candidates: parents of U.S. citizens or legal resident aliens over
the age of 21 were exempted from the quota system.

Restrictions have been imposed, periodic repatriation
campaigns have been launched, and public furor over what are
increasingly seen as lax immigration policies in general and
illegal immigration in particular has mounted. But the virtually unchecked flow of illegal immigration continues. And the
immigrants are not only Mexican nationals: more and more
migrants from poor, overpopulated, and politically unstable
Central and South American countries are using Mexico as a
back door for illegal entry to the United States.

As noted previously, 808,000 people were admitted to the
United States under some sort of permanent immigrant status in
1980, and from 800,000 to 1 million Mexican nationals have come
into the United States illegally. With the number of illegal
aliens already in the United States estimated to be between 8
and 12 million, predictions are that an additional 700,000 or
so immigrants will be legally admitted in 1984 and that the
number of successful clandestine border crossings will push
toward the 1 million mark. Some of these illegals will eventually return to Mexico, but many will stay.

The U.S. birth rate has been declining since 1960, and now
stands at about 16 per thousand, with a rate of natural population increase of 0.7 percent a year. If these figures remain
fairly steady, the United States can expect to experience a
natural population growth of about 40 million--from 230 to 270
million--by the year 2005. If both legal and illegal immigration numbers also remain fairly steady, however, the population
of the United States could easily reach 325 million by 2005.

Once here, Mexican migrants are likely to be greeted with
suspicion, if not outright hostility. With unemployment and

inflation on the rise and social welfare programs on the decline, with racial tensions growing and ethnic conflicts (such
as those that erupted in bloody violence in Miami in 1980 over
the influx of Cuban refugees) gathering steam, with the problems of resettling hundreds of thousands of Asian boatpeople
still appearing, and with crime rising in urban ghettos and
barrios and spreading to suburbia, life in the United States
is not what it was but a decade ago. The land of opportunity
is running out of frontiers. And, as Senator Alan Simpson,
Chairman of the Senate Subcommittee on Immigration and Refugee
Policy, puts it, Americans have become victims of "compassion
fatigue."

In 1977, a Roper poll found that 91 percent of those polled
were in favor of an "all-out effort" to stop illegal immigration; 75 percent wanted to reduce legal immigration to less
than 400,000 per year. In 1980, the same poll shows that 91
percent still favored forceful action on illegal immigration,
but the number calling for decreased immigration rose to 80
percent. With such a hostile reaction to immigration in general
and illegal immigration in particular, why do so many Mexicans
continue to migrate to the United States?

It is not because it is easy: Mexican illegals always
cross at the risk of apprehension and often at the risk of their
lives. But Mexican migration has become a family, community,
and national tradition in Mexico and an agricultural and industrial tradition in the United States. As long as economic
factors in Mexico and the United States continue to interact,
the border will remain "open."

Nearly all Mexican migration to the United States originates
in Mexico's impoverished, densely populated central plateau
region. There, young men are often given a crash course in
Americanization, are assisted with fund-raising for their trip,
and sent off to earn income for their families. An estimated
50 percent or more of all wage-earning males in the region have
spent at least one work period in the United States, usually as
illegals. Many of these young men, and increasing numbers of
women and children, travel for as long as two months to get to
the border. Many of the first-time migrants who go through
fences into California and Arizona and wade or swim across the
Rio Grande into Texas are apprehended. The U.S. border patrol
picks up about 1,500 border violators a day; undocumented aliens
are turned back. But counterfeit Social Security cards can be
purchased in Tijuana for $50 to $100. And the border patrol
guarding the 2,000-mile-long border is drastically understaffed:
a total of only 550 agents patrol the critical 66-mile stretch
from the Pacific Ocean inland. Although most of the migrant
traffic is concentrated on the 12-mile strip of border fronting
Tijuana between the ocean and Mt. Otay, and the greatest number
of illegals enter along a five-mile-long area in the Chula Vista
District in California, there just are too few border patrol
agents to do the job. Although President Reagan has asked for

an INS budget increase in fiscal 1983 of $96 million, recent
budget decreases have cut severely into border operations. To
save gasoline money, the patrol has had to limit its travel
along the border to 20 miles per eight-hour shift.

An estimated two of five illegals are caught at the point
of entry. Of those apprehended, nearly all will regroup and
try again, often the very next night. Likewise, illegals
rounded up inside the United States and returned to Mexico
also usually turn right around and enter again. Inconvenient
as this revolving-door activity is, it is nothing compared to
the horrors that befall many migrants on their trips northward.

Migrants who can afford it often enlist the services of
coyotes, Tijuana smugglers who charge up to $500 for guaranteed
delivery to the United States. And the coyotes do deliver.
Once they have reached the Arizona desert, however, migrants
have been known to be relieved of their valuables by their
coyotes and then abandoned to die of thirst. Even the Mexican
police and customs officials have been known to extract their
share of outward-bound cash and valuables before allowing the
migrants to go on their way. Along the California section of
the border, groups of Mexican banditos terrorize vulnerable
migrants. In recent years, incidences of robberies, rapes,
murders, and kidnappings carried out by banditos have become
so frequent that the San Diego police department has set up a
border crime task force just to deal with them. And yet they
come, migrant workers and migrant families, risking their lives
for a better economic life in the United States. Most of them
leave Mexico not because they want to; the people of the central plateau region tend to be deeply traditional. They leave
because they cannot afford to stay.

AGRARIAN REFORM

Although Mexico is generally considered to be an agrarian
society, it is rapidly converting to a dualistic society with
favored investment emphasis given to the urban industrial
sector. As the disparity between rich and poor in the country
grows, the middle class is squeezed from both sides. In the
scramble for survival within the expanding lower class, economic
pressure is intensified. Since the 1910 revolution, the poorest
of the rural poor, who cannot afford the expense of a journey
to the United States, have migrated in spurts and floods to
both major cities and rural marketing communities within Mexico.
Many of these urban centers have been filled to unmanageable
levels. Mexico City, which for centuries has stood proudly as
the revered cultural center of Mexico, is now ringed with
shanties, plagued by breakdowns in basic service systems,
destabilized by unemployment, and terrorized by crime. Aware
that no jobs exist in their own cities, members of the country's
rural intermediate class take the only way open to them: they
flee to the United States.

Ironically, Mexico boasts the world's longest-running agrarian reform program. Since its inception in 1915, however, the program has become progressively weaker. Today it founders in bureaucratic inefficiency and outright corruption. The people at whom the program is aimed, the rural peasant population, have no voice in either its development or administration.

Mexican agriculture is divided into three major groups: the *ejidatarios*, or communal farmers, the proprietors, and the agricultural workers. The ejidatarios are poor and are on about the same economic level as the smallest proprietors of redistributed land. The small and medium-sized landowners form the rural middle class, whereas the large landowners form an agricultural elite. Since 1915, more than 75 million hectares of land have been transferred by the government of Mexico to about three million peasant farm families. Most of the land redistributed, however, was in thr form of tiny, often arid plots beyond the reach of irrigation projects. And 9,000 acres of land designated for dispersal to peasant farmers in 1970 were never turned over at all; the would-be recipients did not even learn of the land gift until 1977.

The agricultural elite, meanwhile, continues to hold about 84 percent of all privately owned land. It is interesting to note, for example, that Secretary of Agrarian Reform Toledo Corro owns some 45,000 acres of prime Mexican cropland. That land, wealth, and politics go hand in hand in Mexico was further illustrated by the *Washington Post* on August 29, 1981:

> *Mexican President Jose Lopez Portillo has turned down the legal gift of a $2.4 million ranch. He made his decision public in an open letter after a newspaper columnist wrote, 'The ostentation of a gift of this kind will contrast with the poverty millions of our compatriots suffer every day.'*
>
> *Gov. Jorge Jimenez Cruz of the State of Mexico had planned to offer the president the 147-acre ranch in Tenancingo, 50 miles south of Mexico City, when he completes his six-year term on Dec. 1, 1982.*

Due to agrarian reform failures and high population growth rates in rural Mexico, the proportion of adult rural landowners fell from 42 percent in 1940 to 33 percent in 1970. And the trend toward more concentrated land ownership continues, particularly in regions where mechanization, irrigation, and commercial agriculture have become dominant. Smaller farmers, who lack the capital necessary to compete with large-scale enterprises, have taken to selling or leasing their land to larger producers. For the poor Mexican farmer, at least, land reform never really began.

For the past 60 years, the most stable factor in Mexican life has been the government. Although elections were held every four years until 1928, when the single-term presidency was extended to six years, election results were easy to forecast: each president in effect appointed his successor. Then, in 1929, a peculiar, nearly unique single-party system came into being when what is now known as the Partido Revolucionario Institucional (PRI, or Institutional Revolutionary Party) was formed by the powerful and charismatic former president, Calles. Regular presidential elections continue to be held, and the outcomes continue to be entirely predictable. Not surprisingly, presidents tend to choose as their successors men whose political and economic philosophies are compatible with their own. In other words, developmental trends have been institutionalized along with the one-party system.

But beneath this facade of stability, silent resentment, viewed by many as akin to the ominous lull before a storm, has been simmering for years among Mexico's increasing numbers of rural and urban poor. Meanwhile, the government's development plans continue to emphasize the elite sector and often exclude the poor and shrinking middle classes altogether.

For 40 years, successive Mexican presidents have earmarked public investments for irrigation projects designed to nourish a trend toward large-scale, mechanized, export-oriented agriculture. This has resulted in a widening gap between farm productivity in such agricultural oases as the cotton- and wheat-growing regions of the North—known in Mexico as "the United States' backyard"—and the rest of the country. Although Mexico imports enormous quantities of grain from the United States each year, rich northern farmers are subsidized by the government to grow such lucrative export crops as winter vegetables, cocktail onions, strawberries, and other truck crops destined for U.S. markets. The feeling that the U.S. economy is responsible for peasant poverty is a growing factor in rural migration to the United States.

Government financing of large-scale irrigation has enabled larger landowners with political pull to use their access to good land, investment capital, and marketing systems to introduce green revolution technologies. Their increased production from modern high-yield seeds, fertilizers, and pesticides has further enabled them to sink an enormous amount of capital into labor-saving machinery. This has resulted in increased exports of agricultural products, even in the face of growing internal food deficits, accelerated mechanization, widened income inequalities, an even greater concentration of landownership, and increased internal migration from rural to urban areas. At the other end of the economic scale, an attempt to introduce mechanization into a system of accelerated collectivization of peasant farmers into ejidatarios threatens to reduce even further the labor demand in the ejidal sector.

Under President Luis Echeverría (1970-76), support prices were raised for basic agricultural commodities for the first time since 1963 and, during the 1975-76 period, a large labor-intensive rural road-construction program was carried out.

PIDER, a large-scale integrated rural development program, was launched in 1973 with financing from the Mexican government, the World Bank, and the Inter-American Development Bank. So far, PIDER has benefited about a fifth of Mexico's rural population by providing small-scale irrigation systems in about eight *municipios* (counties). With a budget that grew from $88.3 million in 1973 to $500 million in 1980, the program, however, does not operate in arid or semiarid areas deemed to lack the criteria of growth potential; it does not reach the most depressed rural areas in which the bulk of U.S.-bound emigrants originate.

Of some $2 billion invested in agriculture each year during the Portillo administration (1976-82), only about $500-600 million per year is used to benefit the small landowner. Basic imbalances in terms of access to irrigation, credit, and modern technologies were not redressed. In 1976, when President Portillo stated that since there was not enough land to go around, and production was the country's prime consideration, he was setting the country's future on a familiar historical course. According to Herberto Castillo, leader of the recently formed opposition group known as the Mexican Workers' Party, rapid development will lead to "corruption and U.S. enslavement," since many Mexican leaders thrive on business investments in the United States. Whichever course Mexico will take to try to bring about agrarian reform now rests with President Miguel de la Madrid.

OIL: ECONOMIC BENEFITS, POLITICAL LIABILITIES

Crucial to both Mexican and American interests is the development of the vast and virtually untapped oil and natural gas reserves lying along Mexico's Gulf Coast. By spring of 1981, Mexico had become the world's fourth largest oil producer, with proven hydrocarbon reserves of 67 billion barrels and potential reserves estimated to range upward from 200 billion barrels. Whether the influx of oil and natural gas revenues will help to cure the country's socioeconomic woes or will lead directly and quickly to even greater economic imbalances and political destabilization depends on the current price of oil and the foreign debt, as well as the Mexican government's willingness to use any profits to benefit Mexican society as a whole.

So far there is not a great deal to be optimistic about. As the *Economist* of London reported on February 17, 1979:

> After months of debate, the Mexican government has come down clearly on the side of massive industrialization rather than labour-intensive projects. The country's chronic unemployment and underemployment . . . is to be solved as a by-product of industriali-

*zation, rather than as an objective in itself. So
at best, the government admits, the problem will not
be resolved before the beginning of the next century. . . .*

First, however, the government will have to tackle its
foreign debt which, in 1982, stood in the $82-85 billion range,
the highest in the developing world. Capital expenditures by
Pemex accounted for over half of all government investment,
and nearly 30 percent of the entire public sector budget in
1978. Billions have been borrowed externally to finance oil
exploration, drilling, and processing. Meanwhile, while oil
and natural gas accounted for two-thirds of Mexico's export
earnings in 1980, the country's imports jumped by 55 percent
and manufactured goods rose by only six percent. On top of all
that, Mexico, with its enormous population of 71 million, is
oil dependent: the country depends on oil for more than 90
percent of its energy use, and increased development and consumerism will strengthen that oil dependency.

Adding to Mexico's developmental problems is the fact that
the capital-intensive petro-industry is not labor-intensive.
For example, it may take 5,000 laborers to construct a refining
plant, but only 2,000 workers to run it. While diverting
capital from more labor-intensive sectors, it may also eventually create an employment boom quickly followed by a rapid
decline in the labor force.

Over the past three years, however, Mexico has moved from
an economic recession into rampant inflation. During 1981, oil
and gas exports accounted for 74 percent of Mexico's foreign
exchange earnings. A flow of oil wealth and plans for a
developmental and economic boom brought about a new climate
in Mexican-U.S. relations: the Mexican government was no longer
willing to let its neighbor to the north dictate policies for
the Western Hemisphere. Disputes over international waters and
fishing rights have broken out between the two nations. In
1979, demands by the United States for lowered natural gas
import prices sparked anti-U.S. feelings throughout Mexico;
and Cuban President Fidel Castro's official visit to Mexico
deeply wounded Washington. What was good for the United States
was no longer viewed as being necessarily good for Mexico.

Then came the 1981 OPEC oil glut. Mexico's oil sales to
such major importing countries as Japan, France, and Spain fell
so drastically that Mexico's oil income during 1981 was $5 bil-
lion short of the expected $20 billion. The Mexican government
had cut back its overall expenditures by an unprecedented four
percent, and the drop in its oil exports precipitated a rush
for dollars: estimates of between $4 and $5 billion were
exchanged for the suddenly wobbly pesos. By late February,
1984, the exchange rate was 166 pesos per dollar, compared to
a 1981 exchange rate of 27.5 pesos per dollar.

Meanwhile, on August 21, 1981, as Saudi Arabia promised an
oil price freeze at $32 a barrel and announced an oil production

cut of 10 percent, the United States went public with plans to purchase nearly 110 million barrels of Mexican crude oil over a period of five years for its strategic petroleum reserve. The sale marked an attitudinal turnabout for Mexico: just the year before, negotiations by the United States for the sale of Mexican crude at market prices were turned aside by Pemex which said it had no oil available. This time, however, Mexico was happy to sell, and at market prices.

President Portillo stood firm in his determination to hold Mexican oil output down to 2.2 million barrels a day (1.4 million barrels of which are earmarked for export) to ease the impact of sudden influxes of petrodollars on an economy lacking the economic infrastructure to absorb them.

As both the revenues from the oil and the value of the peso declined, Mexico suddenly found itself unable to make the payments on its $82 billion foreign debt. After several frantic meetings in September and October of 1982 between officials of the Mexican Treasury, U.S. banks, and the International Monetary Fund (IMF) the bailout of $2 billion in credit guarantees from the U.S. government and a $4 billion loan from the IMF was received.

Although Mexico has been able to temporarily hold off bankruptcy, a continued decline in oil revenues along with unchanging internal economic and social policies threatens the country with added instability.

Neither Mexico nor the United States can afford the danger of political disruption that economic mismanagement might eventually bring to Mexico. The United States' increasing dependence on Mexican oil and Mexico's increasing need to export its unemployed masses cannot help but be antithetical to the long-term best interests of both countries. If allowed to continue, the result would be an increase in violence against Hispanic immigrants, an even heavier dependency on energy consumption in the United States, and deepening income disparity and political unrest in Mexico.

In a world in which the scramble for rapidly depleting reserves of irreplaceable fossil fuels is turning friend against friend, relations between Mexico and the United States are critical to the national security of each. And even in a world characterized by a widening gap between have and have-not nations, Mexico's economic disparities loom large. Mexico's equitable development is as vital to the United States as it is to the Mexican leadership's stability and to the masses it is finding increasingly difficult to appease.

THE POPULATION PROBLEM

The biggest and oldest problem facing the Mexican government is overpopulation. National family planning efforts have succeeded in reducing the nation's population growth rate from

more than 3.0 percent to 2.5 percent each year. But at the
present rate of growth, Mexico's population, which more than
doubled between 1940 and 1970, will double again in just 28
years from 70 million to 140 million by the year 2009. At the
same time Mexico City, which is already beleaguered by gross
overpopulation, will become the largest metropolis in the
world with a population of more than 32 million, a size comparable to Poland's current population of 36 million! And, if
migration to Mexico City continues, its population numbers
will grow even higher.

Although the trends are reversed, Mexico's population
dilemma can be likened to its oil problem: whether the country's oil reserves are programmed to last 20 or 60 years, the
fact is Mexico's oil eventually will be gone. Similarly, even
if the country manages to reduce its population growth rate
further over the next few years, and thereby extends the
doubling time, Mexico's population eventually will double.

Forty-two percent of Mexico's population is under 15 years
of age; even if the country's fertility control efforts were
to spread like wildfire, a baby boom could not be avoided in
the near future. The vast majority of these babies will be
born into poverty, to parents living beyond the reach of public
health and contraceptive services. And the first of these
babies will be born to young, often teenaged, mothers: the
mean age of women at the time of marriage is 18.4; 85 percent
of all Mexican women are married by the age of 21.

Overall improvements in public health conditions in Mexico
over the past 30 years have pushed life expectancy up to an
average of 65 years and have led to a reduction in the overall
annual mortality rate of from 26 per 1,000 in 1930 to 8 per
1,000 in 1981. The country's infant mortality rate, however,
still hovers around 70 per 1,000 live births as compared to
the U.S. mortality rate of 13 per 1,000 infants born. And
whereas three percent of deaths occurring in the United States
each year are among children from one to five years of age, 43
percent of the deaths in Mexico occur among children under the
age of five.

Families living in the rural areas of Mexico or in urban
slums and shantytowns often live without electricity, running
water, or sewage disposal. Malnutrition is endemic; about 60
percent of the population is undernourished. Since such high-
protein foods as beef (which requires heavy grain inputs for
its production) and seafood are prime export items, the amount
of protein available to Mexicans is decreasing each year. The
nation's housing shortage is critical and growing: at least
69 percent of the country's families live in one- or two-room
houses, often with dirt floors and roofs of thatched palm.
The nation is critically short of water, hospitals, and schools.
In 1979, 61 percent of the population was functionally illiterate.

About half of the nation's potential wage earners are
either unemployed or seriously underemployed. Economists

estimate that 45 percent of the active work force is under-employed; underemployment runs as high as 60 percent in the agricultural sector and 58 percent among those aged 12 to 29. The country already has far more people than it can feed, service, and sustain.

At the time of the 1970 presidential election in Mexico, it was obvious to anyone who could read, count, or see, that the country's runaway birth rate, coupled with a reduced death rate, was leading to disaster. Many, including a significant portion of the nation's Catholic Church hierarchy, blamed the country's high fertility patterns on traditional adherence to the church's outdated and divisive ban on effective contra-ception. Others blamed it on the political left's Marxist view that the concept of overpopulation is but a reflection of capitalistic failures, and can be solved by reorganizing society into a collective mode of production where the produc-tive forces of the people would increase more rapidly than their numbers.

In any case, Echeverría adopted a distinctly pronatalist stance prior to his election with such statements as "To govern is to populate" and "I do not know whether Mexican mothers understand the effectiveness of the contraceptive pill. What I do know is that we need to populate our country . . . we do not want to control our population." And his pro-natalist stance did appeal to the Marxist left, which had begun to question the validity of the PRI government and of former Secretary of the Interior Echeverría's ordering of the shooting of students rioting against the government in 1968, an event that came to be known as the Tlatelolco Massacre.

In 1971, Mexico's GNP growth rate fell below its popula-tion growth rate for the first time. Rising disenchantment with the revolutionary establishment erupted in student riots and outbursts of street fighting in Mexico City. In the countryside, guerrilla activities flared. Duly warned, Echeverría took a new tack in 1972 by announcing the formation of a strong national population policy and stating: "Popula-tion growth could win out over economic development. Failure to make an intense, sustained effort could condemn the country to frustration and dependency." Even before the national policy was announced, Echeverría's wife had opened the govern-ment's first series of family planning education lectures sponsored by Mexico's National Institute for the Protection of Children. And soon after her husband's policy shift had been made public, Sra. Echeverría, herself a mother of eight, remarked: "If in my day there had been talk of family planning, I would have taught courses in it."

In a surprisingly progressive move, a collective pastoral of the 80 Mexican bishops also announced its support of the new family planning policy on the basis of a reinterpretation of the *Humanae Vitae* of 1968, in which the Pope reiterated the church's traditional ban on artificial contraception. Having reinterpreted the *Humanae Vitae* in light of "what is the very real and excruciating emergency for most Mexican families: the population explosion," the bishops praised the government's family planning efforts as "a humane measure, wholly consistent with the Church's belief in the primacy of conscience and its concern for the family unit." The government's new policy was nurtured into action.

In 1974, family planning was made a constitutional right of all couples. Then, under President Portillo, the Nacional de Planficacion Familiar, one of the most comprehensive family planning programs ever established by any government, was formed in 1977. Its aim: to provide free family planning services and supplies to all couples who needed them and to reduce the country's population growth rate to 2.5 percent per year by 1982, to 1.8 percent in 1988, to 1.3 percent in 1994, and to 1.0 percent by the year 2000. So far, the program is ahead of schedule: between 1975 and 1978 the country's total fertility rate declined from 6.0 children per woman to 5.2. And by mid-1980, the country's population growth rate had dropped from an estimated high of 3.3 percent per year in 1974 to its present level, 2.5 percent. To achieve a one percent growth rate by the end of the century, however, will mean that the average family size must drop to two children within the next 22 years, quite a feat considering the large number of young people now in or entering their childbearing years.

Family planning efforts still suffer from both a lack of sufficient personnel and health staff motivation. Many clinic workers have become disinterested in carrying out the extra work entailed in the provision of contraceptive supplies and information, and some are even actively opposed to the very idea of birth control. The program is further hindered by the overall lack of education among those in greatest need of con-traception, since it is generally true that better educated people tend to want fewer children.

From now on, the job of reducing the country's still dangerously high population growth rate will depend on more than simply making contraceptives available. There is a feel-ing that people have become reluctant to change the way they feel about their fertility until they can change the way they feel about their lives. Poverty is self-perpetuating: poor people tend to have—and *want* to have—large families.

Despite the fact that Mexico's poor cannot afford to feed or educate their children, they consider children to be gifts from God. They believe that, one way or another, God will provide for His children who, in turn, are expected to take care of their parents in their old age. There is even a chance that a child will be granted legal permanent residence in the United States and thereby ease the rest of his or her family through the golden door.

Machismo also plays an important role in overpopulation. An illustration of the widespread force of machismo is the

Mexican family planning slogan, "Don't stand in a corner like
a loaded shotgun." The slogan refers to the machismo philosophy
that a woman, like a shotgun, should be kept loaded (pregnant)
and at home.

Until national development is aimed at the provision of a
better life for *all* Mexicans, it will succeed only in reducing
the quality of life for all.

Immigration and U.S. Society

The migratory flow of legal and illegal Mexican aliens acts
both as a safety valve for Mexico's ever building population
and economic pressures and as a damper on structural changes
necessary for the country's long-term development and political
stability.

As a result, the United States has been caught up in a
border game which, in the long run, no one can win. A decision
to control illegal immigration effectively would not be a cost-
free decision for the United States. The short-term benefits
of a policy of strict border control, however, could be dramatic, particularly in the economically depressed Texas and
California border cities where illegals work for below-standard
wages. There, black, Hispanic citizens and legal Hispanic immigrants, women, teenagers, and handicapped who must compete
with illegals for low-skill, low-status jobs throughout the
country, are at a particular disadvantage. And over the long
run, restrictions on migrant labor could be equally beneficial
for the country as a whole, despite initial rises in the cost
of many agricultural products and other consumer goods that
would undoubtedly result.

Migrant labor is not always cheap; illegals are often paid
more than the minimum wage by employers in the country's
industrial sector. In Los Angeles, for example, migrants making up about 80 percent of the garment industry's labor force
are often paid $7 an hour and up.

By the very nature of their illegality, migrants tend to
work scared; they are eager to do the most menial jobs for
minimum pay and are willing to work nightshifts and on weekends.
When a particular job ends, they are prepared to move on to
another job or another area. In short, they seem ready, willing, and happy to do jobs in factories, restaurants, hospitals,
and private homes that are considered to be financially unre-
warding to native-born U.S. citizens. In the agricultural
sector, Mexican migrants seem willing to work for little pay
and live under conditions that the native U.S. migrant work
force will not endure, and at the constant risk of further
exploitation by wily migrant-camp supervisors.

Employers throughout the U.S. industrial and service sectors are as dependent on nonunion migrant labor as sweatshop
owners who manage to keep their operations one step ahead of

the law. Although not all of the jobs filled by illegals are
directly related to production, they all are, nevertheless,
built into industrial and service systems. Their absence could
require plant reorganization and/or a substantial upgrading of
working conditions and wages to attract the native-born unemployed. The sudden disappearance of a readily available migrant
work force could even force some small industrial firms out of
business, even though the jobs filled by illegals may be ultimately dispensable.

For the sake of convenience, Mexican nationals entering
the United States beyond quota limitations can be divided into
four categories: short-term temporary migrants; chronic
temporary migrants; borderland "commuters"; and long-term or
permanent migrants. Most short-term temporary migrants enter
clandestinely without legal documentation of any sort. They
are typically young males in their mid-20s who are either
unmarried or traveling without dependents. Because they come
primarily from the rural central plateau region of Mexico and
have had little or no previous work experience, they seek
employment as unskilled farm or service workers. They tend to
make one to three trips to the United States during their
lifetime, usually for a specific purpose (to make enough money
to renovate their house in Mexico, for example).

Chronic migrants, who make at least five or six trips to
the United States during their lifetime, tend to be somewhat
older and more experienced. By becoming old hands at crossing
the border, they are less likely to be apprehended and more
likely to find better-paying jobs. Some eventually seek
permanent resident alien status; others, who leave their
dependents at home, tend to view temporary migration as a
means of supplementing their family income and as an alternative to being unemployed and desperate in Mexico. More and
more of these migrants are finding employment in construction
or light industry and in urban service work.

Borderland commuters cross the border legally, using so-
called border crossing cards or shopping cards. This card
(INS form I-186) permits the holder to remain in the country
for up to 72 hours to shop or conduct business inside a zone
extending 25 miles from the border. Although shopping cards
do not permit the holders to work, many illegals use these
cards for entry and employment in the country's interior. And
they are not difficult to come by; over 2.2 million of these
cards were issued by U.S. immigration officials from 1960 to
1969, and thousands of additional cards are still issued each
month. Other commuter migrants enter with legal employment
status. These people are permitted to travel regularly from
their homes in Mexico to nearby jobs as seasonal agricultural
workers, and household help.

Long-term migrants, most of whom apply for permanent alien
visas (but not for U.S. citizenship), include the largest
numbers of females and children. Since many enter for the

purpose of joining relatives already living in the United
States, this is often in effect a family reunification type of
migration. Most of these migrants find steady urban employment and end up the best paid of all categories.

Illegal migration from Mexico to the United States is not
only the most critical issue affecting Mexican-American relations, but it is also the most financially complex problem
facing the two nations. The short-term economic benefits of
the virtual open border can be neither overlooked nor over-
estimated. The cash flow from migrant-labor remittances to
Mexico and from illegal migrant contributions to U.S. consumerism and tax coffers is staggering. Sudden, effective
restrictions on migration would involve billions of dollars
in the form of money returned to Mexico for use primarily in
the neglected Mexican countryside. Although most of this
income is channeled into non-income-producing activities (for
example, the construction of new homes, which creates only a
temporary spurt of local commercial industry, or children's
education, which often leads to increased rural-urban migration) the remittances provide a vital lifeline for impoverished
rural dwellers. In 1956 and 1957, an estimated 2,250,000
people, about 11 percent of the total rural population in
Mexico at the time, were dependent on income earned by participation in the bracero program. By 1978, an estimated 13.6
million Mexicans, more than 21 percent of the country's entire
population, were dependent to some extent on migrant remittances.

On the other side of the border, the migrant force's contribution to the U.S. GNP and to relatively low consumer
prices in some areas of the economy are only part of the cash-
flow picture. Illegals do tend to make use of the country's
unemployment compensation program. But, although income tax
and social security payments are withheld from the wages of
illegally documented workers as well as legal migrants, few
illegals, either from fear of apprehension or ignorance of U.S.
tax procedures, ever apply for income tax refunds or use the
social security system.

The current U.S. emphasis on capital-intensive supply-side
economics, fossil-fuel stockpiling, and military buildup is
putting a strain on U.S. life.

At a time when inflation is whittling at the American dream
and increasing numbers of U.S. poor and aged find themselves
alienated by their society, the U.S. social security program is
financially strapped. And each year, tax earnings from migrant
contributions generate more U.S. federal income than the entire
tourist industry does.

Proposals for Revising U.S. Immigration Law

Unemployment rates in the United States, particularly among
ethnic minorities, women, and teenagers, are now very high. In

1983 overall unemployment was 10.2 percent, and non-white
unemployment was 14.7 percent. As a result, people in the
United States are strongly urging government officials to set
higher standards of enforcement for illegal immigration.

The Reagan Administration's response to the nation's immigration crisis is familiar. Heated debates inside and outside
of government have split the administration and raised calls
for strict controls from economists, environmentalists, sociol-
ogists, and population experts alike. The issue is explosive;
President Reagan's immigration policy proposals barely serve
to cool debate, much less redress the problem (such as the
proposal of raising the ceiling on legal immigration from
270,000 to 310,000, a number designed to raise the annual quota
for Mexican and Canadian immigrants to 40,000).

Plans for an extension of amnesty to all illegals already
in the country are viewed by many as making a mockery of U.S.
laws and as a quasi-official way of opening the door to even
greater waves of clandestine immigration. Illegals who entered
the country before January 1, 1980, will be permitted to stay
on a temporary basis, providing they have jobs and no records
of criminal convictions. Although these temporaries will be
ineligible for welfare and unemployment benefits, their children will be permitted to attend public schools.

Eventually the temporaries will qualify for permanent
resident alien status on the basis of an English language test.
Once they become permanents, their relatives will qualify for
entry under the priority system which gives visa preference to
relatives of permanent alien residents or, in the case of
immediate family members, under provisions for nonquota entry.
Adult brothers and sisters of U.S. citizens qualify for preference visas, for example; once legally entered, these immigrants'
own spouses and unmarried children become eligible for preferen-
tial visas. The implications for an upward-spiraling increase
of legal immigration activity are clear; the family reunification feature of the amnesty plan could eventually overwhelm the
entire immigration system.

It is the crackdown on illegal immigration, however, that
is the real sore point between the United States and Mexico.
Although the administration's proposals in this area offer a
step in the right direction, they also demonstrate the injus-
tices inherent in policies designed to protect the production-
oriented status quo on both sides of the border. A proposed
increase in the INS budget for fiscal 1983 of $96 million,
part of which went toward the hiring of more border patrol
agents, comes as a breath of fresh air to border-control
advocates. The apprehending of illegals in the country's
interior, however, is a much more difficult task and may very
well fan the fires of ethnic hostility among U.S. citizens
already fearful of what they see as a growing Hispanicization
of America.

Under the proposed plan, businesses with four or more
employees will be fined up to $1,000 for each illegal hired.

To protect employers, alien job seekers will be required to produce two forms of identification and sign a form swearing to legal entry into the United States. The plan's critics raise the specter of increased job discrimination against all Hispanics and an increased production of bogus I.D. cards to accompany the counterfeit Social Security cards already available in Tijuana.

The Reagan proposal causing the greatest frustration among control advocates is the guest worker program. The adoption of this program will permit 50,000 Mexican guest workers to enter the United States each year for a period of from 9 to 12 months. Although they will not be allowed to bring their dependents, the guest workers will be guaranteed the minimum wage and health care. Opponents charge that the program offers little that is new in the way of solutions. They point to the failures of Germany's *gastarbiter* program of the 1960s, which was discontinued in 1973 when unemployment in that country rose to five percent, to America's own bracero program which from 1942 to 1964 served to legalize a portion of illegal immigration while greatly increasing economic dependency on migration by both the United States and Mexico.

In 1978, a House Select Committee on Population concluded that "Decisions must be made about the future size of the U.S. population, and population policy cannot be made without a corresponding immigration policy." In 1981, the President's Task Force on Global Resources, Environment and Population proposed that "the United States develop a national population policy which addresses the issues of population stabilization . . . and just, consistent, enforceable immigration laws. . . ."

Today, the need to stabilize the population of the United States at a number consistent with resource availability and economic viability becomes crucial to both sustainability and security. Unless the United States bases its population and economic policies on schemes directed toward raising living standards and improving opportunities for its own lower economic classes, the quality of life for all of its citizens could be adversely affected.

During the first congressional hearings on population issues in July 1981, H.R. 907 was introduced to help achieve national population stabilization. Democratic Representative Richard Ottinger of New York, who sponsored the bill, commented,

> *H.R. 907 seeks to have the federal government for the first time adopt a population policy and assure that federal agencies address the effects of population changes on their programs and policies. . . . The bill addresses the need to plan for the sweeping demographic trends which are now changing the face of the nation. . . . While our birth rate has dropped, the population continues to grow by more than two million annually.*

Well over half of the annual U.S. population growth comes from immigration, legal and illegal. Meanwhile, about 30 million U.S. citizens live below the poverty line. Many of these are senior citizens who are direly affected by federal budget cuts and find they can no longer subsist on inflation-eroded fixed incomes in the country they helped to build.

By trying to reconcile the principles of compassion and economic self-interest in the confusion of immigration policies and nonpolicies, the United States has failed to preserve either. The nation's immigration crisis in fact exposes weaknesses in the very foundations of the system. In light of the worldwide population and energy crises, it becomes evident that the United States can preserve its own freedom and affluence—its own national security—only by committing itself to the rights of humankind in general.

The century-long U.S. acceptance of Mexico's overflow population has done nothing to promote the human rights of Mexico's impoverished millions; it can no longer even promote the stability of the Mexican government on which U.S. access to Mexico's hydrocarbons depends. Overpopulation diminishes human value and perpetuates mass poverty.

Mexico is a powder keg. Yet the United States continues to defuse Mexican incentives for population stabilization and equitable economic reform on the one hand while raising the economic expectations of burgeoning numbers of potential migrants on the other. Eventually this attitude may bring Mexico and the United States into conflict, thereby affecting the national security of each country.

The U.S. Committee for Refugees reports that by January 1, 1981, a worldwide total of 12.6 million refugees had still not been resettled. Most of these refugees come from vastly over-populated countries; all of them are fleeing from economic and/or political oppression. Although the United States has taken in many more of these uprooted persons than any other country on earth, and continues to do so, there are obvious limits on the nation's ability to accept and assimilate the world's desperate millions. As Zero Population Growth staff member Phyllis Eisen points out in the July 1981 edition of the *ZPG Reporter*:

> *Limits are not unique to [U.S.] immigration policy. We are a country known for pursuit of individual liberties and freedoms. But we have not avoided the need for limits in our lives and actions. Our liberties and freedoms today are based on our respect for personal, social and legal limits. In a society governed by laws, we make choices every day about limits on personal and collective action, as well as their enforcement. In a democratic society, those limits must serve the well-being of the society as a whole and the improved opportunities of all its members.*

Like the earth itself, there are limits to the number of people the United States can support. And its capacity for providing for the well-being of its traditionally upwardly mobile society is already being severely strained.

From the late 1940s to the early 1970s, U.S. society experienced an economic and cultural dynamism unparallelled in the history of humanity. People in the United States came to depend on an expanding economy and to cherish the freedoms it brought. The affluent, freewheeling land of opportunity became a magnet for increasing numbers of impoverished and uprooted people around the world.

But the U.S. society had also been molded around the availability of cheap and plentiful oil. With the Arab oil embargo of 1973 and subsequent OPEC oil price hikes, the United States was forced into an awareness of the finiteness of worldwide oil reserves and of the precarious and inflationary effect of foreign control over a major portion of the country's fuel supplies.

Although the United States continues to import large quantities of oil each year (in 1980, it imported 7.5 million barrels of oil a day at a daily cost of $240 million) it cannot be expected to seek oil imports indefinitely. In 1982, oil imports were down less than 4 million barrels per day. The call for fuel self-sufficiency can be met only by increased domestic exploration and output, by oil conservation and an eventual federal commitment to the vigorous development of environmentally safe and renewable energy alternatives from solar, wind, and water sources. As U.S. dependency on oil evaporates, most of the rationale for a virtual open-door policy between Mexico and the United States will wither.

Meanwhile, job opportunities at all levels of the labor pyramid are drying up. Moreover, the products of the U.S. postwar baby boom, which peaked in 1954, are now making their numbers felt on the job market. Under these conditions, Mexico's continuing dependence on the U.S. labor market to absorb increasingly large numbers of its unemployed and underemployed people cannot help but be self-defeating for both the Mexican government and the impoverished Mexicans who become economic hostages in a high-risk game of nations.

A sudden unilateral sealing of the Mexican-American border, either physically or by economic sanction (e.g., a case of a U.S. refusal to sell wheat to Mexico as long as illegal immigration continues), could be deeply painful for Mexico. Hundreds of thousands of migrant workers would be forced onto Mexico's stagnating labor market; the problems of reintegration and of an even sharper decline in the country's socioeconomic mobility could be overwhelming.

By allowing the Mexican government to postpone vital policy decisions necessary for the overall well-being of its citizenry, the United States is in effect suppressing structural changes that could make Mexican migration to the United States decrease.

Whether or not strict controls eventually stem the tide of
Mexican migration, Mexico will soon reach the point of economic
crisis where change is inevitable. The facts dictate against
Mexico's attempts to develop on the model of the post-industrial
revolution United States; Mexico's population is too great and
its infrastructure too undeveloped to support a lopsided leap
to mechanization.

In a mere 28 years at its present rate of population growth,
Mexico will have twice as many people as it does now. The
implications of such an inexportable crush of humanity on an
economy totally unprepared for it are as critical to the United
States as they are to Mexico itself. Unless Mexico's development plans are structured to emphasize rural development based
on effective and equitable agrarian reform, labor-intensive
industrialization and the encouragement of the small-business
sector, greatly expanded public health and educational services,
and population stabilization via a vigorous and comprehensive
program to dramatically reduce the country's high fertility
rate, the country will have no control over the direction that
inevitable change takes.

Learning How to Pull and When to Push

The problem of migrant workers is by no means limited to
the United States and Mexico. Some 20 million persons, not
including refugees and other displaced persons, are employed
around the world in a variety of guest-worker schemes. Most
of these programs, however, have run into serious trouble for
the same reasons that the United States' virtual open-door
policy with Mexico is in trouble; changing economic, social,
and political conditions call for changing immigration policies.

Migrants who are "pulled" to another country by expectations
of laying away financial nest eggs and gaining new skills for
upgrading their employment prospects in their own country are
frequently displaced when an economic slowdown in a receiving
country reverses the pull factor. In this case, an unplanned
migration back to the sending country takes place as it did
in Europe after the 1973 oil embargo. In 1974-75, over 600,000
migrant laborers were unexpectedly "pushed" home to Turkey,
Yugoslavia, Italy, and Spain.

Similarly, social reactions to large numbers of foreigners
occur throughout the world, even when the private sector of an
economy is eager to maintain the receiving country's migrant
work force. An illustration of this is the Seventh National
Plan for Economic Development, adopted by France in 1977, which
stopped the formerly huge immigration of temporary workers from
Algeria. Ethnic tensions aggravated by political change also
can dramatically alter the demographic and economic character
of a country, as it did in Uganda in 1972.

Other recent examples of reversed economic, social, and
political push factors at work are the expulsions of the

Chinese from Indonesia, the Ibo from Nigeria, and the Indian Tamils from Sri Lanka. Large numbers of foreign workers, many of them U.S. citizens, fled Iran after the fall of the Shah. And growing political and economic instability in other parts of the Middle East point to the possibility of future waves of return migration to such large labor exporters as Yemen and Jordan.

Push factors in sending countries also sometimes shift into reverse to pull migrants back. Many Portuguese workers, for example, migrated back to Portugal upon the independence of such former colonies as Angola. Even more recently, thousands of black Rhodesian migrants and refugees have returned to their homeland since the shift from white to black rule in the newly renamed Zimbabwe.

Push and pull factors dictating migratory flows, however, are generally predictable; their reversal can be programmed rather than being left to fate and crisis management. The most successful guest-worker programs have been characterized by strict control over migrant numbers and a coordinated system for preparing migrants for reintegration into their own societies. Since 1974, for example, the Netherlands has been working on a development assistance program based on research concluding that projects focusing only on return migration do not succeed unless the general employment situation in the migrants' home countries are substantially improved. Concentrating on six migrant-sending countries, Turkey, Yugoslavia, Portugal, Morocco, Tunisia, and the Cape Verde Islands, the Dutch Ministry of Development Cooperation has tied its developmental assistance to the specific needs of the particular regions in which migration originates. Assistance thus based on exhibited need and aimed at the areas affecting and affected by Holland's migratory flow, serves the long-range interests of all nations concerned while skirting the stigma of colonial-style interference. The Dutch program might very well have practical implications both for the phasing down of Mexican migration and for offering a way for the Mexican government to accept area-focused technical assistance without a U.S. frustration of Mexico's desire to maintain political distance from the United States. Were such a program of technical assistance funded by the taxation of both oil exports and migrant wages, the program could work even faster to stem the migrant tide.

The question of a taxation system for international migration has been debated for years; some countries have already imposed such taxes. While Germany's guest-worker program was operating, migrant employers were required to pay a fee to cover the recruitment and round-trip travel costs of migrant laborers. A migration tax has been used in France to provide social services for the workers.

A scheme for the employment-generating transfer of industrial capacity to labor-exporting countries has already proved successful for the United States. About 83,000 workers are

employed in maquiladora plants established in Mexico under U.S.
Tariff Code 807. These labor-intensive plants operate on a
franchise-type basis, with the manufactured goods directed to
distribution centers in the United States. This scheme is also
widely used in South Korea, the Philippines, Hong Kong, and
Colombia. And in 1975, West Germany transferred a complete
steel mill and its Yugoslavian employees to a heavy migrant-
sending region of Yugoslavia.

OUTLOOK FOR THE FUTURE

The symbiosis that exists between Mexico and the United
States in dealing with their job and energy needs has pushed
these nations into a precarious position. The longer Mexico
waits to address the underlying causes of its migratory flow,
the less people its weak economy will be able to support. At
the same time, the United States, in failing to control its
energy and immigration problems, is endorsing its excessive
consumption of energy, as well as opening the door to overpopulation problems.

As long as the Mexican and U.S. governments continue to
support these attitudes, the population and energy symbiosis
will remain. Neither a larger border patrol, work permit
system, amnesty for illegals, nor penalties for employers hiring
illegals will be effective in breaking this destructive bond
between the United States and Mexico.

Only with an efficient leadership in Mexico, bringing about
significant change in the areas of land reform, income distribution, education, health, and family planning will there be a
healthy economy and thus a more stationary population. At the
same time, the United States needs to break its dependence on
Mexican oil and labor supplies. The development of more lucrative alternate energy resources, along with stronger incentives
for hiring U.S. citizens would be a beneficial approach in
bringing about a more independent relationship between Mexico
and the United States.

REFERENCES

Center for the Study of Democratic Institutions. 1977. "Mexico
—The Special Case." *Center Magazine* (Santa Barbara, California) 10, no. 4.

Cernea, Michael M. 1979. *Measuring Project Impact: Monitoring
and Evaluation in the PIDER Rural Development Project--
Mexico.* World Bank Staff Working Paper, no. 332.

Coale, Ansley J. 1978. "Population Growth and Economic Development: The Case of Mexico." *Foreign Affairs* 56, no. 2.

"Controls for an Alien Invasion." 1981. *Time*, August 3.

Cornejo, Gerardo, Alan Keller, Susana Lerner, and Leandro
    Azuara. 1975. *Law and Population in Mexico*. Medford,
    Massachusetts: Fletcher School of Law and Diplomacy.

Cornelius, Wayne A. 1979. "Mexican and Caribbean migration
    to the United States." Study prepared for the Ford Foun-
    dation, New York.

Fox, Robert W. 1975. "Mexico: Methodology for Projection
    of Total Population of Urbanized Areas." In *Urban Popula-
    tion Growth Trends in Latin America*. Washington, D.C.:
    Inter-American Development Bank.

Gay, Lance. 1981. "Immigration: Out of Control?" *Washing-
    ton Star*, May 5, 6, 7, and 8.

Haub, Carl. 1979. "Mexico." *Intercom* (Washington, D.C.:
    Population Reference Bureau) 7, nos. 11 and 12.

Heer, David M. 1979. "What is the Annual Net Flow of
    Undocumented Mexican Immigrants to the United States?"
    Demography 16, no. 3.

Huessy, Peter R. 1980. "Illegal Immigration: Foreign
    Population and Its Impact on the American Future."
    National Forum (Louisiana State University, Baton Rouge:
    Phi Kappa Phi Honorary Society) 60, no. 2.

Kelly, Orr. 1979. "On a Raid with U.S. Agents—Nabbing 29
    'Illegals' in One Illinois Town." *U.S. News and World
    Report*, July 4.

Martin, Philip L. 1980. "Immigration Reform: The Guestworker
    Option." Paper prepared for the Giannini Foundation Con-
    ference on Temporary Labor Migration in Europe: Lessons
    for the American Policy Debate, Belmont, Maryland, June 12-
    14.

Martin, Philip L., and Judith A. Sorum. 1980. "Guestworkers
    and Immigration Policy." University of California, Davis,
    Department of Agricultural Economics, Working Paper no.
    80-6.

Morris, Leo, et al. 1981. "Contraceptive Prevalence Surveys:
    A New Source of Family Planning Data." *Population Reports*
    (Baltimore, Maryland: Population Information Program,
    Johns Hopkins University) series M, no. 5.

Nagel, John S. 1978. "Mexico's Population Policy Turnaround."
Population Bulletin (Washington, D.C.: Population Reference Bureau) 33, no. 5.

North, David S. 1970. *The Mexican Border Crossers: People
Who Live in Mexico and Work in the United States.* Washington, D.C.: TransCentury Foundation.

Population Reference Bureau. 1981. "Birth Control, Overpopulation, and the Catholic Church." *Intercom* (Washington,
D.C.) 9, no. 3.

Rhoda, Richard E. 1979. *Development Activities and Rural-
Urban Migration: Is it Possible to Keep Them Down on the
Farm?.* Washington, D.C.: Office of Urban Development,
Agency for International Development.

Rodríguez-Barocio, Raúl, José García-Nuñez, Manual Urbina-
Fuentes, and Deirdre Wulf. "Fertility and Family Planning
in Mexico." *International Family Planning Perspectives* 6,
no. 1.

Sinkin, Richard. 1980. "Return Migration and Reintegration:
Implications for AID Programs and Policies." Study prepared
for the Agency for International Development, University
of Texas, Austin.

United States Committee for Refugees. 1981. *1981 World
Refugee Survey.* New York.

U.S., Departments of Justice, Labor, and State. Interagency
Task Force on Immigration Policy Staff Report. 1979.
Compendium of papers prepared by the U.S. Departments of
Justice, Labor, and State for use by the Select Commission
on Immigration and Refugee Policy. Washington, D.C.

Warren, Charles W., Jack C. Smith, José García-Nuñez, Roger W.
Rochat, and Jorge Martinez-Manautou. 1981. "Contraceptive
Use and Family Planning Services Along the U.S.-Mexico
Border." *International Family Planning Perspectives.* (New
York) 7, no. 2.

Westinghouse Health Systems and the Coordinacion del Programa
Nacional de Planificacion Familiar. 1978. *Mexico:
Contraceptive Prevalence Survey Summary Report.* Mexico
City.

Index

Agriculture: of Bangladesh: agrarian, 207–12; agricultural growth, 212–13; crop shortage, 208–09; drought, 208; groundwater, 209, 212–13; irrigation, 213; main crop, 172; of Egypt: agricultural land, 159; agricultural shortages, 151–54; irrigation, 151; of India: food production, 39, 47; high value crops, 47; irrigation, 47, 41; of Mexico: agrarian industry, 221, 226; agrarian irrigation, 227; agrarian reform programs, 225–26; agrarian society, 225; green revolution, 227; of Philippines: exports, 135–39; farmers, 135–39

Birth rate: of Bangladesh, 189, 207; of Egypt: and population growth, 148–49; of India: annual births, 56, 57; birth rate drop, 83; of Philippines: 127, 129

Budget: of Bangladesh: educational budget, 182; food budget, 207–08, 210; of Philippines: budget rise, 117

Children's issues: of Bangladesh: early marriage, 185–86; education, 180–82; mortality rate, 179–80; status, 191; value of children, 187; of Egypt: child marriage, 160; infant death rate, 158; of India: child disease, 91–92; child mortality rate, 23–24; educa-

tion, 15–16; of Mexico: infant mortality rate, 231

Colonial period: of India: British era, 8–9; Dutch influence, 7–8; French and English, 7–8; of Mexico: Irish, 220; Scandanavian, 220; of Philippines: American period, 105–06; Spanish period, 102–04

Contraception in Bangladesh: oral contraception, 197; in Egypt: contraceptives, 149; IUD, 163–64; oral contraceptives, 163; in India: 66; acceptors chart, 88–89; coitus interruptus, 90; condoms, 62–70, 87; depo-provera, 66; IUD, 62, 65, 86–87; in Mexico: contraceptives, 321; public health, 231; in Philippines: acceptors, 116; artificial contraceptives, 122–23; oral contraceptives, 114

Culture: of Bangladesh, 179; purdah, 183–85, 189, 190, 191; of India: class, 5–6; untouchables, 5, 13; of Philippines: Barangays, 102; cultural center, 109; economic class, 104

Death rates: of Bangladesh: 179–80; women's, 186; of India: 2, 21; annual death rates, 92; of Mexico: annual death rates, 231; of Philippines: infant mortality, 129. See also Children's issues.

Demographics: of Bangladesh: annual growth rate, 172, 188; growth rate, 216; of

247

About the Author

GEORGIA LEE KANGAS was born in 1931. She earned a B.A. degree in English literature from the University of California and embarked on a career in free-lance writing that took her from northern California to Nuremberg, West Germany in the late 1950s.

In 1960, she married Lenni Kangas and, although her husband's various positions in the Office of Population for USAID took them to such diverse places as Cairo, New Delhi, and Manila, she was able to continue with her writing career.

Ms. Kangas immersed herself in the social and cultural atmosphere of each country in which she lived. In addition to her active participation in the Cairo Family Planning Association she also worked as a tour manager for archeological sites. In India, she was a contributing editor for *News Circle Magazine* and a reporter-feature writer for *Dateline, Delhi*. In the Philippines she served as the president of both the Association of College Women and the Manila Theater Guild and was the editor of *Fact and Fancy*, a small English-language publication.